WITHDRAWN

PENGUIN  CLASSICS

ANCRENE WISSE

A12901 225790

ILLINOIS CENTRAL COLLEGE
PR1808.W48 1993
STACKS
Ancrene wisse :

A12901 225790

ANCRENE WISSE (*Guide for Anchores*)
of a religious order, perhaps a Dominica
remains unknown. He may also be the au
works related by date and dialect to *Ancrene Wisse*. Recent scholarship
suggests that he wrote *Ancrene Wisse* in the second quarter of the
thirteenth century for a group of anchoresses living in the north
Herefordshire/south Shropshire region.

HUGH WHITE is Lecturer in English at University College London.
He has written several articles on medieval English literature and a
book, *Nature and Salvation in Piers Plowman*.

W9-AMX-453

Ancrene Wisse

GUIDE FOR ANCHORESSES

Translated and with an Introduction and Notes by
HUGH WHITE

I.C.C. LIBRARY

PENGUIN BOOKS

84605

PR
1808
.W48
1993

PENGUIN BOOKS

Published by the Penguin Group
Penguin Books Ltd, 27 Wrights Lane, London w8 5tz, England
Penguin Books USA Inc., 375 Hudson Street, New York, New York 10014, USA
Penguin Books Australia Ltd, Ringwood, Victoria, Australia
Penguin Books Canada Ltd, 10 Alcorn Avenue, Toronto, Ontario, Canada m4v 3b2
Penguin Books (NZ) Ltd, 182–190 Wairau Road, Auckland 10, New Zealand

Penguin Books Ltd, Registered Offices: Harmondsworth, Middlesex, England

Published in Penguin Books 1993
1 3 5 7 9 10 8 6 4 2

Translation copyright © Hugh White, 1993
All rights reserved

The moral right of the translator has been asserted

Filmset in 9.5/12.5 pt Monophoto Garamond
Typeset by Datix International Limited, Bungay, Suffolk
Printed in England by Clays Ltd, St Ives plc

Except in the United States of America, this book is sold subject
to the condition that it shall not, by way of trade or otherwise, be lent,
re-sold, hired out, or otherwise circulated without the publisher's
prior consent in any form of binding or cover other than that in
which it is published and without a similar condition including this
condition being imposed on the subsequent purchaser

LCC LIBRARY

Contents

Introduction

It has often been thought desirable that it should be printed, in order that the interesting information to be derived from it with regard to the state of society, the learning and manners, the moral and religious teaching, and the language of the period in which it was written might become more generally accessible.

So wrote James Morton in his 1853 edition and translation of the *Ancrene Wisse*.[1] Since Morton's time various editions, translations and selections have made the work in its different versions increasingly accessible, and the publication of a translation in Penguin Classics continues that process.[2]

The interest Morton found is certainly present in *Ancrene Wisse*, and what he said would of itself bring readers to the work. Others, though, might sense a certain coldness in that 'interesting information' and suspect that here is matter for the antiquarian only. This, however, would be wrong. A warmer recommendation is to be found in the Introduction to Geoffrey Shepherd's brilliant edition of part of the text of *Ancrene Wisse*. A hundred years after Morton, Shepherd writes:

It shows – as does no other early writing in English   the temper and intensity of the noblest aspirations of English people in the twelfth century. At the same time in a vernacular mirror is reflected a whole complex of new spiritual ideas which belonged to Europe as well as to England.[3]

Furthermore, this record of the past is a literary masterpiece:

Few English writers have commanded the wit, liveliness and sentiment [of the author]. He writes with the simplicity of extreme sophistication. He was not the first of the great writers of English prose, but he is certainly not the least.[4]

Shepherd's enthusiastic commendations of various aspects of the work should indicate that there is something more here than a heap of literary bones.

Nevertheless, there are adjustments to be made and barriers to be overcome in reading *Ancrene Wisse*, even in a modern translation. That the medieval title seems odd to us is not, I think, simply a matter of its being Middle English – it is as much a matter of our unfamiliarity with the idea of an anchorite, an unfamiliarity which is symptomatic of the extent to which our assumptions about the proper ends of living have altered since the Middle Ages.

What, then, is an anchorite? The word anchorite is derived from the Greek *anachoretes*, meaning 'one who has withdrawn'. This, though, does not tell us how an anchorite is different from other practitioners of a withdrawn life, such as monks or hermits. Anchorites, unlike monks, do not simply withdraw from the world into a community set apart; they withdraw into an essentially solitary life.[5] This vocation to solitude they share with hermits, but whereas the hermit is not bound to a single location the anchorite is committed to living in a single place for life, a commitment enforced by enclosure in a small cell.

In medieval England such a cell would often, though not always, be attached to a church. This is the situation envisaged in *Ancrene Wisse*.[6] Good examples of such anchorholds can still be seen on churches at Chester-le-Street in Durham and at Hartlip in Kent, and there are remains elsewhere in England.[7]

Within the anchorhold many hours a day were spent in spiritual endeavour. It has been calculated that the set devotions detailed in Part One of *Ancrene Wisse* would take some four hours, on top of which the anchoresses would listen to services in the church.[8] Then there were their own private prayers and meditations and their devotional reading. As if enclosure and the rigorous programme of prayer were not enough, privation and pain through fasting, vigils, the wearing of uncomfortable clothing and flagellation would be embraced. Total sexual abstinence was required. As Shepherd says:

Such a life, deliberately based on the cultivation of physical suffering, inhibitions and frustrations, may well seem strange and remote to us.[9]

Indeed, the anchoritic ideal may well call forth from us condemnation and revulsion. For does it not involve a perverse, unhealthy thwarting of natural impulse? Is it not a waste of life?

Some vestigial traces of a sympathy with ascetic practices are to be found in our culture. There is still some observance of Lenten abstinence, for instance; but the vapidity of much of that abstinence is testimony to how much we have lost an understanding of the ascetic life. So, too, is the attempt sometimes heard from the pulpit to persuade congregations to exchange abstinence and ascesis at Lent for some supposedly more positive devotional effort. Yet for many centuries the importance of ascetic practice for the spiritual life was taken for granted. *Ancrene Wisse*'s vivid testimony to lives of extreme asceticism is a particularly sharp reminder of the validity of the ascetic principle for many Christians in the past, for if, in absolute terms, relatively few medieval people became solitaries, most would have accepted the worth of a life completely devoted to prayer and the pursuit of holiness. We might prefer to regard anchorites as eccentrics, given that their way of life asks a set of rather awkward questions of our own, but for many medieval people – as the extensive sponsorship of anchorites makes clear[10] – the extremity of the anchoritic life was the extremity not of a margin but of a peak.

Many New Testament texts can be brought forward to justify particular ascetic practices, such as fasting and keeping vigil.[11] A more general vindication of the ascetic life is to be found at Mark 8.34, where Jesus says, 'If any man would come after me, let him deny himself and take up his cross and follow me.' Anchoritic practice fulfils the demands of self-denial and suffering, and *Ancrene Wisse* constantly sees the sufferings of the anchorites in relation to the sufferings of Christ – the suffering *is* the following of Christ. Again, the anchorite could point to Jesus' saying at Matthew 10.39, 'He who finds his life will lose it, and he who loses his life for my sake will find it', or at John 12.25, 'He who loves his life loses it, and he who hates his life in this world will keep it for eternal life.' Anchorites were such people. It is not just appalled moderns for whom enclosure in the anchorhold is a being buried alive, a living death. *Ancrene Wisse* speaks of the anchorhold as a tomb,[12] and the ritual of enclosure might involve the celebration of a Requiem Mass.[13] Dust might be scattered on the anchorite as if a corpse were being buried. But this surrender of life – and the asceticism of the anchorite can be regarded as a martyrdom[14] – this commitment to the living death of enclosure is a full-blooded response to central Christian paradoxes about life and death.

For St Paul the inclinations of the Old Adam are kept at bay through ascetic practices.[15] Anchorites attempted to counter within themselves the inclinations to sin in fallen human nature. These inclinations were in medieval times attributed in large measure to the body, the impulses of which were generally seen as liable to distort the proper operations of the soul. Sexuality was especially problematic. In broad terms, for the medieval Church acceptable sex was marital sex aiming at procreation – and even then the act tended to remain under something of a moral cloud. Much better than sex was chastity and in particular virginity. This medieval attitude to sex is deeply embedded in *Ancrene Wisse*, and it constitutes one of the strongest challenges offered by the text to our own culture, so much more positive in its attitudes to sex and the body.

Besides allowing an imitation of Christ and being a means of restraining the Old Adam, the asceticism of the anchorhold is also a way of undergoing the punishment God, in his justice, imposes on sin. So *Ancrene Wisse* asks why, in view of the sufferings of the sinless Christ, sinners should expect not to suffer:

God the Father Almighty, how bitterly did he beat his precious Son, Jesus Christ Our Lord, who never had any sin, only because he bore flesh like ours, which is full of sin – and we are to be spared, who bear on us his Son's death? The weapon which slew him, that was our sin.[16]

If the flesh is full of sin, the world is no better. To the Johannine remark on hatred for life in this world we might add a text from the Epistle of James which opposes even more sharply this world and God:

You ask and do not receive, because you ask wrongly, to spend it on your passions. Unfaithful creatures! Do you not know that friendship with the world is enmity with God?[17]

Plainly the anchoritic flight from the world and the anchorite's commitment to the denial of 'passions' are an extreme version of the hostility to the world here implicitly enjoined. *Ancrene Wisse* itself uses a text from James to describe the religion of the anchoresses:[18] they are of the

Order of St James because they follow his description of pure religion in keeping themselves clean from the world.

In this attitude to the world may lie more difficulties for the modern reader. Keeping oneself clean – is it not a bit negative, timid and indeed selfish? We are perhaps more likely to see the world as a place full of sufferings which are to be pitied rather than of spiritual dangers which are to be feared. We are more likely to feel that we are called to save the world – is this not, after all, an imitation of Christ's mission? – than to reject it. How does the cultivation of one's own holiness away from the pressures of the world, but also from its needs, help one's neighbour? The religious heroes of our culture often have about them something of the social worker or the political activist. And this is sufficiently in tune with the James text which the author of *Ancrene Wisse* uses to define his anchoresses' religion. We might, indeed, feel some surprise that he uses this text at all. In its entirety James 1.27 reads:

Religion that is pure and undefiled before God and the Father is this: to visit orphans and widows in their affliction, and to keep oneself unstained from the world.

To us this naturally appears as a programme of Christian living which makes works of active, practical charity incumbent on all, as well as a properly adjusted personal morality. But the author sees the James text as specifying two possible, and different, kinds of pure religion. If we are prepared to call the second kind selfish, perhaps that has to do with a diminished sense of sin and a loss of the fear of damnation. The pressing urgency of holiness is much reduced if what we do makes no difference to our ultimate end, and, unless it can be shown to promote visible practical results, sanctity may well appear as a sort of optional extra. But, in fact, the medieval life of prayer was not something exclusively turned inwards and solely for the benefit of those who did the praying. The standard medieval division of society into three estates – workers, warriors and people who pray – indicates a recognition of society's need for a class of people specifically committed to prayer – to intercession, certainly, where praying is clearly an act of love for one's neighbour, but also to the rendering to God of the debt of praise on behalf of society at large.

If we are inclined to think of the virtue of the anchorites as a timid, self-protective, stay-at-home kind of virtue, this may be because we do not take very seriously the battle against temptation in the limited arena of the anchorhold – what harm can these shut-away people do, after all? But this would be an unmedieval way of looking at things. For medieval people the spiritual world was acutely real and significant, and the physical and social limitations of the anchorhold did not imply that the struggle against temptation conducted within it was of limited importance. Quite the reverse, in fact. Because of their contempt for the flesh and the world, the third adversary of the life of the spirit, the devil, would, according to *Ancrene Wisse*, be particularly anxious to work the overthrow of the anchoresses[19] – to claim them would be a great victory for him. The Rule of St Benedict speaks of

the Anchorites or Hermits, that is those who not in the first fervour of their conversion, but after long probation in a monastery, having learnt in association with many brethren how to fight against the devil, go out well-armed from the ranks of the community to the solitary combat of the desert.[20]

In this view anchorites are the spiritual crack-troops, particularly heroic operatives in the fight against the forces of evil. It is a view that would have been widely shared.[21] And we should note that, since this battle against the devil is one that everybody has to fight, the personal combat of the anchorite may be regarded as the engagement of a common enemy, and as such an activity not wholly directed to the welfare of the self.

As to the charge of negativeness, we should remember the purpose of ascetic practice; the mortification of the flesh and the subjugation of the will in renunciation of worldly pleasure and ambition and in commitment to a strict form of living have as their end the love of God, for which those practices better fit the soul. So the section on penance in *Ancrene Wisse* leads into that on love, where the work as a whole reaches its climax.

Vocations to this life of intense spiritual discipline and struggle were felt throughout the Middle Ages. People in Britain seem to have been particularly drawn to it. The solitary life was a prominent feature of the spirituality of the Celtic Church. Bede records that, prior to a conference around the year 602 with St Augustine, British churchmen consulted an anchorite about whether to abandon their Celtic Church traditions for the Roman practices which Augustine was seeking to introduce. St Cuthbert lived as a solitary on the island of Farne for eight years from 676. Towards the end of the seventh century, Guthlac, related by blood to the royal house of Mercia, withdrew from the monastery at Repton to an island in the Lincolnshire Fens, where he lived for some fifteen to twenty years. His *Life*, composed not long after his death, records alarming physical combat with the forces of evil and suggests that the solitary life was by no means for the faint-hearted escapist:

He suddenly saw the whole tiny cell filled with horrible troops of foul spirits; for the door was open to them as they approached from every quarter; as they entered through floor-holes and crannies, neither the joints of the doorways nor the openings in the wattle-work denied them entry, but, bursting forth from the earth and sky, they covered the whole space beneath the heavens with their dusky clouds. For they were ferocious in appearance, terrible in shape with great heads, long necks, thin faces, yellow complexions, filthy beards, shaggy ears . . .

An extensive catalogue of further unpleasant physical attributes follows and then:

Without delay they attacked and burst into his home and castle, and quicker than words they bound the limbs of the said man of God and took him out of the cell; and leading him away, they plunged him into the muddy waters of the black marsh. Then they carried him through the wildest parts of the fen, and dragged him through the dense thickets of brambles, tearing his limbs and all his body . . . And once again they took whips like iron and began to beat him. When, after innumerable kinds of torments, after beatings with iron whips, they saw him persist unmoved . . . they began to drag him through the cloudy stretches of the freezing skies to the sound of the horrid beating of their wings.[22]

Naturally, Guthlac survives and triumphs.

Anchorites were involved in the production of the Lindisfarne Gospels around the beginning of the eighth century. In the ninth century Plegmund was called from his life as a solitary to become archbishop and assist Alfred with his programme for the restoration of Christian culture in England. A later archbishop, Dunstan (*c*.909–88), had spent a period of seclusion in Glastonbury Abbey. The European religious reform movement of the eleventh and twelfth centuries which was so potent in the revivification of monastic practice seems to have led to a burst of solitary vocations. To cite just two examples out of many from twelfth-century England, Godric of Finchale (Durham) and Wulfric of Haselbury (Somerset) were among the so-called *loricati* who wore chain-mail next to the skin. Godric wore out three suits. Wulfric, we are told, would recite the whole Psalter nightly sitting in a tub of cold water.[23] In the thirteenth century Loretta, Countess of Leicester, retired into enclosure after the death of her husband, as did Katherine, Lady Audley, of Ledbury (Herefordshire), in the early fourteenth century. They were instances of the considerable number of cultivated women, among whom were the original addressees of *Ancrene Wisse*, who became anchoresses, though there were also women of lesser education. In the fourteenth century Richard Rolle, who seems himself to have led a wandering eremitic existence, wrote the *Form of Perfect Living* for his friend Dame Margaret, an anchoress, and Walter Hilton composed at least part of the *Scale of Perfection* for a woman recluse. Richard II, on his way to meet the leaders of the Peasants' Revolt of 1381, made a confession to the anchorite of Westminster. Julian of Norwich, whose account of the visions, or *shewings*, granted to her during a period of illness constitutes another of the great masterpieces of English spiritual writing, was an anchoress: she was, it seems, still alive in the second decade of the fifteenth century and able to offer counsel to Margery Kempe, whose *Book* provides memorable testimony to her own unorthodox – and unreclusive – spirituality.[24] All in all, we have evidence for the existence of 780 anchorites on some 600 sites in England between 1100 and 1539, when Henry VIII dissolved the monasteries and brought English anchoritism to an end.[25] Women were more numerous than men among the anchorites, considerably so in the thirteenth century. No doubt it was generally felt that enclosure was the proper form of the solitary life for women.

That anchorites counselled kings is testimony to the high esteem in which the vocation was held. Wulfric had dealings with Henry I and Stephen, Robert of Knaresborough (Yorkshire) with King John. Nor was this esteem a regal quirk: Margery Kempe's visit to Julian of Norwich shows that anchorites were sought out as counsellors by commoners, too. Here is another way in which the apparently anti-social and self-absorbed anchorites turn out to be at the service of others. In fact, the anchorhold tended to become something of a broadcasting station for local gossip: 'From mill and from market, from smithy and from anchor-house, people bring the news',[26] runs a proverb quoted in *Ancrene Wisse*. The kind of thing from which the author seeks in the last part of his work to protect the anchoresses[27] – basically requests for safe-keeping – shows that demands were often made of anchorites by those outside the anchorhold. Clearly the solitary life was not in practice absolutely solitary, and the anchorites not beyond the reach of the society that surrounded them. In reality, practical necessity demanded otherwise. We are told that the anchorites of the Egyptian desert were provided for miraculously by animals and, nearer home, that Elgar, the Welsh solitary, was fed on Bardsey Island by eagles,[28] but such provision was not taken for granted. Anchoresses usually had maidservants. The author of *Ancrene Wisse* regards two, an inside one and an outside one, as appropriate and envisages, naturally, a fair amount of converse between mistress and servants.[29]

Provision for the original anchorites of *Ancrene Wisse* seems to have been secure:

For I know no anchoress who has all that she needs with more ease and with more dignity than you three have – Our Lord be thanked for it. For you do not think at all about food or clothing for yourselves or for your maids; each of you has from a single friend all that she needs, and the maid need not look further for bread or food than at his hall.[30]

Other anchorites were supported by living patrons, but there was also much giving in the form of bequests by people of widely different social standing: anchorites were approved of across the community.[31] Adequate support was one of the things the ecclesiastical authorities had to consider before licensing an anchorite; there were those who took to the enclosed life without the sanction of the ecclesiastical authorities, but a prospective anchorite was supposed to have the permission of the bishop of the diocese. The consent of incumbent and patron had to be obtained for living in an anchorhold at a church.

The anchoritic life is obviously not one to be undertaken by any except those utterly committed to it and it is reassuring to read of the trouble taken by John Thoresby, Bishop of Worcester (1349–52), to have Lucy de Newchirche's candidature properly examined. He writes to his archdeacon as follows:

Lucy de Newchirche has approached us many times with earnest and humble devotion, as was clear to us from her appearance and demeanour, asking to be enclosed in the hermitage of St Brandan at Bristol in our diocese. But as we have no knowledge of the life and conversation of the said Lucy, we commit to you, in whose trustiness, diligence, and caution we have full confidence, an enquiry from men and women worthy of credit with regard to the conversation of this Lucy, and whether you would consider her to be of pure and praiseworthy life, and whether she excels in those notable virtues which ought to prevail in persons who give up the life of the world. And if at a day and time appointed ... for her examination, you should find her to be resolutely and firmly set on the pure purpose with regard to which we have burdened your conscience in the presence of God, we commit to you our power ... of enclosing her, either personally or by deputy as an anchoress in the aforesaid hermitage.[32]

But though excellence in notable virtues was looked for in an anchorite and though the anchorites of England could provide authentic examples of the life of ascesis and spiritual struggle, it would be naïve to suppose that all anchorites made a spiritual success of their vocations. *Ancrene Wisse* shows an acute consciousness of the sort of things that might go wrong. Or we might cite Ælred of Rievaulx (1110–67) who wrote a Rule of Anchoritic Life for his sister (a rule known and used by the author):[33]

But many, either not knowing about or not caring about the purpose of this way of life, think that it is enough to confine within walls their bodies alone, while not only is the mind let loose to wander, dissipated among cares and worries and agitated as well with impure and illicit desires; but the tongue also all day long runs through villages and towns, markets and public places, through the lives, behaviour and deeds of men, and discourses on things not just profitless, but shameful as well.

You will hardly find a single anchoress before whose window there is not a garrulous old female or a rumour-mongering woman who besieges her with stories and feeds her on rumours and backbitings, describes the shape, features and behaviour of some monk or other, or a clerk, intersperses certain enticements, and depicts the lasciviousnesses of girls and the licence of widows, for whom what is allowed is what pleases them, and the cleverness of wives in deceiving their husbands and getting their fill of pleasures. The mouth dissolves in cackles of laughter and the poison drunk in as a sweet drink spreads through the limbs and entrails.

Thinking about what has been said disturbs the anchoresses' devotions and there follow discussions as to 'when and with whom she may fulfil what she contemplates. The cell is turned into a whore-house: the window is somehow made bigger and either she goes out or the adulterer comes in.'[34] Later in the Middle Ages we find the anchorhold at Whalley in Lancashire in acute moral crisis. Of it we are told that

Dyvers that have been anchores and recluses ... contrary to theyre own oth and profesyon have brokyn out of the seyd plase wherein they were reclusyd and departyd therfrom wythout eny reconsylyation ... And divers of the wymen, that have been servents ther and attendyng to the recluses afortym, have been misgovernyd and gotten with child withyn the seyd plase halowyd.[35]

In the light of these passages *Ancrene Wisse*'s apparently rather alarmist reaction to the prospect of a touch of hands between anchoress and male visitor may seem less unreasonable than one might initially suppose.[36] But falling away would not necessarily have been spectacular: one can easily imagine loss of zeal overtaking the anchorite charged with the iteration of what might well come to seem a monotonous regime, how the hours would pass unsaid, the time for meditation go by in unproductive wool-gathering.

Certainly, then, there were abuses and failures, but equally there would have been many who lived out the rigorous demands of this life with some success. And for these the satisfaction of feeling themselves closer to God, growing in holiness, would have provided succour against what would surely at times have been the tedium and the keenly felt frustration of their lives. But there would be other rewards − or perhaps the same differently perceived. For in a somewhat paradoxical way the life of enclosure permitted and encouraged the exploration and development of the self in a freedom probably greater than that available amid the pressures of society outside the cell. Here, perhaps, self-denial issues in a kind of self-indulgence, but it is a kind of which our own culture approves. Indeed, it may be that our own culture, in its enthusiasm for individualism, is deeply indebted to the medieval anchorites. Shepherd puts it thus:

Their habits of introspection, their techniques for the control of thought, their attempts to clutch at the irreducible core of personality – at the very 'spark of the soul' . . . have given a stamp and character to the mentality of Europeans. Not only had they their own souls to save; they were colonizing kingdoms of the mind not yet constituted.[37]

If we turn from these longer perspectives back to *Ancrene Wisse*, can we say anything more specific of the anchorites for whom it was written? We find the following passage:

There is much talk of you, what well-bred women you are, desired by many on account of your goodness and generosity, and sisters of one father and of one mother, who have in the blossoming of your youth, renounced all the joys of the world and become anchoresses.[38]

As this suggests, these original three sisters were women of some cultivation: they had books in French and English,[39] and could at least recite a large body of prayers in Latin (though the general practice in the text of translating Latin quotations may suggest that their command of this language was imperfect). They were also capable of copying books (some women in the Middle Ages could read but not write).[40] Whether all members of the expanded community of which *Ancrene Wisse*'s revised version speaks would have been similarly accomplished is open to question.[41]

Further than this, attempts have been made to identify the sisters addressed in the text with anchoresses known from other sources. The most impressive so far is that of Eric Dobson in his *The Origins of Ancrene Wisse*. Using a wide variety of evidence and drawing on an unparalleled knowledge of the various versions of *Ancrene Wisse*, Dobson argues that the anchoresses were enclosed near Limebrook in Herefordshire, and also that the author was an Augustinian canon[42] of nearby Wigmore Abbey called Brian of Lingen. The evocative medieval traces at Lingen, Wigmore and Limebrook deserve to be associated with a masterpiece, but Dobson's brilliant construction has recently been called into question at certain points by Bella Millett who, reviewing what the author says about the practice of his order, argues that he was probably a Dominican rather than an Augustinian.[43]

But though his theory in its full ramifications seems unsustainable, Dobson will not have been far wrong over place and time. The literary dialect used by the author of *Ancrene Wisse* and its first copyists seems to belong to the northern Herefordshire/southern Shropshire region; it indicates that the author will have had close connections with this area, but where he wrote and where exactly within the area his text was copied for its early users is uncertain. As to date, if the work is indeed Dominican, the original version cannot have been written before 1216, when the Dominicans were founded – and probably not before 1221, when they first arrived in England. In a passage added to the version of the text translated here there may be a reference to the Dominican priory at Chester.[44] This would provide evidence of date, since the Chester priory was not founded until 1236. These dates are somewhat later than those favoured by Dobson, but are reconcilable with the linguistic and palaeographical evidence.[45]

It is possible that we have other works by the same author. *Ancrene Wisse* is one of a set of works closely related by dialect, verbal and thematic parallels and manuscript. These comprise three Saints' *Lives*, of Katherine, Margaret and Juliana,[46] a letter on virginity now referred to as *Hali Meiphad* (Holy Virginity) and *Sawles Warde* (The Custody of the Soul), an allegorical treatise. There are also four lyrical meditations focusing particularly on Christ's love for the soul. Analysis reveals some variation in style and language between these works,[47] but it may still be that some or all of them were written by the author of *Ancrene Wisse*. If we are not dealing with a single author, it seems very likely that we should think of a single centre, much concerned with the instruction of female religious, and that the original audiences for the various works overlapped considerably.

The task of instruction is carried out with the help of Latin material rendered into English – for these pieces are not totally independent original compositions. In the case of *Ancrene Wisse* the sources are numerous and of many kinds (though how much of the author's knowledge of them was direct and how much derived from compilations is unclear). There is of course the Bible, and more specifically the

Psalms. There is also the large body of interpretation with which the Bible had been surrounded. There are Augustine, Jerome and particularly Gregory. There is *Lives of the Fathers*. There is the *Prayers and Meditations* attributed to St Anselm of Canterbury. This last is a work of the twelfth century, the spirituality of which was dominated by the piety of the Cistercians, itself largely moulded by St Bernard of Clairvaux. Bernard is frequently cited in the text, which also draws upon other writers of the order, among them Ælred of Rievaulx. Bernard's influence is very apparent in the use of meditations on Christ in his humanity, as a man, as a stimulus to love of God.[48]

Ancrene Wisse is indebted to the twelfth century, too, in the use it was able to make of various aids to biblical exegesis. According to Shepherd:

Not only was the gloss being systematized, but learned clerks were producing alphabetic handbooks (*Distinctiones*) of keywords ... with moral and symbolic meanings, dictionaries of interpretations of names, collections of synonyms or of allegories, classified handbooks of birds and beasts and flowers and precious stones and numbers (each with a moral meaning attached).[49]

The style of the exegesis which is such an important component of *Ancrene Wisse* seems strange to us. The work's preparedness to depart from the literal meaning of a text in favour of allegory and etymology depends on an understanding of the Bible as very directly the word of God and therefore a work which signifies in immensely rich and complex ways. Hand in hand with this attitude to the Bible went an understanding of the physical world as a treasury of symbols of moral and allegorical import, freighted by God with dense significations for the edification of humankind. One would not expect easily to fathom the depths of meaning in texts and objects. This sense of richness of meaning legitimates and encourages the imagistic gymnastics which is one of the most striking things about *Ancrene Wisse* and which offers a pleasure akin to that to be found in following through the extended conceits of the Metaphysical Poets.

We may take it that the dexterity with which the often traditional allegorical images are handled is in considerable measure attributable to the author himself. Though he is constantly indebted to sources, his treatment of them where sources can be established proves to be free, creative, moving with or away from the source as a matter of choice rather than being constrained to a slavish reproduction of the original. The author seems to take some pride in his literary abilities, drawing attention to the careful organization of the parts of his work:

Now, my dear sisters, I divide this book into eight distinctions, which you call parts, and each, without mingling, speaks all by itself of separate things; and nevertheless each one comes properly after the other and the next is always joined to the one before.[50]

In fact, though, the pressure of formal division, whether of the book into parts or the part into subdivisions, is not as powerful as these remarks might suggest. This is perhaps a good thing: there is a certain deadness about the relentless pursuit of enumerated categories by means of which many medieval devotional and instructional works seek to cover their subjects. In *Ancrene Wisse*, although this kind of categorization is employed, it often has to give way to the unfolding of a line of thought beyond what is required by the category, so that the experience of reading tends not to be a matter of running up against the hard lines of a conceptual grid. Rather, one often finds oneself following a sinuous path along a sequence of somewhat opportunistically connected points where it is not always easy to trace a clear relation to a controlling expository design. Not that this is a failing: if the text is to move people to the love of God, it does well not to bore them with too rigid an exposition. Indeed, one effective way of engaging the attention is to develop material unpredictably.

But the author has at his command a panoply of devices for maintaining interest and making sure his moral doctrine drives home. Like many another medieval writer of religious instruction he tells stories, drawing largely on the Bible and *Lives of the Fathers*. He is a master of the allegorical vignette, vivid realizations of doctrine – God as a mother teasing her child, or the sins as functionaries in the devil's court, or Christ as a knight-suitor.[51] He uses imaginary dialogue in which a vigorous colloquial register is often employed. He plays with words. It would seem that he was well versed in the techniques taught in rhetorical treatises, and modern critics have been able to use the terminology of these works to analyse the style of *Ancrene Wisse*.[52] Particularly numerous are figures of repetition.[53] The prominence of this kind of figure probably has to do with the fact that the book was written to be read aloud – for even solitary reading would at this time most likely not have been silent.

The appeal to the ear also explains a kind of repetition which has attracted the interest of literary historians, the alliteration. Old English poetry consists of pairs of 'half lines' usually containing two stresses, the members of the pair linked by alliteration. The Old English prose homilists Ælfric (c.955–c.1020) and Wulfstan (d. 1023) use somewhat similar rhythmical/alliterative patterns and so do *Ancrene Wisse* and its companion pieces. Critics nowadays are less ready than was R. W. Chambers to use *Ancrene Wisse* as a totem of English national identity, a conductor of the tradition of a specifically English prose running from Old English literature to Thomas More and beyond,[54] because it is evident that in both content and style it owes a considerable debt to Latin literature.[55] Nevertheless, that there is some relationship between the rhythmical and alliterative practices of Old English literature and the style of these Early Middle English works seems clear. In this the text displays its geographical origins, for in the West of England Old English habits of composition survived the Norman Conquest with some vigour, albeit much modified, as is witnessed not only by *Ancrene Wisse* and its companion texts but also by the poetry of Laȝamon (who was a priest at Areley Kings, near Stourport-on-Severn, at around the time that *Ancrene Wisse* was written) and by the Alliterative Revival of the fourteenth century, which had its roots in the West and which produced such poetic masterworks as *Sir Gawain and the Green Knight* and William Langland's *Piers Plowman*.

This indicates briefly the place of *Ancrene Wisse* in literary history. What, then, of its specific influence? It was a popular work in the Middle Ages, repeatedly copied, translated and adapted. There is a Latin version and two Anglo-Norman ones; one Latin text was transcribed as late as the sixteenth century. The work was adapted to make it suitable for male religious. There was what seems to be a Lollard revision in the fourteenth century, and the *Tretyse of Love* and the *Treatise of the Five Senses*, written in the fifteenth century, use material from *Ancrene Wisse*. To it, then, the spiritual life of many men and women has been indebted.

And it is with the spiritual life that we should end. Whilst it can be recommended as a literary masterpiece or as a fascinating document of social and cultural history, we ought to remember that *Ancrene Wisse* was written to help people to live good lives. It would be to this end, finally, that the author, whatever his sense of himself as a skilled literary craftsman, would have wished his work to be read – not for the play of images in themselves but for the teaching that that play seeks to enforce. One ought to stress, too, that *Ancrene Wisse* can still function effectively as moral teaching. The author anticipated the expansion of his readership;[56] he might not have anticipated being read eight centuries after he wrote. But the passage of those centuries will not prevent modern readers finding their own moral embarrassments clearly reflected and sharply anatomized in the text. It may be also that they will find effective help offered for these difficulties. *Ancrene Wisse* certainly has a way with words – but it also has wisdom.

This Translation

In translating there is always a tension between achieving fidelity to the original and producing a readable version in the new language. In the case of *Ancrene Wisse* this tension is rendered more acute by its being a work of rhetorical artistry, part of the value of which lies in the ways it chooses and orders words. A translation ought to try to make these ways evident in some degree to the reader. It is obviously not always possible in modern usage even to get near to reproducing the relations between the words and sounds of the Middle English; but I have had it in mind to stay as close as I reasonably might to its linguistic patterns. Accordingly, I have not sought to smooth out what may be felt nowadays as awkwardnesses in cases where this would require an unnecessary departure from the original. For instance, my paragraphing follows indications in the manuscript, even though this sometimes produces sections of text of a length perhaps uncomfortable for modern readers. (However, to have adopted its punctuation system would have made the translation too hard to read.) It seems to me that we are likely to get closer to the experience of reading the original by seeking to follow the way in which it disposes its words than by adapting it to our canons of good style. Awkwardnesses may perhaps disappear if we think of ourselves as reading the text out loud, as the early audience of *Ancrene Wisse* would probably have done.

The positioning of inverted commas may occasionally seem strange: when translating a Latin passage the author sometimes continues without a break into what seems to be his own comment rather than a representation of the original text. It is possible that we should take the comment to be something the cited authority is imagined saying, but I have generally closed the inverted commas where the translating ends and the commenting begins. I tend to render the original's subjunctives with modern English subjunctive forms rather than with a combination of auxiliary verb (e.g. 'should') and verb or with indicatives, though both these would probably be more comfortable for the modern reader. I also allow into my translation certain formulations which would not be admissible were I writing an original piece in modern literary English. There are several occasions when a double subject is followed by a singular verb or when the number (singular or plural) of a pronoun or possessive adjective is not the same as that of its antecedent; an antecedent not explicitly expressed may have to be supplied from the context; an either/or construction may use an order of words strictly incorrect in modern English. Sometimes the translation preserves a seriously disruptive change of construction, as with the change from a relative construction to a conditional in the sentence beginning 'And is not someone a foolish trader' on p. 99.

I have kept the Latin quotations (with the manuscript's inconsistencies of spelling) in the main text and given translations at the foot of the page. To have supplied translations in the main text might have given a false impression of the way the work operates. If modern readers find themselves not comprehending the Latin fully, they will probably be experiencing this aspect of the text rather as many of its early readers did. These would presumably, if nothing else, have responded to the air of dignity possessed by the language of the Church. With such a response in mind, and given that the biblical quotations come from a Latin version close to the Vulgate, I have based my translation of biblical material on the Douai Bible. This version translates the Vulgate into a language the archaic quality of which seems equipped to evoke in modern readers a response analogous (up to a point) to that of their medieval predecessors confronted with the Scriptures in Latin. I use the Vulgate numbering of the Psalms; I style Revelation Apocalypse, The Song of Songs Canticles, and 1 and 2 Samuel 1 and 2 Kings (with the King James Bible's 1 and 2 Kings becoming 3 and 4 Kings). For the forms of biblical names, I use what I take to be the versions most familiar nowadays.

Much of the Latin in the text is from non-biblical authorities, and where the sources of such quotations have been established I give them. Readers should be aware that *Ancrene Wisse* may be indebted to

Latin authorities even in places where a Latin quotation does not make that clear. However, I have not generally noted passages to which the author is, or may be, indebted where there is no Latin quotation.

My preparation of this translation and its apparatus of commentary has been much facilitated by several previous versions, which I have come to admire greatly for their different virtues, and by the researches of very many scholars. I am conscious of owing too many debts at too many points for them to be individually acknowledged. I am, however, particularly grateful to have been able to consult the recent translation by Anne Savage and Nicholas Watson (see Further Reading, which follows this section). Their fine volume appeared when my translation was almost complete, but I have nevertheless been able to profit from it, especially in making my annotations. Also of great help was Sister Ethelbert Cooper's unpublished Birmingham University dissertation, 'Latin Elements of the *Ancrene Riwle*' (1956).

I should like to thank the Master and Fellows of Corpus Christi College, Cambridge, for allowing me to consult their MS 402, which contains the version of the *Ancrene Wisse* here translated, and also the Council of the Early English Text Society for permission to base this translation on J. R. R. Tolkien's edition of the Corpus version (EETS 249, London, 1962). I should also like to acknowledge help and support of various kinds from my colleagues Valerie Adams, Philip Horne, Michael Mason and Henry Woudhuysen – and from members of my family, even though for them my concern with anchoresses has at times had its penitential aspects.

Further Reading

Besides the text on which this translation is based, the Early English Text Society has published most of the other surviving texts of *Ancrene Wisse* in their original languages. Selections from the Corpus Christi version are printed in *Ancrene Wisse: Parts Six and Seven*, ed. Geoffrey Shepherd (London, 1959; repr. Exeter, 1985) and in *Medieval English Prose for Women*, ed. Bella Millett and Jocelyn Wogan-Browne (Oxford, 1990). Shepherd's edition contains an excellent Introduction and Notes. Millett and Wogan-Browne's volume contains Parts Seven and Eight of *Ancrene Wisse* and also *Hali Meiþhad, Seinte Margarete* and *Sawles Warde*, all with facing translation. There are Notes and Introduction and a Glossary. The Prologue and Part One have been edited separately (with facing translation, Introduction and Notes) by Robert W. Ackerman and Roger Dahood as *Ancrene Riwle: Introduction and Part 1* (Binghamton, N.Y., 1984).

James Morton edited and translated the version in the British Library Cotton MS Nero A. xiv for the Camden Society as *The Ancren Riwle* (London, 1853). M. B. Salu translated the Corpus version in *The Ancrene Riwle* (London, 1955; repr. Exeter, 1990). Most recently a new translation of the Corpus version by Anne Savage and Nicholas Watson has appeared in the Classics of Western Spirituality Series published by the Paulist Press in a volume entitled *Anchoritic Spirituality: Ancrene Wisse and Associated Works* (New York, 1991). This includes translations of all the texts associated with *Ancrene Wisse* with full Introductions, comprehensive annotation and helpful Indexes.

On anchorites in medieval England, particularly informative are R. M. Clay, *The Hermits and Anchorites of England* (London, 1914) and Ann K. Warren, *Anchorites and their Patrons in Medieval England* (Los

Angeles and Berkeley, 1985); see also F. D. Darwin, *The English Mediaeval Recluse* (London, 1944) and Sharon K. Elkins, *Holy Women of Twelfth-Century England* (Chapel Hill, 1988). For a theological consideration of the secluded religious life, see Andrew Louth, *The Wilderness of God* (London, 1991). A useful collection of essays is *Monks, Hermits and the Ascetic Tradition*, ed. W. T. Shiels (Oxford, 1985). A good general history of monasticism is C. H. Lawrence, *Medieval Monasticism* (London, 1984).

Books on *Ancrene Wisse* include E. J. Dobson, *The Origins of Ancrene Wisse* (Oxford, 1976) – on which, see Bella Millett, 'The Origins of Ancrene Wisse: New Answers, New Questions', *Medium Aevum* 61 (1992), pp. 206–28; Janet Grayson, *Structure and Imagery in Ancrene Wisse* (Hanover, 1974); and Linda Georgianna, *The Solitary Self: Individuality in the Ancrene Wisse* (Cambridge, Mass., 1981). Roger Dahood writes on *Ancrene Wisse* and related works in '*Ancrene Wisse*, the Katherine Group and the *Wohunge* Group', *Middle English Prose: A Critical Guide to Major Authors and Genres*, ed. A. S. G. Edwards (New Brunswick, N.J., 1984).

For various aspects of the background to *Ancrene Wisse* the following might be consulted: Robert L. Benson and Giles Constable (eds.), *Renaissance and Renewal in the Twelfth Century* (Oxford, 1982); J. A. W. Bennett, *Middle English Literature*, ed. Douglas Gray (Oxford, 1986); M. T. Clanchy, *England and its Rulers, 1066–1272* (London, 1983); David Knowles, *The Monastic Order in England* (rev. ed. Cambridge, 1949); Angela M. Lucas, *Women in the Middle Ages* (Brighton, 1983); Elizabeth Salter, *English and International: Studies in the Literature, Art and Patronage of Medieval England*, ed. Derek Pearsall and Nicolette Zeeman (Cambridge, 1988); and E. Gilson, *The Mystical Theology of St Bernard* (London, 1940).

The *Prayers and Meditations* attributed to St Anselm have been translated for Penguin by Benedicta Ward (Harmondsworth, 1973). There is a translation of St Ælred's *The Eremitical Life* by Mary Paul MacPherson in the volume *Treatises and the Pastoral Prayer*, Cistercian Fathers Series 2 (Kalamazoo, 1971). Many works by St Bernard and other Cistercian writers are available in translation in this series, and see also *The Cistercian World: Monastic Writings of the Twelfth Century*, ed. Pauline Matarasso (Harmondsworth, 1993). Some of the writings of Augustine, Jerome and Gregory are fairly readily available in translation, Augustine being better served than the other two with popular paperback editions of some of his works (particularly the *Confessions* and *The City of God*). For the Desert Fathers, see *The Sayings of the Desert Fathers*, translated by Benedicta Ward (Oxford, 1975) and *The Lives of the Desert Fathers*, translated by Benedicta Ward and Norman Russell (Oxford, 1974).

Preface

In the name of the Father and of the Son and of the Holy Ghost, here begins the Anchoresses' Guide.

Recti diligunt te (in Canticis[1] *sponsa ad sponsum). Est rectum grammaticum, rectum geometricum, rectum theologicum, et sunt differencie totidem regularum. De recto theologico sermo nobis est, cuius regule due sunt: una circa cordis directionem, altera uersatur circa exteriorem rectificationem. Recti diligunt te*[2a] – 'Lord,' says God's bride to her precious bridegroom, 'the right love you.' They are right who live according to a rule. And you, my dear sisters, have for many a day requested a rule from me. There are many kinds of rule, but among them all there are two of them of which I shall speak, at your request, with God's grace. The one rules the heart and makes it even and smooth without the lumps and pits of a conscience crooked and accusing, which says, 'Here you sinned', or 'This has not yet been atoned for as well as it ought to be'. This rule is always within and rights the heart. *Et hec est caritas quam describit Apostolus:*[3] *de corde puro et consciencia bona et fide non ficta*[b] – this rule is the charity of a pure heart and clean conscience and true faith. '*Pretende*,' *inquit Psalmista*, '*misericordiam tuam scientibus te*' *per fidem non fictam*, '*et iusticiam tuam*' – *id est, uite rectitudinem* – '*hiis qui recto sunt corde*' – *qui scilicet omnes uoluntates suas dirigunt ad regulam diuine uoluntatis. Isti dicuntur*

---

a The right love thee (the bride to the bridegroom in Canticles [1.3]). There is a grammatical right, a geometrical right, a theological right, and there are as many differences in the rules for each. Our discourse is about theological right, for which there are two rules: one deals with the directing of the heart, the other with the making right of outer things. The right love thee.

b And this is the charity which the Apostle describes: from a pure heart and a good conscience and an unfeigned faith (1 Timothy 1.5).

1

'*boni*' *antonomastice.*[4] *Psalmista:* '*Benefac, Domine, bonis et rectis corde*'; *istis dicitur ut glorientur testimonio uidelicet bone conscientie:* '*Gloriamini, omnes recti corde*' – *quos scilicet rectificauit regula illa supprema rectificans omnia; de qua Augustinus:* '*Nichil petendum preter regulam magisterii*'; *et Apostolus:* '*Omnes in eadem regula permaneamus.*'[5 a] The second rule is all outside and rules the body and bodily deeds. It teaches everything about how one must conduct oneself on the outside, how to eat, drink, dress, sing, sleep, wake. *Et hec est exercitio corporis que iuxta Apostolum modicum ualet, et est quasi regula recti mechanici, quod geometrico recto continetur.*[b] And this rule is only for serving the other; the other is like a lady, this like her handmaiden. For all of the second, outside, one that is ever done is only done to rule the heart within.

Now you ask what rule you anchoresses must keep. You must in all ways, with all your might and strength, keep the inner – and the outer for her sake. The inner is always the same, the outer is variable. For each must keep the outer according as she may best serve the inner with it. Now, then, it is the case that all anchoresses can properly keep one rule, *quantum ad puritatem cordis circa quam uersatur tota religio*[c] – that is, all can and ought to keep a rule in respect of purity of heart, that is, clean and pure inner judgement (*consciencia*),[6] without the guilt of sin which has not been atoned for through confession. This the lady rule does, which rules and directs and smooths the heart and the conscience of sin, for nothing makes it crooked except sin alone. Righting it and smoothing it are the goodness and all the strength of each religious profession and each order. This rule is made not by man's invention,

a 'Extend,' says the Psalmist, 'thy mercy to them that know thee' by true faith, 'and thy justice' · that is, rightness of life – 'to them that have a right heart' (Psalm 35.11) – those, in fact, who direct all their will in accordance with the rule of the divine will. These are called 'good' antonomastically. The Psalmist: 'Do good, Lord, to those that are good and to the right of heart' (Psalm 124.4); they are told that they should glory – in the witness of a good conscience, that is: 'Glory, all ye right of heart' (Psalm 31.11) – those whom, in fact, that supreme rule making everything right has made right; on which Augustine: 'Nothing must be sought contrary to the rule of authority'; and the Apostle: 'Let us all continue in the same rule' (Philippians 3.16).

b And this is bodily exercise which according to the Apostle is profitable to little (1 Timothy 4.8), and is, as it were, the rule of right mechanics, which is contained in right geometry.

ɔ In respect of purity of heart, with which all religion is concerned.

but by God's command. Therefore it is always the same without change, and all ought to keep it the same always. But all cannot keep one rule, and need not and ought not keep the outer rule in one way, *quantum scilicet ad obseruantias corporales*[7][a] – that is, in respect of bodily observances, according to the outer rule, which I called the handmaiden and which is man's invention, established for nothing else but to serve the inner. It makes people fast, keep vigil, wear cold and harsh clothes – other such hardships which the flesh of many can endure, of many not. Therefore this rule may change variously in accordance with each one's condition and nature. For one is strong, another weak and may very well be excused and please God with less. One is a scholar, another not and must work the more and say her prayers in another way. One is old and frail and the less feared for; another is young and lovely and needs to be better guarded. Therefore each anchoress must observe the outer rule according to the advice of her confessor, and whatever he commands and orders her under obedience, who is familiar with her condition and knows her strength. He may change the outer rule as wisdom dictates, as he sees that the inner may be best kept.

No anchoress, on my advice, shall make a profession – that is, take vows of obligation – except to three things, which are obedience, chastity and fixity of place – that she shall never more change that place, except out of necessity only (such as violence and fear of death, obedience to her bishop or his superior). For whoever takes a thing in hand and vows to God under obligation to do it, she binds herself to it and commits deadly sin in the breaking of it if she breaks it willingly. If she does not vow it, she may still do it and leave off whenever she wishes – for example, with food, with drink, forgoing flesh or fish – all other such things; with clothing, with sleeping, with the hours, with other prayers – saying so many, or in such a way. These and others of the kind are all matters of free choice, to be done or left off while one wishes and when one wishes, unless they have been vowed. But charity – that is, love and humility and patience, faithfulness and keeping the ten old commandments, confession and penitence – these and others like them, some of which are of the old law, some of the new, are not

a In respect, that is, of bodily observances.

3

the invention of man or a rule which man has established but are God' commandments, and therefore everyone has necessarily to keep them, and you above all, for these rule the heart. What I write is nearly all about its ruling – except at the beginning of the book and at the final conclusion. The things that I write here about the outer rule – you keep them all, my dear sisters, Our Lord be thanked, and shall do so, through his grace, better and better the longer you go on. And yet I do not wish that you should vow to keep them as obligations, for after that, whenever you broke any of them, it would hurt your heart too much and make you so afraid that you might soon – which God prevent from happening to you – fall into despair, that is, into a lack of hope and a lack of trust in being saved.[8] Therefore what I write for you, my dear sisters, about outer things in the first part of your book concerning your devotions, and especially in the last part, you must not vow; but have it in your heart and do it as if you had vowed it.

If any ignorant person asks you of what order you are, as some do, you tell me, who strain out the gnat and swallow the fly, answer 'Of St James's' – who was God's Apostle and for his great holiness called God's brother.[9] If such an answer seems to him remarkable and strange, ask him what order is and where he can find in Holy Writ religion more openly described and made apparent than in St James's canonical epistle. He says what religion is and what right order is: *Religio munda et immaculata apud Deum et Patrem hec est: uisitare pupillos et uiduas in necessitate sua, et immaculatum se custodire ab hoc seculo*[a] – that is, 'Pure and spotless religion is to visit and help widows and fatherless children and to keep oneself pure and unspotted from the world.' Thus St James describes religion and order. The latter part of his saying applies to recluses, for there are two parts, for the two kinds of religious there are: to each applies its part, as you may hear. Some good religious are in the world, especially prelates and faithful preachers, who have the first part of what St James said; they are, as he said, those who go to help widows and fatherless children. The soul is a widow who has lost her husband, that is, Jesus Christ, through any mortal sin;

---

a Religion clean and undefiled before God and the Father is this: to visit the fatherless and widows in their tribulation, and to keep oneself unspotted from this world (James 1.27).

similarly, he is fatherless who has through his sin lost the father of heaven. To go to visit such and comfort them and help them with the food of holy teaching – this is right religion, says St James. The latter part of this saying applies to your religious profession, as I said before, which protects you, above other religious, pure and unspotted from the world.[10] Thus the Apostle James, who describes religion, mentions neither white nor black in his order.[11] But many strain out the gnat and swallow the fly – that is, find great significance where there is the least. Paul, the first anchorite,[12] Antony[13] and Arsenius,[14] Macarius[15] and the others – were they not religious and of St James's order? Also St Sarah[16] and St Syncletica[17] and other such, both men and women, with their coarse mattresses and their hard hairshirts – were they not of a good order? And were they white or black, as foolish people, who think the order resides in the cloak, ask you? None the less, God knows, they were in fact both. Not, however, in respect of clothes, but in the way God's bride sings about herself, *Nigra sum, sed formosa*[a] – 'I am black and, nevertheless, white,' she says: uncomely without, pure within. In this way answer those who ask about whether your order is white or black. Say you are both of them, through God's grace, and of St James's order, as he wrote in the latter part: *Immaculatum se custodire ab hoc seculo*[b] – that is, as I said before, to keep oneself pure and unspotted from the world. Herein is religion, not in the wide hood, or in the black cape, or in the white surplice, or in the grey cowl. Where many are gathered together, there, for the sake of unanimity, one ought to attach great significance to uniformity of clothing and of other matters to do with outer things, so that the uniformity without may signify the uniformity of one love and of one will which they all have in common within. With their habit, which is one, which each has the same as the next, and also in other things, they cry out that they all have together one love and one will, each like the next. Look out that they do not lie! Thus it is in a community, but wherever a man or a woman lives on their own, hermit or anchorite, there is not much significance in things on the outside, from which scandal cannot come. Listen to Micah: *Indicabo tibi, O homo, quid sit*

a   I am black but beautiful (Canticles 1.4).
b   To keep oneself unspotted from this world (James 1.27).

...um et quid Deus requirat a te: utique facere iudicium et iusticiam et sollicite ambulare cum Domino Deo tuo [a] – 'I shall show,' the man says – the holy Micah, God's prophet – 'what is good, and what religion and what order, what holiness God asks of you.' See this; understand it. Do well and judge yourself weak all the time, and with fear and with love walk with God your Lord. Where these things are, there is right religion, there is true order, and to do all the rest and leave this is only trickery and a false deception. *Ve uobis, Scribe et Pharisei, ypocrite, qui mundatis quod deforis est calicis et parapsidis, intus autem pleni estis omni spurcitia similes sepulcris dealbatis.* [b] All that good religious do or wear in accordance with the outer rule, all of it together is for this. It is all only like a tool to build towards this; it is all only like a handmaiden to serve the lady in ruling the heart.

This one book is divided into eight smaller books.

Now, my dear sisters, I divide this book into eight distinctions,[18] which you call parts, and each, without mingling, speaks all by itself of separate things; and nevertheless each one comes properly after the other and the next is always joined to the one before.[19]

The first part speaks entirely about your devotions.

The second is how, through your five senses, to protect your heart, in which is order and religion and the soul's life. In this distinction are five chapters, like five pieces corresponding to the five senses, which protect the heart like watchmen, wherever they are faithful; and it speaks of each sense separately in order.

The third part is about birds of a certain kind which David in the Psalter likens himself to, as if he were an anchorite, and how the nature of these birds is like anchorites.

The fourth part is about both fleshly and spiritual temptations, and comfort in the face of them, and about their remedies.

The fifth part is about confession.

The sixth part is about penance.

a I will show thee, O man, what is good and what the Lord requireth of thee: verily, to do judgement and justice, and to walk solicitous with the Lord thy God (Micah 6.8).

b Woe to you, Scribes and Pharisees, hypocrites, who make clean the outside of the cup and of the dish, but within you are full of all uncleanness, like to whited sepulchres (Matthew 23.25, 27).

The seventh is about the pure heart, why one ought to and why one must love Jesus Christ, and what deprives us of his love and prevents us from loving him.

The eighth part is entirely about the outer rule. First, about food and drink and about other things which are to do with that. After that, about the things which you may accept and what things you may look after and possess. After that, about your clothing and about such things as are to do with that. After that, about your work, about hair-cutting and blood-letting, about your maids' rule. Lastly, how you must teach them lovingly.

PART ONE
Devotions

Here begins the first book, about hours and prayers which are good to say.[1]

When you first rise, bless yourself and say *In nomine Patris et Filii et Spiritui Sancti, Amen*,[a] and begin at once *Veni, Creator Spiritus*[2][b] with eyes and hands raised up to heaven, bending forward on your knees upon the bed; and say the whole hymn through like this, with the versicle *Emitte Spiritum tuum*[c] and the prayer *Deus, qui corda fidelium*.[d] After this, putting on your shoes and dressing, say *Pater noster*[e] and *Credo*.[3][f] *Iesu Criste, Fili Dei uiui, miserere nobis, qui de uirgine dignatus es nasci, miserere nobis*.[g] Say these words all the time until you are completely ready. Make much use of these words and keep them in your mouth often on every occasion that you can, whether you are sitting or standing.

When you are completely ready, sprinkle yourself with holy water, which you should always have, and think about God's flesh and his precious blood, which is above the high altar,[4] and fall down towards it with these greetings:

> *Ave, principium nostre creationis,*
> *Ave, precium nostre redemptionis,*

a In the name of the Father and of the Son and of the Holy Spirit, Amen.
b Come, Creator Spirit.
c Send forth thy Spirit (Psalm 103.30).
d O God, who [didst teach] the hearts of the faithful.
e Our Father.
f I believe.
g Jesus Christ, Son of the living God, have mercy on us, thou who deignedst to be born of a virgin, have mercy on us.

Aue, viaticum nostre peregrinationis,
Ave, premium nostre expectationis,
Aue solamen nostre sustentationis.

Tu esto nostrum gaudium,
Qui es futurus premium.
Sit nostra in te gloria
Per cuncta semper secula.

Mane nobiscum, Domine,
Noctem obscuram remoue,
Omne delictum ablue,
Piam medelam tribue.

Gloria tibi, Domine,
Qui natus es de uirgine
Cum Patri, et cetera.[5a]

You must do likewise when the priest holds it up at the mass and before
the *Confiteor*,[b] when you are to receive communion. After this, fall on
your knees to your crucifix with the five greetings in remembrance of
God's five wounds.

Adoramus te, Christe, et benedicimus tibi, quia per sanctam crucem redemisti
   mundum.[c]

Tuam crucem adoramus, Domine. Tuam gloriosam recolimus passionem.
   Miserere nostri, qui passus es pro nobis.[d]

---

a Hail, foundation of our creation,/ Hail, price of our redemption,/ Hail, viaticum
   of our pilgrimage,/Hail, reward of our expectation,/ Hail, consolation of our
   waiting.
   Be thou our joy,/ Who will be our reward./ May our glory be in thee/Through all
   time, always.
   Remain with us, Lord,/ Remove dark night,/ Wash away all sin,/ Give holy relief.
   Glory to thee, Lord,/ Who wert born of a virgin/ With the Father, etc.
b I confess.
c We adore thee, Christ, and bless thee, because through the holy cross thou hast
   redeemed the world.
d We adore thy cross, Lord. We commemorate thy glorious passion. Have mercy
   on us, thou who suffered for us.

Salue, crux sancta,

Arbor digna,

Cuius robur preciosum

Mundi tulit talentum.[a]

Salue, crux, que in corpore Christi dedicata es et ex membris eius tanquam margaritis ornata.[b]

O crux, lignum triumphale,

Mundi uera salus, uale.

Inter ligna nullum tale

Fronde, flore, germine.

Medicina christiana,

Salua sanas, egras sana.[6c]

And beat on your breast with these words: *Quod non ualet uis humana sit in tuo nomine.*[d] Whoever does not know these five should say the first, *Adoramus te,*[e] kneeling, five times. And bless yourself at each of these greetings and with these words: *Miserere nostri, qui passus es pro nobis,*[f] beat your heart and kiss the earth, having crossed it with your thumb. After that, go to the image of Our Lady and kneel with five *Aues.*[g] Lastly, bow your knee to the other images and to your relics, especially to the saints to whom you have, out of love, dedicated your altars, particularly so if any of them has been consecrated.

After that immediately, Our Lady's Matins; and say it in this way. If it is a work day, fall to the earth;[7] if it is a holy day, bowing down a little, say *Pater noster* and *Credo*, both quietly. Stand up after that and say *Domine, labia mea aperies.*[h] Make a cross on your mouth with your thumb. At *Deus, in adiutorium,*[i] a large cross with your thumb and your

---

a Hail, holy cross,/ Worthy tree,/ Whose precious strength/ Bore the price of the world.

b Hail, cross, thou who wert dedicated to the body of Christ and decorated with his limbs as if with pearls.

c O cross, triumphant wood,/ True salvation of the world, hail./ Among trees there is none such/ In leaf, in flower, in seed./ Christian medicine,/ Save the healthy, heal the sick.

d What human strength cannot do, in thy name, let it be.

e We adore you.

f Have mercy on us, who didst suffer for us.

g Hail [Mary]s.

h Lord, thou wilt open my lips (Psalm 50.17).

i God, [come] to [my] assistance (Psalm 69.2).

two fingers from above the forehead down to the breast and fall to the earth, if it is a work day, with *Gloria Patri*,[a] or bow down if it is a holy day until *Sicut erat*.[b] Thus at each *Gloria Patri* and at the beginning of the *Venite*[c] and in the *Venite* at *Venite adoremus*[d] and at the *Aue Maria*[e] and wherever you hear Mary's name uttered and at any *Pater noster* that occurs in your hours and at the *Credo* and at the collect for every hour and at the last verse of every hymn and at the last verse but one of the psalm *Benedicite, omnia opera Domini, Domino*.[8][f] At all these, if it is a holy day, bow down a little; if it is a work day, fall to the earth. At the beginning of every hour, at *Deus, in adiutorium*, make the sign of the cross, as I taught earlier. At *Veni, Creator*[g] bow or kneel, depending on what day it is. At *Memento, salutis auctor*,[h] always fall down and at these words, *Nascendo formam sumpseris*,[i] kiss the earth and likewise in the *Te Deum laudamus*[j] at these words, *Non horruisti uirginis uterum*,[k] and at the mass in the great *Credo*[9] at *Ex Maria uirgine et homo factus est*.[l]

Let everyone say her hours as she has written them down[10] and say each hour separately, as far as you can at its own time – rather too soon than too late, if you ever cannot keep to the time. Matins by night in winter, in summer at daybreak (this winter shall begin at the day of the Holy Cross in Autumn[11] and last until Easter). Prime in winter early, in summer by mid-morning; *Pretiosa*[12][m] after that. If because of any emergency you need to speak, you must say it immediately before and after Matins, if there be such a need. None always after food (and when you sleep, after sleep), while summer lasts, except when you fast. In winter before food, when you are all fasting all the time – Sundays,

a Glory [be to] the Father.
b As it was [in the beginning].
c Come, [let us praise the Lord] (Psalm 94).
d Come, let us adore (Psalm 94.6).
e Hail Mary.
f Bless the Lord, all ye works of the Lord.
g Come, Creator [Spirit].
h Remember, author of salvation.
i In being born thou didst assume [our] form.
j We praise thee, O God.
k Thou didst not abhor the Virgin's womb.
l [And was incarnate] of the Virgin Mary and was made man.
m Precious [in the sight of the Lord is the death of his saints] (Psalm 115.15).

however, after food, for you eat twice. At the first psalm you must stand, if you are well able, and at the other sit, and always at *Gloria Patri* stand up and bow. Whoever can stand all the time in honour of Our Lady, let her stand in God's name. At all the seven hours, say *Pater noster* and *Aue Maria* both before and after; *Fidelium anime*[a] after each hour before the *Pater noster*. At three hours, say *Credo* with the *Pater noster*: before Matins and after Prime and after Compline; and from your Compline until after *Pretiosa*, keep silence.

After Evensong,[13] say your *Placebo*[14][b] at once each night, when you are well able, unless it is the holy night for a feast of nine lessons which is to come in the morning.[15] Before Compline or after Matins, *Dirige*[16][c] with three psalms and with three lessons, every single night. On anniversaries of your dearest friends, say all nine; instead of *Gloria* at the end of each psalm, *Requiem eternam dona eis, Domine, et lux perpetua luceat eis.*[d] At *Placebo*, sit until *Magnificat*[e] – likewise at *Dirige*, except at the lessons and at the *Miserere*,[f] and from *Laudate*[g] to the end. Say *Requiescant in pace*[h] instead of *Benedicamus*[i] at the end. In the morning or at night after the suffrages of Matins, say the Commendation,[17] the psalms sitting, the prayers kneeling or standing. If you do this each night except Sunday night only, you will do much the better. On a one-meal day we[18] say both *Placebo* and *Dirige* after the food graces, on a two-meal day after None – and you may do likewise.

Say the Seven Psalms[19] sitting or kneeling with the Litany. Say the Fifteen Psalms[20] in this way: the first five for yourself, the second five for the peace of all Holy Church, the third five for all Christian souls. After the first five, *Kyrie eleison, Christe eleison, Kyrie eleison; Pater noster ... et ne nos; Saluos fac seruos tuos et ancillas tuas, Deus meus, sperantes in te. Oremus: Deus, cui proprium est.*[j] After the second five

a The souls of the faithful.
b I will please [the Lord] (Psalm 114.9).
c Direct, [Lord] (Psalm 5.9).
d Eternal rest grant them, Lord, and let light perpetual shine on them.
e [My soul doth] magnify [the Lord] (Luke 1.46–55).
f Have mercy on me (Psalm 50).
g Praise ye [the Lord] (Psalm 148).
h May they rest in peace.
i Let us bless [the Lord].
j Lord, have mercy, Christ, have mercy, Lord, have mercy. Our Father ... and

likewise, *Kyrie eleison, Christe eleison, Kyrie eleison; Pater noster ... et ne nos; Domine, fiat pax in uirtute tua, et abundancia in turribus tuis. Oremus: Ecclesie tue quesumus, Domine, preces placatus.*[a] After the third five, which you must say without *Gloria Patri, Kyrie eleison iii; Pater noster ... et ne nos; A porta inferi erue, Domine, animas eorum. Oremus: Fidelium, Deus, omnium.*[b] Say the Seven Psalms and the Fifteen in this way about noon, for about the time that mass is sung in all religious orders and Our Lord suffered pain upon the cross,[21] you ought especially to be at prayers and supplications, and also from Prime until mid-morning when priests in the world[22] sing their masses.

You may, if you wish, say your *Pater nosters* in this way: 'Almighty God, Father, Son, Holy Ghost, as you three are one God, so you are one power, one wisdom and one love; and yet power is referred to you particularly in Holy Writ, you precious Father, to you wisdom, blessed Son, and to you love, Holy Ghost.[23] Give me, one Almighty God, threefold in three persons, these same three things – power to serve you, wisdom to please you, love and will to do it; power so that I can do it; wisdom to know how to do it; love so that I wish to do always what is dearest to you. As you are full of each good, so there is no good wanting where these three, power, wisdom and love, are joined together: may you grant me them, Holy Trinity, in your honour.' Three *Pater nosters; Credo*; the versicle *Benedicamus Patrem et Filium cum Spiritu Sancto; laudemus et super exaltemus eum in secula. Oremus: Omnipotens sempiterne Deus, qui dedisti famulis tuis in confessione uere fidei eternae gloriam agnoscere. Alpha et Omega,*[24][c] whoever has it – or let them say another of the Holy Trinity if they want.

'Ah, Jesus, your mercy, Jesus for my sins hung on the cross, for

[lead] us not ... Save thy servants and thy handmaids, my God, who hope in thee. Let us pray: God, whose property it is [to have mercy].

a Lord, may there be peace in thy strength, and abundance in thy towers (Psalm 121.7). Let us pray: We beseech thee, Lord, mercifully receive the prayers of your Church.

b From the gate of hell, deliver, Lord, their souls. Let us pray: God, [Creator and Redeemer] of all the faithful.

c Let us bless the Father and the Son with the Holy Spirit; let us praise him and exalt him above all for ever. Let us pray: Almighty, eternal God, who hast granted to your servants to acknowledge in confession of the true faith the glory of the eternal [Trinity]. Alpha and Omega.

those five wounds[25] from which you bled on it, heal my bleeding soul of all the sins with which, through my five senses, it is wounded. In the remembrance of them, may it be so, precious Lord' – five *Pater nosters*; the versicle *Omnis terra adoret te et psalmum dicat nomini tuo. Oremus: Iuste Iudex*[a] if you know it, or another of the Cruces:[26] *Deus, qui unigeniti tui Domini nostri Iesu Christi pretioso sanguine uexillum sancte crucis*[b] – this is one of the best.

'For the seven gifts of the Holy Ghost,[27] that I may have them, and for the seven hours which Holy Church sings,[28] that I may share in them whether I sleep or wake, and for the seven supplications in the *Pater noster*[29] against the seven capital and deadly sins,[30] that you should protect me against them and all their offspring and give me the seven happy blessednesses[31] which you have, Lord, promised to your chosen in your blessed name' – seven *Pater nosters*; *Emitte spiritum tuum. Oremus: Deus, cui cor omne patet. Ecclesie tue quesumus, Domine. Exaudi quesumus, Domine, supplicum preces.*[c]

'For the ten commandments which I have broken, some or all, and whatever there may be of other things unfaithfully tithed by myself to you – in remedy of these breaches, to reconcile myself to you, precious Lord' – ten *Pater nosters*; the versicle *Ego dixi, Domine, miserere mei. Oremus: Deus, cui proprium est miserere.*[d]

'In honour, Jesus Christ, of your twelve Apostles, that I may in all things follow their teaching, that I may have through their prayers the twelve boughs which blossom from Charity, as St Paul writes,[32] blessed Lord' – twelve *Pater nosters*; the versicle *Annuntiauerunt opera Dei et facta eius intellexerunt. Oremus: Exaudi nos, Deus, Salutaris Noster, et Apostolorum tuorum nos tuere presidiis.*[e]

a Let all the earth worship thee and sing a psalm to thy name. Let us pray; Just Judge.

b God, who by the precious blood of thine only begotten [Son], Our Lord Jesus Christ, [didst wish to sanctify] the standard of the holy cross.

c Send forth thy spirit [and they shall be created and thou shalt renew the face of the earth] (Psalm 103.30). Let us pray: God, to whom every heart is open. We beseech thee, Lord, [hear the prayers] of thy Church. Hear, we pray, Lord, the prayers of suppliants.

d I have said, Lord, have mercy upon me. Let us pray: God, whose property it is to have mercy.

e They declared the works of the Lord and understood his deeds. Let us pray: Hear us, Lord, Our Saviour, and watch over us with the protection of thine Apostles.

The saints whom you love best, in their honour say either less or more, as your heart inclines, and the versicle afterwards with their collect.

'For all those who have done me, said to me, or wished me any good, and for all those who do the six works of mercy,[33] merciful Lord' – six *Pater nosters*; the versicle *Dispersit, dedit pauperibus. Iusticia eius manet. Oremus: Retribuere dignare.*[a] Let whoever wishes say the psalm *Ad te leuaui*[b] before the *Pater nosters* and *Kyrie eleison, Christe eleison, Kyrie eleison.*

'For all the souls who have departed in the faith of the four Gospels which hold up all Christendom on four sides, that you should give them the four marriage-gifts in heaven,[34] merciful Lord' – four *Pater nosters*. If you say nine, as there are nine hosts of angels,[35] that God through his mercy may hasten them out of pain into their fellowship, you do still better. And here also, if you wish, say *De profundis*[c] before the *Pater noster*, and *Kyrie eleison* three times; the versicle *A porta inferi. Oremus: Fidelium.*[d]

During the day some time, or the night, gather in your heart all the sick and sorrowful who endure misery and poverty, the pains that prisoners endure and feel where they lie, heavily fettered with iron, especially of the Christians who are in heathen parts, some in prison, some in as great servitude as an ox or an ass is. Have pity on those who are under severe temptations. Set all their sorrows in your heart and sigh to Our Lord that he take pity on them and look towards them with the eye of his mercy. And if you have time, say the psalm *Leuaui oculos*;[e] *Pater noster*; the versicle *Conuertere, Domine – usquequo? Et deprecabilis esto super seruos tuos. Oremus: Pretende, Domine, famulis et famulabus.*[f]

In the mass, when the priest raises up God's body, say this verse

---

a He hath dispersed, he hath given to the poor. His justice remaineth for [ever]. Let us pray: Deign to reward.

b To thee have I lifted up [my eyes] (Psalm 122).

c Out of the depths [I have cried to thee] (Psalm 129).

d From the gate of hell [deliver, Lord, their souls]. Let us pray: [God, Creator and Redeemer of all] the faithful.

e I have lifted up my eyes [unto the hills] (Psalm 120).

f Return, Lord: How long? And be open to the prayers of thy servants. Let us pray: Stretch forth, Lord, to [thy] servants and handmaids [the right hand of thy heavenly help].

standing: *Ecce salus mundi, uerbum Patris, hostia uera, riua caro, deitas integra, uerus homo,*[a] and then fall down with these greetings:

> *Ave, principium nostre creationis,*
> *Aue, precium nostre redemptionis,*
> *Aue, viaticum nostre peregrinationis,*
> *Aue, premium nostre expectationis,*
> *Aue, solacium nostrae sustentationis.*
>
> *Tu esto nobis gaudium,*
> *Qui es futurus premium.*
> *Sit nostra in te gloria*
> *Per cuncta semper secula. Amen.*
>
> *Mane nobiscum, Domine.*
>
> *Gloria tibi, Domine.*[b]

Set quis est locus in me quo ueniat in me Deus meus, quo Deus ueniat aut maneat in me, Deus qui fecit celum et terram? Itane, Domine, Deus meus, est quicquam in me quod capiat te? Quis michi dabit ut uenias in cor meum et inebries illud et unum bonum meum amplectar te? Quis michi es? Miserere ut loquar. Angusta est tibi domus anime mee. Quo uenias ad eam, dilatetur abs te. Ruinosa est; refice eam. Habet que offendant oculos tuos – fateor et scio – set quis mundabit eam? Aut cui alteri preter te clamabo? Ab ocultis meis munda me, Domine, et ab alienis parce famule tue. Miserere, miserere. Miserere mei, Deus, secundum magnam[36 c] – and so all the psalm to the end with *Gloria Patri; Christe*

---

a Behold, the salvation of the world, the word of the Father, the true victim, living flesh, complete godhead, true man.

b Hail, foundation of our creation,/Hail, price of our redemption,/Hail, viaticum of our pilgrimage,/Hail, reward of our expectation,/Hail, consolation of our waiting.

Be thou our joy,/Who will be our reward./May our glory be in thee/Through all time, always. Amen.

Remain with us, Lord.

Glory to thee, Lord.

c But what is the place in me where my God may come into me, where God may come or remain in me, God who made heaven and earth? Is there, Lord, my God, anything in me that may contain thee? Who will grant me that thou come into my heart and make it drunk and that I embrace thee, my one good? What art thou to *audi nos*[a] twice; *Kyrie eleison, Christe eleison, Kyrie eleison; Pater noster; Credo ... carnis resurrectionem et uitam eternam. Amen. Saluam fac famulam tuam, Deus meus, sperantem in te. Doce me facere uoluntatem tuam, quia Deus meus es tu. Domine, exaudi orationem meam et clamor meus ad te ueniat. Oremus: Concede, quesumus, omnipotens Deus, ut quem enigmatice et sub aliena spetie cernimus, quo sacramentaliter cibamur in terris, fatie ad fatiem eum uideamus eo sicuti est ueraciter et realiter frui mereamur in celis, per eundem Dominum.*[b] After the mass-kiss,[37] when the priest consecrates, there forget all the world, there be entirely out of the body, there in gleaming love embrace your beloved, who has alighted into the bower of your breast from heaven, and hold him tight until he has granted you all that ever you ask.[38] This prayer before the great cross is of great strength.

About midday, whoever can (whoever cannot then, at some other time), let her think about God's cross as much as ever she knows how or is able, and of his terrible pain, and begin after that those same five greetings that are written above,[39] and also kneel at each one and bless herself, as it says there, and beat her breast and make a prayer of this sort: *Adoramus te Christe. Tuam crucem. Salue crux, que. O crux lignum.*[c] Arise then and begin the antiphon *Salua nos, Christe Saluator, per uirtutem sancte crucis*[d] with the sign of the cross and say standing the psalm

me? Have mercy so that I may speak. The house of my soul is narrow for thee. So that thou mayst come to it, let it be enlarged by thee. It is in ruins; remake it. It has what may offend thine eyes – I know it and confess it – but who will purify it? Or to whom other than thee shall I cry? Cleanse me from my secret faults, Lord, and from those of others spare thy servant. Have mercy, have mercy. Have mercy on me, God, according to [thy] great [mercy] (Psalm 50).

a Glory [be] to the Father; Christ, hear us.

b Lord have mercy, Christ have mercy, Lord have mercy. Our Father; I believe [in] ... the resurrection of the body and the life everlasting. Amen. Save thy servant, my God, who hopes in thee. Teach me to do thy will, because thou art my God. Lord, hear my prayer and let my cry come unto thee. Let us pray: Grant, we beseech [thee], omnipotent God, that him whom we discern obscurely and under another form, on whom we feed sacramentally on earth, we may see face to face, and deserve to enjoy him in heaven as he is truly and really, through the same Lord.

c We adore thee, Christ. [We adore] thy cross. Hail, cross, thou who [wert dedicated to the body of Christ]. O cross [, triumphant] wood.

d Save us, Saviour Christ, through the power of the holy cross.

Iubilate[a] with *Gloria Patri*, and then always say the antiphon thus: *Salua nos, Christe Saluator, per uirtutem sancte crucis* and bless yourself at *Qui saluasti Petrum in mare, miserere nobis*[b] and beat the breast and then fall down and say *Christe audi nos, Iesu Christe audi nos; Kyrie eleison, Christe eleison, Kyrie eleison; Pater noster . . . et ne nos,*[c] the versicle *Protector noster aspice, Deus, et respice in faciem Christi tui. Oremus: Deus qui sanctam crucem*[d] as before. Afterwards begin *Adoramus,*[e] all five as before. *Salua nos, Christe;*[f] the antiphon as before; the psalm *Ad te leuaui,*[g] the antiphon as before to the end, and then, as before, fall to the earth. *Oremus: Christe, audi nos*[h] twice; *Kyrie* three times; *Pater noster . . . et ne nos*; the versicle *Protector noster*[i] as before. *Oremus: Adesto, quesumus, Domine, Deus noster, et quos sancte crucis letari facis;*[j] the third time just the same and the fourth time and the fifth. Change nothing except the psalms and the prayers: the first psalm *Iubilate*, the second *Ad te leuaui*, the third *Qui confidunt,*[k] the fourth *Domine, non est exaltatum,*[l] the fifth *Laudate Dominum in sanctis eius*[m] – and in each there are five verses. The five prayers are: *Deus qui sanctam crucem*; *Adesto, quesumus, Domine*; *Deus, qui pro nobis Filium tuum*; *Deus, qui unigeniti*; *Iuste Iudex;*[n] with *O beata et intemerata*[o] – and whoever does not know these five prayers, say one all the time. And whoever thinks it too long, leave out the psalms.

a Be joyful (Psalm 99).
b Thou who savedst Peter on the sea, have mercy on us.
c Christ hear us, Jesus Christ hear us; Lord have mercy, Christ have mercy, Lord have mercy; Our Father . . . [lead] us not.
d Behold, God, Our Protector, and look upon the face of your Christ. Let us pray: God, who [didst ascend] the holy cross.
e We adore.
f Save us, Christ
g To thee have I lifted up [my eyes] (Psalm 122).
h Let us pray: Christ, hear us.
i [Behold, God,] Our Protector.
j Let us pray: Be present, we beseech [thee], Lord, Our God, and those thou makest rejoice in [the honour of] the holy cross [defend also by its perpetual aid].
k They that trust (Psalm 124).
l Lord, [my heart] is not exalted (Psalm 130).
m Praise ye the Lord in his holy places (Psalm 150).
n God, who [didst ascend] the holy cross; be present, we beseech [thee], Lord; God, who [didst consent that] thy Son [should suffer] for us; God, who [with the precious blood] of thy only begotten [Son]; Just Judge.
o O blessed and undefiled.

'Lady St Mary, for that great joy[40] which you had within you at that time when Jesus, God, God's Son, after the angel's greeting took flesh and blood in you and of you, accept my greeting with the same *Aue*[a] and make me take little account of each outer joy, but comfort me within and send me those of heaven. And as surely as in that flesh which he took of you there was never sin, nor in yours, as we believe, after that taking, whatever there may have been before,[41] cleanse my soul of fleshly sins.' Begin the *Aue* until *Dominus tecum*[b] as one begins the antiphon, and then the psalm, and after the psalm right through five times – and thus for each psalm – *Aue Maria, gratia plena, Dominus tecum*; *Magnificat*;[c] *Aue Maria* right through five times.

'Lady St Mary, for the great bliss which you had when you saw that blessed babe born of your pure body for the healing of mankind, without any breach,[42] with virginity intact and a virgin's honour, heal me who am all broken, so I fear, through my will, whatever the case with my deeds, and grant me to see in heaven your blessed face and at least to behold the virgins' honour, if I am not worthy to be blessed in their company.' *Aue Maria, gratia plena, Dominus tecum*; *Ad Dominum cum tribularer*; *Aue*[d] as before, five times.

'Lady St Mary, for that great bliss which you had when you saw your dear precious Son after his terrible death arise to blessed life, his body seven times brighter than the sun, grant that I may die with him and arise in him, die to the world, live in the spirit, share his pain in fellowship on earth so as to be his fellow in heaven. For that great bliss that you had, Lady, in his blessed arising after your great sorrow, after the sorrow in which I am here, lead me to your bliss.' *Aue Maria, gratia plena, Dominus tecum*; *Retribue seruum tuum*; *Aue*[e] – five times.

'Lady St Mary, for that great bliss which you had when you saw your bright blessed Son, whom the Jews thought to stifle in the tomb, so gloriously and so powerfully ascend on Holy Thursday to his bliss, into his kingdom of heaven, grant that I with him may cast all the

a Hail [Mary].
b The Lord is with thee.
c Hail Mary, full of grace, the Lord is with thee; [My soul] doth magnify [the Lord] (Luke, 1.46–55).
d Hail Mary, etc.; In my trouble I [cried] to the Lord (Psalm 119); Hail [Mary].
e Hail Mary, etc.; Give bountifully to thy servant (Psalm 118.17ff.); Hail [Mary].

world under foot and ascend – now, in my heart; when I die, in spirit; on Judgement Day, in the body, to heavenly joys.' *Aue Maria, gratia plena, Dominus tecum; In conuertendo; Aue*[a] – five times.

'Lady St Mary, for that great bliss which filled all the earth when he received you into immeasurable joy and with his blessed arms set you on the throne and a queen's crown on your head, brighter than the sun, high heavenly queen, so receive these greetings from me on earth that I may blessedly greet you in heaven.' *Aue Maria, gratia plena, Dominus tecum; Ad te leuaui; Aue*[b] – five times and then the versicle *Spiritus Sanctus superueniet in te et uirtus Altissimi obumbrabit tibi. Oremus: Gra'iam tuam.*[c] Antiphon:

> *Ave, Regina celorum,*
> *Aue, Domina angelorum,*
> *Salue, Radix Sancta,*
> *Ex qua mundo lux est orta.*
> *Vale, ualde decora,*
> *Et pro nobis semper Christum exora.*[d]

Versicle: *Egredietur uirga de radice Iesse et flos de radice eius ascendet. Oremus: Deus, qui uirginalem aulam.*[e] Antiphon:

> *Gaude, Dei genetrix, Uirgo inmaculata,*
> *Gaude, que gaudium ab angelo suscepisti,*
> *Gaude, que genuisti eterni luminis claritatem,*
> *Gaude, mater,*
> *Gaude, sancta Dei genetrix Uirgo,*
> *Tu sola mater innupta,*
> *Te laudat omnis Filii tui creatura, genetricem lucis,*
> *Sis pro nobis pia interuentrix.*[a]

a Hail Mary, etc.; [When the Lord] brought back [the captivity of Sion] (Psalm 125); Hail [Mary].
b Hail Mary, etc.; To thee have I lifted up [my eyes] (Psalm 122).
c The Holy Spirit shall come upon thee and the power of the Most High shall overshadow thee (Luke 1.35). Let us pray: [Pour forth] thy grace.
d Hail, Queen of heaven,/ Hail, Lady of angels,/ Greetings, Holy Root,/ From whom light has risen for the world./ Hail, most fair,/ And always beseech Christ for us.
e There shall come forth a rod out of the root of Jesse and a flower shall rise up out of his root (Isaiah 11.1). Let us pray: God, who [deigned to choose] the virginal hall.

Versicle: *Ecce, uirgo concipiet et pariet filium et uocabitur nomen eius Emmanuel. Oremus: Deus, qui de beate Marie uirginis utero.*[b] Antiphon:

> *Gaude, Uirgo,*
> *Gaude, Dei genetrix,*
> *Et gaude, gaudium, Maria, omnium fidelium.*
> *Gaudeat ecclesia in tuis laudibus assidua,*
> *Et, pia Domina, gaudere fac nos tecum ante Dominum.*[c]

Versicle: *Ecce, concipies in utero et paries filium et uocabis nomen eius Iesum. Oremus: Deus, qui salutis eterne beate Marie uirginitate fecunda humanum genus.*[d] Antiphon:

> *Alma Redemptoris Mater, que peruia celi*
> *Porta manes et stella maris, succurre cadenti*
> *Surgere qui curat populo; tu que genuisti*
> *Natura mirante tuum sanctum genitorem,*
> *Uirgo prius ac posterius, Gabrielis ab ore*
> *Sumens illud Aue, peccatorum miserere.*[43][e]

Here sit for the *Aues*, fifty or a hundred, or more or less, depending on the time there is. Finally, the versicle *Ecce ancilla Domini. Fiat michi*

a   Rejoice, mother of God, immaculate virgin,/Rejoice, thou who didst receive joy from the angel,/Rejoice, thou who didst beget the clarity of eternal light,/Rejoice, mother,/Rejoice, holy mother of God, Virgin,/Thou alone mother and Virgin,/Every creature of thy Son praises thee, begetter of light,/May thou be for us a gracious intercessor.

b   Behold, a virgin shall conceive and bear a son, and his name shall be called Emmanuel (Isaiah 7.14). Let us pray: God, who from the womb of the blessed Virgin Mary.

c   Rejoice, Virgin,/Rejoice, mother of God,/And rejoice, Mary, joy of all the faithful./Let the Church rejoice without ceasing in thy praises,/And, gracious Lady, make us rejoice with thee before the Lord.

d   Behold, thou shalt conceive in thy womb and bear a son and shalt call his name Jesus (Luke 1.31). Let us pray: God, who through the fruitful virginity of Mary [didst secure the reward] of eternal salvation for mankind.

e   Bountiful Mother of the Redeemer, who of heaven the open/Gate art always and star of the sea, help the falling/People, who look to rise; thou who didst beget,/While Nature marvelled, thy holy begetter,/Virgin before and after, from Gabriel's mouth/Receiving that 'Hail!', have mercy on sinners.

secundum uerbum tuum. Oremus: O sancta Uirgo uirginum.[44][a] Whoever wishes may stop before, immediately after the first prayer, *Gratiam tuam*,[b] and let her then say her sum of *Aues* after the last psalm, *Ad te leuaui.*[c] Before the psalm always begin an *Aue* to *Dominus tecum*[d] and say the psalm standing. The psalms are chosen in accordance with the five letters of Our Lady's name,[45] if you look carefully, and all this prayer to do with her five highest blisses runs by fives. Reckon up in the antiphons and you will find in them five greetings. The prayers which I have only indicated are written everywhere, except the last. Have written on a scroll whatever you do not know. I sometimes begin my *Aues* like this:

'Lady, sweet Lady, sweetest of all ladies, Lady, dearest Lady, loveliest Lady, *O pulcherrima mulierum,*[e] Lady St Mary, precious Lady, Lady queen of heaven, Lady queen of mercy, Lady show me mercy, Lady maiden mother, maiden, God's mother, Jesus Christ's mother, mother of mercy, mother of grace.

> *O Uirgo uirginum,*
> *Maria, mater gratie,*
> *Mater misericordie,*
> *Tu nos ab hoste protege*
> *Et hora mortis suscipe.*
> *Per tuum, Uirgo, Filium,*
> *Per Patrem, Paraclitum,*
> *Assis presens ad obitum*
> *Nostrumque mundi exitum.*
> *Gloria tibi, Domine,*
> *Qui natus es de uirgine, et cetera.'*[f]

a Behold the handmaid of the Lord. Be it done unto me according to thy word (Luke 1.38). Let us pray: O holy Virgin of virgins [, who didst bring forth thy Son, the vanquisher of Satan].

b [Grant us] thy grace.

c To thee have I lifted up [my eyes] (Psalm 122).

d The Lord is with thee.

e O most beautiful of women.

f O Virgin of virgins,/Mary, mother of grace/Mother of mercy,/Thou protect us from the enemy/And support us at the hour of death./Through thy Son, Virgin,/Through the Father and the Paraclete,/Be present at our passing/

And fall to the earth and kiss it at this last verse, whoever is in good health, and then *Aues*, in tens together, the tenth always going like this: *Aue Maria, gratia plena, Dominus tecum. Benedicta tu in mulieribus et beatus fructus uentri tui. Spiritus Sanctus superueniet in te et uirtus Altissimi obumbrabit tibi. Ideoque et quod nascetur ex te sanctum uocabitur Filius Dei. Ecce ancilla Domini, fiat michi secundum uerbum tuum*[a] – and kiss the earth at the end, or a step or a bench or something higher, and begin 'Lady, sweet Lady', as previously the first ten. The first ten kneeling up and down; the second kneeling upright, still, except at the *Aue Maria* some small movement with the other knee a little; the third ten down and upon the elbows right to the ground. The fourth the elbows on a step or on a bench, and always for the *Aue* bow with the head. The fifth ten standing; and afterwards begin the sequence as at the beginning.

All that you ever say of other prayers of this sort, such as *Pater nosters* and *Aues* in your own way, psalms and prayers – I am well pleased. Let each one say them as her heart most inclines: reciting verses of the Psalter, reading of English or of French,[46] holy meditations, your kneelings – whenever you can, attend to them, before food and after. Always as you do more, so may God increase further for you his precious grace. But look, so I beg you, that you are never idle,[47] but work or read or are at prayer, and thus are always doing something from which good may arise. If you want to say the hours of the Holy Ghost,[48] say each hour of them before the hour of Our Lady.

Listen to the priest's hours as far as you can;[49] but you must not recite verses or sing so that he can hear it. Your graces standing, before food and after, as they are written for you, and at the *Miserere*[b] go before your altar and there end your graces. Whoever wants to drink between meals, let her say: *Benedicite. Potum nostrum Filius Dei benedicat, in nomine Patris*[c] and bless herself afterwards. *Adiutorium nostrum in*

And at our going forth from the world./Glory to thee, Lord,/Who wast born of a virgin, etc

a Hail Mary, [etc.]. Blessed art thou among women and blessed is the fruit of thy womb (Luke 1.42). The Holy Spirit shall come upon thee and the power of the Most High shall overshadow thee. And therefore also that holy thing which shall be born of thee shall be called the Son of God (Luke 1.35). Behold the handmaid of the Lord, be it done unto me according to thy word (Luke 1.38).

b Have mercy [on me, Lord] (Psalm 50).

c Bless [the Lord]. May the Son of God bless this drink, in the name of the Father.

nomine Domini, qui fecit celum et terram. Sit nomen Domini benedictum, ex hoc nunc et usque in seculum. Benedicamus Domino. Deo gratias.[a]

Whenever you go to your bed at night or in the evening, fall on your knees and think in what you have during the day angered Our Lord, and cry to him earnestly for mercy and forgiveness. If you have done any good, thank him for his gift, without whom we cannot either do well or think well, and say *Miserere* and *Kyrie eleison, Christe eleison, Kyrie eleison, Pater noster . . . et ne nos;*[b] the versicle *Saluas fac ancillas tuas, Deus meus, sperantes in te. Oremus: Deus, cui proprium est*[c] and standing *Visita, Domine, habitationem istam*[d] and lastly then *Christus vincit* † *Christus regnat* † *Christus imperat* †[e] with three crosses with the thumb upon the forehead and then *Ecce crucem Domini; fugite partes aduerse; vicit leo de tribu Iuda, radix David; Alleluia.*[f] A large cross, as at *Deus, in adiutorium,*[g] for *Ecce crucem Domini*[h] and then four crosses on four sides with these next four sentences:

> *Crux* † *fugat omne malum,*
> *Crux* † *est reparatio rerum.*
> *Per crucis hoc signum* †
> *Fugiat procul omne malignum,*
> *Et per idem signum* †
> *Saluetur quodque benignum.*[501]

a Our help is in the name of the Lord who made heaven and earth. May the name of the Lord be blessed from this time forth. Let us bless the Lord. Thanks [be] to God.

b Lord have mercy, Christ have mercy, Lord have mercy; Our Father . . . [lead] us not.

c Save thy handmaids, my God, who hope in thee. Let us pray: God, whose property it is [to have mercy].

d Visit, Lord, this dwelling.

e Christ conquers. Christ reigns. Christ rules.

f Behold the cross of the Lord; flee, enemy forces; the lion of the tribe of Judah, the root of David, has conquered; alleluia.

g God, [come] to [my] assistance (Psalm 69.2).

h Behold the cross of the Lord.

i The cross puts to flight all evil,/The cross is the restoration of things. By this sign of the cross/Let every malign thing flee,/And by the same sign Let all that is benign be kept safe.

Lastly yourself, and over the bed as well, *In nomine Patris et Filii*.[a] In bed, as far as you can, neither do nor think anything, but sleep.

Whoever either does not know Matins or cannot say it, let her say instead of Matins thirty *Pater nosters*, and *Aue Maria* after each *Paternoster*, and *Gloria Patri* after each *Aue*. Lastly, *Oremus*:[b] (whoever knows it) *Deus, cui proprium est*; *Benedicamus Dominum*; *Anime fidelium*.[c] Instead of Evensong let her say twenty, instead of every other hour fifteen in this way, except that at Evensong, whoever knows it shall say first *Domine, labia mea aperies et os meum*; *Deus, in adiutorium*[d] and at Compline *Conuerte nos, Deus, salutaris*; *Deus, in adiutorium*.[e] At all the other hours *Deus, in adiutorium*.

Whoever is unwell, let her cut out from Matins ten, from each of the others five – half of each if she is iller. Whoever is very sick, let her be free of all. Let her take her illness not only patiently, but very gladly, and all is hers that Holy Church reads or sings.

Though you ought to think of God at all times, you should most, however, in your hours, so that your thoughts are not floating about then. If through carelessness you get words wrong or mistake a verse, make your *Venie*[11][f] with only your hand down on the earth. Fall right down for great mistakes and often make plain in confession your carelessness about this.

This is now the first part, which has spoken to this point of your devotions. Whatever may be the case with those now, I would wish that these following rules were kept by everyone as they are, through God's grace, by you.[52]

a In the name of the Father and of the Son.
b Let us pray.
c God, whose property it is [to have mercy]; Let us bless the Lord; The souls of the faithful.
d Lord, thou wilt open my lips, and my mouth [shall declare thy praise] (Psalm 50.17); God, [come] to [my] assistance (Psalm 69.2).
e Turn us, God Our Saviour; God, [come] to [my] assistance.
f Pardons.

PART TWO
Protecting the Heart through the Senses

Here begins the second part, about the guarding of the heart through the five senses.

Omni custodia serua cor tuum, quia ex ipso uita procedit[a] – 'With all kinds of guarding, daughter,' says Solomon, 'keep your heart well, for the soul's life is in it', if it is well locked up. The heart's guardians are the five senses, sight and hearing, taste and smell, and feeling in each part of the body. And we shall speak about them all, for whoever guards these well does Solomon's bidding. He guards his heart and his soul's health well. The heart is a most wild beast and makes many a light leap, as St Gregory says: *Nichil corde fugatius*[b] – 'Nothing flees a man sooner than his own heart.' David, God's prophet, complained on one occasion that it had escaped from him: *Cor meum dereliquit me*[c] – that is, 'My heart has fled from me' – and afterwards he blesses himself and says that it had come back: *Inuenit seruus tuus cor suum*[d] – 'Lord,' he says, 'my heart has come back again; I have found it.' When so holy a man, so wise and careful, let it escape from him, another person may worry a great deal about its flight. And where did it break out from David, the holy king, God's prophet? Where? God knows, at his eye-window, through a sight that he saw, through his looking at something, as you shall hear after.[1]

Therefore, my dear sisters, love your windows as little as ever you can. Let them all be small, the parlour ones the smallest and narrowest.

a With all watchfulness keep thy heart, because life issueth out from it (Proverbs 4.23).
b Nothing is more fugitive than the heart (*Pastoral Rule* 3.14).
c My heart hath forsaken me (Psalm 39.13).
d Thy servant hath found his heart (2 Kings 7.27).

Let the curtain in them be of double thickness, the curtain black, the cross white, on the inside and the outside. The black curtain signifies that you are black and worthless to the world outside, that the true sun has scorched you[2] outwardly and thus on the outside made you the unattractive creatures you are through the beams of his grace. The white cross pertains to you; for there are three crosses, red and black and white. The red pertains to those who for God's sake are made ruddy and red[3] with the shedding of their blood, as the martyrs were. The black cross pertains to those who do penance in the world for hateful sins. The white pertains properly to white virginity and to purity, which it is great suffering to keep well. (By the cross suffering is always to be understood.) Thus the white cross signifies the protection of white virginity, which it is great suffering to guard well. The black cloth also, besides its signification, does less harm to the eyes and is thicker for keeping out the wind and more difficult to see through, and keeps its colour better against wind and other things. See that the parlour curtain is secured and well fixed on every side. And mind your eyes there, so that your heart does not flee and go out, as his did from David, and your soul sicken as soon as it is out. I write for others much that in no way touches you, my dear sisters, for you do not have a reputation – and shall not, through the grace of God, have it – as peeping anchoresses, nor for enticing glances or for the behaviour that some at times – alas – unnaturally indulge in. For it is against nature and an immensely astonishing wonder that the dead[4] should dote and go mad in sin with living worldly men.

'But, dear sir,' someone says, 'is it in fact so exceedingly evil to peep out?' Yes it is, dear sister; because of the evil that comes of it it is evil, and exceedingly evil for every anchoress, especially for the young – and for the old because they are giving an evil example to the younger ones, and a shield to defend themselves with, since if anyone reproaches them, then they say at once, 'But, sir, they do the same who are better than I am and know better than I what is right for them to do.' Dear young anchoress, often a very skilful smith makes a very weak knife; follow the wise in wisdom and not in folly. What it is right for an old anchoress to do may be wrong for you. But neither of you may look out without evil. Now take note what evil has come of peeping. Not one evil or two, but all the misery that there now is and ever yet was and ever shall be – it all comes of sight. That this is true, here, look, is proof.

Lucifer, because he saw and beheld in himself his own beauty, leapt into pride and turned from an angel into an ugly devil. Of Eve, our first mother, it is written that sin entered first of all through her eyesight: *Vidit igitur mulier quod bonum esset lignum ad uescendum, et pulcrum oculis, aspectuque delectabile, et tulit de fructu eius et comedit, deditque uiro suo*[a] – that is, Eve looked at the forbidden apple and saw that it was beautiful and began to take delight in looking at it and directed her desire to it and took it and ate of it and gave it to her lord. Look how Holy Writ speaks and penetratingly tells how sin began. Thus sight went before and made a path for evil desire, and after that came the deed which all mankind feels.

This apple, dear sister,[5] signifies all that desire and delight in sin turns to. When you look at a man, you are in Eve's situation; you are looking at the apple. Supposing someone had said to Eve when she first cast her eye on it, 'Ah, Eve, turn away, you cast your eye on your death', what would she have answered? 'But, dear sir, you are wrong. Why do you find fault with me? The apple that I'm looking at is forbidden me to eat, not to look at.' Thus would Eve readily enough have answered. O my dear sisters, indeed Eve has many daughters who follow their mother and answer in this way. 'But do you think,' someone says, 'that I am going to leap on a man even if I do look at him?' God knows, dear sisters, stranger things have happened. Eve your mother leapt after her eyes; from the eye to the apple, from the apple in paradise down to the earth, from the earth to hell, where she lay in prison four thousand years and more – she and her husband both – and condemned all her offspring to leap after her to death without end.[6] The beginning and root of all this grief was a casual look. Thus often, as they say, a lot grows from little. Let each feeble woman have great fear when she who was directly made by God's hands was betrayed by a look and brought into a vast sin which spread over all the world.

a So the woman saw that the tree was good to eat, and fair to the eyes, and delightful to behold, and she took of the fruit thereof, and did eat, and gave to her husband (Genesis 3.6).

Egressa est Dyna filia Jacob ut uideret mulieres alienigenas, et cetera.[a] A maiden called Dinah, Jacob's daughter, as it tells in Genesis, went out to look at foreign women'.[7] It does not even say that she looked at men. And what came of that looking, do you think? She lost her virginity and was made a whore. Afterwards, because of it, promises were broken by high patriarchs and a great city burnt down and the king and his son and the citizens killed, the women led away, her father and her brothers, though they were such noble princes, made outlaws. Her look turned out like this. All this the Holy Ghost had written down to warn women about their foolish eyes. And take note of this, that this evil of Dinah's did not come from her seeing Sichem, Hamor's son, whom she sinned with, but from her letting him lay eyes on her; for what he did to her was at the beginning very much against her will.

Likewise, Bathsheba, by uncovering herself in David's sight, caused him to sin with her,[8] though he was such a holy king and God's prophet. Now along comes a weak man – he thinks he is venerable, though, if he has a wide hood and a closed cloak[9] – and wants to see young anchoresses. He has to see, as if he were a stone, how her beauty pleases him – who has not had her face burnt in the sun – and says she can see holy men without hesitation – yes, such as he is because of his wide sleeves. But, proud sir, have you not heard that David, God's darling,[10] about whom he himself said *Inueni uirum secundum cor meum*[b] – 'I have found,' he said, 'a man after my heart' – this man whom God himself by this precious saying declared king and prophet chosen from all men, this man through an eye cast on a woman as she washed herself let out his heart and forgot himself, so that he committed three extreme capital and deadly sins: adultery with Bathsheba, the lady he looked at; treason and manslaughter on his faithful knight, Uriah, her lord. And you, a sinful man, are so very bold to cast foolish eyes upon young women. You, my dear sisters, if anyone is determined to see you, do not ever think good of it, but trust him the less. I do not want anyone to see you unless he has special leave from your director. For all the three sins of which I have just spoken, and all that evil of Dinah's of

a Dinah, the daughter of Jacob, went out to see the foreign women, etc. (Genesis 34.1).

b I have found a man according to my own heart (Acts 13.22).

which I spoke further back – it all came about, not because the women looked foolishly at men, but[11] [through their uncovering themselves in the sight of men's eyes and doing that through which they might fall into sins.

Therefore it was commanded in God's name in the Old Law that a pit was always to be covered, and if any pit were to be uncovered and a beast fall into it, he who uncovered the pit should pay for it.[12] These are very dreadful words for a woman who shows herself to a man's eyes. She is signified by the one who uncovers the pit. The pit is her beautiful face and her white neck and her light eyes – and her hand, if she holds it out in the sight of his eyes; and also her words are a pit, if they are not well enough ordered; and all that is to do with her, whatever it may be, through which foul love might the sooner quicken – all Our Lord calls a pit. This pit he commanded to be always closed and covered, lest any beast should fall into it and drown in sin. The beast is the beastly man who does not think of God and does not use his senses as a man ought to, but seeks to fall into the pit that I spoke of, if he finds it open. But the judgement is very severe on those who uncover the pit, for they must pay for the beast which has fallen into it. She is guilty of the beast's death before Our Lord and must answer for his soul at the Day of Judgement and pay for the loss of the beast, when she has nothing but herself for payment. This is a heavy payment all right! And God's judgement is – and his command – that she should pay it whatever, because she uncovered the pit that it drowned in. You uncover the pit, you who do anything because of which a man is tempted in the flesh on your account, even though you may not know it. Dread this judgement very much. And if he is tempted so that he commits deadly sin in any way, though it is not with you but with desire for you, or if he seeks to carry out with some other the temptation which has been awakened on your account, because of your actions, be quite certain of the judgement: you must pay for the beast, because of the opening of the pit, and unless you confess it, you must, as they say, suffer the rod – that is, suffer for his sins. A dog will happily go in wherever he finds it open. *Inpudicus oculus inpudici cordis est nuncius. Augustinus*[a] – what the mouth cannot for shame, the light eye

a The unchaste eye is the messenger of the unchaste heart. Augustine (from the Augustinian Rule; see Augustine, *Letter* 211).

speaks, and is like an errand-bearer for the light heart. But now, here is a woman who would not for anything desire filthiness with a man, and yet, nevertheless, would never worry if he thought about her and was tempted on her account. But St Augustine puts these two in one set of scales – to desire and to have a desire to be desired: *Non solum appetere, sed appeti uelle criminosum est*[a] – to want someone or to have a desire to be desired by someone – both are capital sins. *Oculi tela prima sunt adultere*[b] – eyes are the arrows and the first weapons of lechery's pricks – and just as men fight with three kinds of weapons – with shot, with spear-point and with the sword-edge – just so with these weapons, that is, with the shot of the eyes, with the spear of wounding words, with the sword of deadly touching, lechery, the stinking whore, fights with the lady of chastity – that is, God's wife. First she shoots the arrows of light eyes, that fly forth lightly, like an arrow that is feathered, and stick in the heart; after that she shakes the spear and advances upon her, and with words which shake[13] gives spear wounds; the sword-blow comes straight down – that is, the touching – for the sword strikes from near at hand and gives the death-blow; and it is truly, alas, nearly over with those who come so near together that they touch one another or feel one another anywhere. Let whoever is sensible and innocent guard herself against the shot – that is, guard her eyes well – for all the evil that ever there is comes from the eyes' arrows.[14] And is she not too stupid and too foolhardy, who holds her head out boldly on the open battlements when the castle is being attacked with bolts from outside? To be sure, our foe, the warrior of hell, he shoots, as I suppose, more bolts at one anchoress than at seventy-seven ladies in the world. The battlements of the castle are her house's windows; let her not lean out from these lest she should get these devil's bolts straight in her eyes before she the least suspects it – for he is always attacking. Let her keep her eyes in; for should she once be blinded, she is easy to fell. Blind the heart and she is easy to overcome and is soon brought to the ground with sin.

Bernardus: Sicut mors per peccatum in orbem, ita per has fenestras intrat in

---

a Not only to desire but to want to be desired is sinful (from the Augustinian Rule; see Augustine, *Letter* 211).

b The eyes are the first weapons of the adulteress.

mentem[a] – 'Just as death came,' says St Bernard, 'into the world through sin, so through eye-windows death has its entry into the soul.' Lord Christ! People would shut up every hole tightly as long as they could shut death out – the death of life in the flesh; and an anchoress will not close her eye-windows against the death of hell and of the soul. And quite rightly may eye-windows be called harm-windows,[15] for they have done much harm to many an anchoress.

All Holy Writ is full of warnings about the eye. David said, *Auerte oculos meos ne uideant uanitatem*[b] – 'Lord,' says David, 'turn away my eyes from the world's error and its fantasy.' Job said, *Pepigi fedus cum oculis meis ut ne cogitarem [quidem] de uirgine*[c] – 'I have,' says Job, 'fixed an agreement with my eyes, so that I do not think ill.' Well now! What is he saying? Does one think with the eyes? God knows, he speaks very well; for after the eye comes the thought and, after that, the deed. That Jeremiah knew well, who lamented and said, *Oculus meus depredatus est animam meam*[d] – 'Alas, my eye has robbed all my soul.' When God's prophet made such a lament about the eyes, what kind of lament, do you think, has come to many men and many women – sorrow on account of their eyes? The Wise Man[16] asks in his book whether anything harms a woman more than her eyes: *Oculo quid nequius? Totam faciem lacrimare facit, et cetera*[e] – 'All the face must flow with tears,' he says, 'for the sight of the eye alone.'

Now, for this reason let all the openings of all your windows, as they have been closed to the view of all men before this, be so afterwards.[17] And if they can be, let them be more firmly closed. The general rule is: all those who close them well, God guards them well. And all those . . . to sin, either with foolish eye, or with mouth, or with hand . . . and many such unseemly and unnatural things[18] – to an anchoress above all,

---

a Bernard: Just as death [entered] the world through sin, so through these windows it enters the soul (*The Degrees of Humility and Pride* 10.28).

b Turn away my eyes, that they may not behold vanity (Psalm 118.37).

c I made a covenant with my eyes, that I would not [so much as] think upon a virgin (Job 31.1). (The '*quidem*' is supplied from the Vulgate text of Job, not appearing in the Nero manuscript.)

d My eye hath wasted my soul (Lamentations 3.51).

e What is more wicked than an eye? It makes the whole face weep, etc. (Ecclesiasticus 31.15).

which would never have come to pass if she had shut her window firmly. And if anyone contradicts this, I bring in her conscience to witness forcefully against her, that should she linger at her window with eye, or mouth, or ever receive a hand and a foolish word, she has been adorned and falsely tricked out in a feigned holiness. Ah, treacherous traitor! 'God, I would not do it to you for any evil, or for any filthiness,' says he – or she; and these same people soil themselves and their accursed eyes anger God who sees] treason within the lecherous heart. Not only all physical touching but also each lecherous word is hateful villainy and worthy of God's anger, even if things develop no further between a man and an anchoress. In fact, by the just vengeance of God it goes on further and further and often arrives – and before it is the least suspected – at that foul sin; we have, alas, heard of it often enough. Let no man trust an anchoress who, to show herself, lets in a man's eye. Above all that is written for you in your rule about outer things, this point, this article about being well concealed, I want to be kept best. To a woman who desires it, open in God's name; if she does not speak about it, leave things as they are, unless you think she will be shocked afterwards. Anchoresses have been tempted by their own sisters. Do not invite any man to look in at your altar. But if his devotion asks it and gets its request, draw well back inside and put the veil down over your breast and soon close the curtain again and fasten it tight. If he looks at the bed or asks where you sleep answer casually, 'Sir, I am well provided for in that', and keep silent. If the bishop comes to see you, hasten to him quickly, but sweetly request him, if he asks to see you, that you may, as to that, conduct yourself towards him as you have done and are doing towards all others. If he will anyhow have a sight of you, see that it is very brief. Put your veil down at once and draw back. One anchoress humbly refused St Martin a sight of her and because of that he honoured her as he never did any other. And because of that her reputation is to this day sustained by Holy Church, for, as we read of her, 'Whoever wants to guard her windows well against the evil must do it also against the good.'[19] Whenever you have to give anything over to any man, your hand should not come out – not yours out or his in. And if it has to come in they should not touch one another. 'She is safe,' says Holy Writ, 'who withdraws herself far from snares', and 'She who loves peril, into peril shall she fall': *Qui caret laqueis securus est, et qui amat periculum incidet in illud.*[a] The devil's snare is often set where one least suspects. No one who is not full of fear is not caught. For God will not guard anyone who is so foolhardy as not to guard herself watchfully against him. Enough has now been said about this sense on this occasion to warn the innocent. We shall, however, soon after this speak more about it.[20]

Speech and taste are both in the mouth, as sight is in the eye, but we shall leave taste until we speak of your food and speak now about speech, and after that about hearing; about both jointly in due course, as they go together.

First of all when you go to your parlour window, find out from your maid who it is who has come. For it may be someone that you should excuse yourself from. When you have after all to come forward, cross your mouth, eyes and ears very carefully and your breast as well, and go forward in the fear of God. To a priest, say first *Confiteor*[b] – and after that he ought to say *Benedicite*.[c] Listen to his words and keep completely silent, so that when he leaves you, he does not know either your good or your evil and does not know whether to blame you or praise you. Some are so learned or speak so wisely that they would like the person sitting and speaking with them to know it, and give word for word and degenerate into scholars when they should be anchoresses, and teach him, who has come to teach them – would like through their conversation to be known and recognized as one of the wise. Recognized she is, for by the very thing by which she thinks to be accounted wise he understands that she is stupid, for she hunts for praise and catches blame. For at the very least when he has gone away he will say, 'This anchoress talks a lot.' Eve in paradise held a long conversation with the snake, told him all the lesson God had taught her and Adam about the apple, and so the fiend, through what she said, understood her weakness immediately and found a way of getting at her for her destruction. Our Lady St Mary acted in quite another way. She did not hold forth to the angel, but asked him briefly what she did not know. You, my dear sisters, follow Our Lady and not the cackling Eve.

a He that is aware of the snares shall be secure (Proverbs 11.15), and he that loveth danger shall perish in it (Ecclesiasticus 3.27).

b I confess.

c Bless [the Lord].

Therefore let an anchoress, whatever she may be, however much she may know, keep silent, not have a hen's nature. The hen when she has laid can only cackle, but what does she get out of that? The jackdaw [21] comes straight away and takes her eggs away from her and eats what should produce live birds. Exactly so the jackdaw devil carries away from cackling anchoresses all the good that they have begotten and which ought, like birds, to carry them up towards heaven, if it were not cackled about. The wretched poor pedlar makes more noise to advertise his soap than the rich mercer all his precious goods – as is told later. It is good that you should ask a spiritual man whom you trust – as you can few – for advice and remedies which he can teach you against temptations, and show him in confession, if he will hear you, your greatest and your smallest sins, so that he may pity you and because of the pity cry more fervently to Christ for mercy for you and have you in his prayers. *Set multi ueniunt ad uos in uestimentis ouium, intrinsecus autem sunt lupi rapaces* [a] – 'But be on your guard and be wary,' says Our Lord, 'for many come to you clothed in lamb's fleece and are raging wolves.' Trust those in the world little, religious still less, and do not desire their acquaintance too much. Eve spoke without fear to the snake; Our Lady was afraid of Gabriel's speech. Our Friars Preacher and our Friars Minor [22] are of such orders that all people might well be amazed if any of them turned his eye towards the wood-glade. [23] Therefore on each occasion that any of them in charity comes to teach you and comfort you in God, if he is a priest, say before he leaves, '*Mea culpa* [b] – I confess to God Almighty and to you that, as I fear, I was never truly penitent for my greatest sins, which I have shown to my father confessors. And though my intent in this is to atone for them, I do it so poorly and commit other sins every day from when I was last confessed, and that was then and by that person' – and name him. 'I have sinned thus' – and say in what way, as it is written for you in your confession book [24] towards the end, and lastly say, 'This and much more', *Confiteor*, and ask him to receive you specially into his good will and thank him for his visit and request him lastly to greet this person and that person, and that they should pray for you.

a But many come to you in the clothing of sheep, but inwardly they are ravening wolves (Matthew 7.15).
b My fault.

Without the witness of a woman or a man who can hear you, do not speak to any man often or long, and, even if it is in confession, let a third always sit in the same house or where they can look in your direction, unless there is no room for the third. This is not said on your account or that of others like you but, still, the truthful person is often mistrusted and the guiltless lied about, as Joseph was in Genesis by the evil lady for want of a witness.[25] The evil are soon believed and the wicked happily lie about the good. Some unfortunates have, when they said they were confessing, confessed most strangely. Therefore the good ought always to have a witness, for two reasons especially: the first is so that the envious cannot lie about them without the witness proving them false; the second is to give an example to others and to deprive the evil anchoress of that unfortunate guile of which I spoke.[26]

Do not hold conversation with anyone through the church window, but reverence it because of the holy sacrament which you see through it, and use the house window for speaking sometimes to your women, to others the parlour window. You ought not to speak except at these two windows.

Silence always at meals. If other religious (as you know) do it, you above all ought to. If anyone has a loved guest, she should have her maids entertain her well, as in her place, and she shall have permission to unfasten her window once or twice and make signs to her of her pleasure. The courtesy of some has turned to their evil; under the appearance of good, sin is often hidden. There ought to be a great difference between an anchoress and the lady of a house. Each Friday of the year keep silence, unless it be a double feast, and then keep it some other day of the week; in Advent and in Ember weeks, Wednesday and Friday;[27] in Lent three days; all Holy Week[28] until noon, and after noon after the meal until evening. You may, however, say to your women in a few words whatever you want. If any good man has come from far, listen to what he says and answer what he asks in a few words.

A great fool would he be, the man who was able for his profit to grind whichever he wanted, chaff or wheat, if he ground the chaff and left the wheat. Wheat is holy speech, as St Anselm says.[29] She who chatters grinds chaff. The two jaws are the two grindstones, the tongue is the clapper. See, dear sisters, that your jaws grind nothing except the soul's food, and your ears drink nothing except the soul's healing. And close not only your ears, but your windows against idle speech. No tale or tiding of the world should come to you.

You shall not on any account curse or swear, except if you say 'certainly' or 'surely', or something of this sort. Do not preach to any man – and no man should ask your counsel, or give you his. Advise women only. St Paul forbids women to preach: *Mulieres non permitto docere*.[a] Do not censure any man or reproach him for his vice, unless he is over-familiar with you. Old and holy anchoresses may do it in certain ways, but it is not a safe thing and is not appropriate for young ones. It is the job of those who are set over others and have them to guard, as the teachers of Holy Church. An anchoress has only herself and her maids to guard. Let each keep to her own job and not take someone else's. Many think to do well, who do very odd things indeed; for, as I said before, under the appearance of good, sin is often hidden. Through this sort of censuring have some anchoresses raised between themselves and their priests either a hypocritical love or a great strife.

Seneca: *Ad summam uolo uos esse rariloquas, tuncque pauciloquas*[30][b] – 'This is the end of the story,' says Seneca the wise. 'I want you to speak seldom and then little.' Many dam up their words so as to let more out, as one does water at a mill. Job's friends did so, who had come to comfort him – sat silent for seven nights;[31] but when they had finally begun to speak, then they could never stop their racket. *Gregorius: Censura silencii nutritura est uerbi.*[c] So it is with many, as St Gregory says: 'Silence is the foster-nurse of words and brings forth chatter.' On the other hand, as he says, *Iuge silentium cogit celestia meditari*[d] – 'Long and well-kept silence compels the thoughts up towards heaven.' Just as you can see that water, when it has been dammed up and well stopped up in front so that it cannot go down, is then compelled to climb back upwards – dam up your words in just this way – stop up your thoughts, as you wish them to climb and rise up towards heaven and not to fall downwards and flow through the world, as does abundant

a I suffer not women to teach (1 Timothy 2.12).
b In sum I want you to be infrequent speakers and then speakers of little.
c Gregory: The discipline of silence is the nurse of speech (*Homilies on Ezekiel* 1. 11, 3 (on chapter 3, verse 16)).
d Continual silence forces one to meditate on heavenly things (*Letters* 28.3).

chatter. When you have to, open up the floodgates of your mouth a little bit, as they do at a mill, and let them down soon.

Words kill more people than swords: *Mors et uita in manibus lingue*[a] – 'Life and death,' says Solomon, 'are in the tongue's hands.' *Qui custodit os suum custodit animam suam*[b] – 'Whoever guards his mouth well guards,' he says, 'his soul.' *Sicut urbs patens et absque murorum ambitu sic, et cetera. Qui murum silencii non habet, patet inimici iaculis ciuitas mentis*[c] – 'Whoever does not keep back his words,' says Solomon the wise, 'he is like a city without a wall which an army can enter on all sides.' The fiend of hell with all his army goes straight through the mouth which is always open into the heart. In *Vitas Patrum* it tells that a holy man said, when some brothers from whom he had heard much speech were praised, *Boni utique sunt, set habitatio eorum non habet ianuam; quicumque uult intrat et asinum soluit*[d] – 'They *are* good,' he said, 'but their dwelling has no gate; their mouths jabber all the time – whoever wants can go in and lead off their ass' – that is, their unwise soul. Therefore St James says, *Si quis putat se religiosum esse, non refrenans linguam suam set seducens cor suum, huius uana est religio*[e] – that is, 'If anyone thinks that he is religious and does not bridle his tongue, his religion is false, he deceives his heart.' 'Does not bridle his tongue' is very well said. A bridle is not only in the horse's mouth, but partly sits over the eyes and goes round the ears, for there is a great need that all these three be bridled. But the iron sits in the mouth and on the light tongue, for there is most need of restraint when the tongue is in motion and has started to gallop.

Often we intend, when we begin to speak, to say little in carefully ordered words, but the tongue is slippery because it wades in wetness and slides on easily from few words into many; and then, as Solomon

a Death and life are in the hands of the tongue (Proverbs 18.21).
b He that guardeth his mouth guardeth his soul (Proverbs 13.3).
c As a city that lieth open and is not compassed with walls[, so is a man that cannot refrain his own spirit in speaking] (Proverbs 25.28). If a person does not have a wall of silence, the city of his mind lies open to the missiles of the enemy (Gregory, *Pastoral Rule* 3.14).
d They are indeed good, but their dwelling does not have a door; whoever wants to enters and lets loose their ass (*Lives of the Fathers* 5.4).
e If any man think himself to be religious, not bridling his tongue but deceiving his own heart, this man's religion is vain (James 1.26).

says, *In multiloquio non deerit peccatum*[a] – 'Much speaking cannot, though it begin never so well, be without sin.' For from true it slides to false, out of good into some evil, from measure into lack of moderation, and from a drop it grows into a great flood that drowns the soul – for with the flowing word the heart flows, so that long afterwards it cannot properly be gathered together. *Et os nostrum tanto est Deo longinquum quanto mundo proximum, tantoque minus exauditur in prece, quanto amplius coinquinatur in locutione.*[b] This is what St Gregory says in his Dialogue: the nearer our mouth is to worldly speech, the further it is from God, when it speaks to him and makes any prayer to him. This is why we often cry upon him and he keeps away from our voice and will not hear it, for it stinks to him of all the world's jabber and of its chatter. Whoever then wishes God's ear to be near her tongue should keep away from the world, otherwise she may long cry before God hears her, and he says through Isaiah, *Cum extenderitis manus uestras, auertam oculos meos a uobis; et cum multiplicaueritis orationes non exaudiam uos*[c] – that is, 'Though you should make your prayers many times to me, you who play with the world, I will not hear you, but I will turn away when you raise your hands high towards me.'

Our precious Lady St Mary, who ought to be an example to all women, spoke so little that nowhere in Holy Writ except four times do we find that she spoke. But because she spoke so seldom her words were weighty and had great power. *Bernardus ad Mariam: In sempiterno Dei uerbo facti sumus omnes et ecce morimur. In tuo breui responso refitiendi sumus, ut ad uitam reuocemur. Responde uerbum et suscipe Uerbum; profer tuum et concipe diuinum.*[d] The first of her words of which we read were those with which she answered the angel Gabriel, and these were so powerful that on her saying, *Ecce ancilla Domini: Fiat michi secundum uerbum tuum;*[e]

a In the multitude of words there shall not want sin (Proverbs 10.19).

b And our mouths are further from God as they are closer to the world, and are heard less in prayer as they are more defiled in speech (*Dialogues* 3.15).

c When you stretch forth your hands, I will turn away my eyes from you; and when you multiply prayer, I will not hear you (Isaiah 1.15).

d Bernard to Mary: In the eternal word of God we are all made and, look, we are dying. In your short answer we are to be remade, so that we may be called back to life. Give the word in reply and receive the Word; offer your own and conceive the divine (*The Praises of the Virgin Mary* 4.8).

e Behold the handmaid of the Lord: be it done unto me according to thy word (Luke 1.38).

at this speech, God's Son – true God also – became man, and the Lord whom the whole world could not contain enclosed himself within her maiden's womb. Her second words were when she came and greeted Elizabeth, her kinswoman. And what power was shown at these words? – What? – A child began to play in response to them – that was St John in his mother's womb. *Idem. Vox eius Iohannem exultare fecit in utero.*[a] The third time that she spoke was at the marriage and there, at her request, was water turned to wine.[32] The fourth time was when she had lost her Son, and afterwards found him.[33] And how great a wonder followed those words? – God Almighty submitted to man, to Mary and to Joseph, to a workman and to a woman, and followed them as their own wherever they wanted. Now take note here and learn carefully from this how infrequent speech has great strength.

Vir linguosus non dirigetur in terra[b] – 'The man of many words,' says the Psalmist, 'shall never lead a right life on earth.' Therefore he says elsewhere, *Dixi: custodiam uias meas, ut non delinquam in lingua mea:*[c] hypallage;[34] and it is as though he said, 'I shall guard my ways through the keeping of my tongue – if I guard my tongue well, I can keep on the way towards heaven well.' For as Isaiah says, *Cultus iusticie silentium*[d] – 'The cultivation of righteousness, that is silence.' Silence cultivates it and, cultivated, it brings forth the soul's eternal food, for it is immortal, as Solomon testifies: *Iusticia immortalis est.*[e] Therefore Isaiah links hope and silence both together and says spiritual strength shall stand in them: *In silentio et spe erit fortitudo uestra*[f] – that is, 'In silence and in hope shall be your strength.' Take note how well he speaks, for whoever is very quiet and keeps silence long, she may confidently hope that when she speaks to God he hears her. She may also hope that she will sing, through her silence, sweetly in heaven. This now is the reason for the linking – why Isaiah links hope and silence and couples them both together. Besides, he says in the same passage that in silence and in

---

a The same [chapter]: Her voice made John leap in her womb (see Luke 1.41).
b A man of many words will not keep a straight course in the world (Psalm 139. 12).
c I said: I will guard my ways, that I sin not with my tongue (Psalm 38.1).
d The cultivation of justice is silence (Isaiah 32.17).
e Justice is immortal (Wisdom 1.15).
f In silence and in hope shall your strength be (Isaiah 30.15).

hope shall be our strength in God's service against the devil's tricks and his temptations. But look for what reason: hope is a sweet spice within the heart, which sweetens everything bitter that the body drinks. But whoever chews spice must keep her mouth shut, so that the sweet scent and the strength of it stays within. But she who opens her mouth with much jabber and breaks silence, she spits hope right out, and the sweetness of it, with worldly words and loses spiritual strength against the fiend. For what makes us in God's service and in temptations strong to endure hardship, to wrestle sturdily against the devil's holds but hope of high reward? Hope keeps the heart healthy whatever the body may endure: as they say, 'If there weren't hope, the heart would break.' Ah, Jesus, your mercy – how does it stand with them who are where all grief and misery are, without hope of getting out, and whose hearts cannot break. Therefore, as you want to keep hope within you, and its sweet scent which gives the soul power, with your mouth shut chew it within your heart, and do not blow it out with jabbering lips, with gaping mouths. *Non habeatis linguam uel aures prurientes*[a] – 'Look,' says St Jerome, 'that you do not have an itching tongue or ears' – that is, that you do not desire either to speak or to listen to worldly speech. To this point we have spoken about your silence and how your speech must be infrequent. *Contrariorum eadem est disciplina.*[b] About silence and about speech there is only one teaching, and therefore in writing they both go together. Now we shall say something about your hearing, against evil speech, so that you shut your ears against it and, if need be, fasten your windows.

To all evil speech, my dear sisters, stop your ears and feel disgust for the mouth that spews out poison. *De omni uerbo otioso, et cetera.*[c] Evil speech is of three kinds: poisonous, foul and idle. Idle speech is evil; foul speech is worse; poisonous is the worst. All from which good does not come is idle and useless, and of this kind of speech, says Our Lord, must each word be reckoned up and reason given why the one said it and the other listened to it; and this is, however, the least evil of the three evils. Well? How then is one to give reasons for the worse? Well?

a You should not have an itching tongue or ears (Jerome, *Letter* 52.14).

b Opposites are the object of the same teaching.

c Every idle word [that men shall speak, they shall render an account for it in the Day of Judgement] (Matthew 12.36).

How for the worst, that is, for poisonous and for foul speech? -- not only the one who speaks it, but the one who listens to it. Foul speech is, for instance, about lechery and about other filthinesses that unwashed mouths sometimes speak. These are all scraped out of an anchoress's rule![36] The person who spits out such filth in any anchoress's ears should have his mouth closed not with sharp babblings but with hard fists.

Poisonous speech is heresy, twisted lying, backbiting and flattery; these are the worst. Heresy – God be thanked – does not hold sway in England. Lying is so evil a thing that St Augustine says that to shield your father from death you should not lie.[37] God himself says that he is truth, and what is more against truth than lying is? *Diabolus mendax est et pater eius*[a] – The devil is a liar and the father of lying. She, then, who stirs her tongue in lying makes of her tongue a cradle for the devil's child and rocks it diligently, as if its nurse.

Backbiting and flattery and egging on to do evil are not man's speech but are the devil's blasts and his own voice. If they ought to be far from all worldly men, well then, how ought anchoresses to hate them and shun them, so that they do not hear them? 'Hear', I say, for whoever speaks them, she is not an anchoress. *Salomon: Si mordet serpens in silentio, nichil minus eo habet qui detrahit in occulto*[b] – 'The snake,' says Solomon, 'stings quite soundlessly, and she who speaks behind a person's back what she would not to his face is not any better.' Do you hear how Solomon likens a backbiter to a stinging snake? So it is, to be sure: she is a snake's offspring and carries poison – she who speaks evil – in her tongue.

The flatterer blinds the man he flatters and puts a pin in his eye. *Gregorius: Adulator ei cum quo sermonem conserit quasi clauum in oculo figit.*[38c] The backbiter chews men's flesh on Friday and with his black bill pecks at living carrion, as one who is the devil of hell's raven. *Salomon: Noli esse in conuiuiis eorum, et cetera, qui conferunt carnes ad uescendum, et cetera.*[d] If

---

a The devil is a liar and the father of lies (John 8.44).
b Solomon: If a serpent bite in silence, he is nothing better that backbiteth secretly (Ecclesiastes 10.11).
c Gregory: The flatterer puts a pin, as it were, in the eye of the person with whom he talks (see John of Salisbury, *Policraticus* 3.4).
d Solomon: Be not in the feasts [of great drinkers], etc., who contribute flesh to eat, etc. (Proverbs 23.20).

he wanted to peck and tear up with his bill rotten stinking flesh, as is the raven's nature – that is, if he wanted to say evil only of those who rot and stink right in the filth of their sin – it would be less outrageous, but he alights on living flesh, dismembers it and tears it apart – that is, speaks ill of those who are alive in God. He is too greedy a raven and too bold altogether. Or again, take note of what two jobs these attendants do for their lord, the devil of hell. It is foul to say, but fouler to be it – and that's how it is in any case. *Ne uideatur hec moralitas minus decens, recolat in Esdra, quod Melchia hedificauit portam stercoris. 'Melchia' enim 'corus domino' interpretatur; 'filius Rechab', id est, 'mollis patris'.*[39] *Nam uentus Aquilo dissipat pluuias et faties tristis linguam detrahentem.*[a] They are the devil's toilet attendants and are always in his toilet. The flatterer's job is to cover the toilet hole, which he does as often as with flattery and praising he covers up for a man his sins, than which nothing stinks fouler. And he covers it and puts a lid on it so that he cannot smell it. The backbiter takes the lid off it and opens up the filth so that it stinks far and wide. Thus they are always busy in this foul job and each strives against the other over it. Men like this stink of their stinking job and make every place stink that they come near. May the Lord prevent the breath of their stinking throats ever coming near you. Other sorts of speaking make foul, but these poison both the ears and the heart. So that you may recognize them better if any comes your way, look, here are their characters. Flatterers are of three kinds: the first are evil enough; the second, though, are worse; the third, though, are worst. *Ve illis qui ponunt puluillos, et cetera. Ve illis qui dant bonum malum et malum bonum; ponentes lucem tenebras et tenebras lucem. Hoc scilicet detractoribus et adulatoribus peruenit.*[b] The first, if a man is good, praises him to his face and soon enough makes him out to be still better than he is, and if he says well or does well raises it up too high with

---

a In case this moralization should seem too indecent, one should recollect that in Esdras Melchias built a dung-gate (see 2 Esdras 3.14). For 'Melchias' means 'north wind of the Lord'; 'son of Rechab', that is, 'of a gentle father'. For the north wind driveth away rain as doth a sad countenance a backbiting tongue (Proverbs 25.23).

b Woe to them that put pillows [under every elbow] (Ezekiel 13.18). Woe to them that call evil good and good evil; that put darkness for light and light for darkness (Isaiah 5.20). This, evidently, applies to detractors and flatterers.

excessive praise. The second, if a man is evil and says and does so much wrong that it is so open a sin that he cannot in any way altogether deny it, he nevertheless to the man's own face makes his evil out to be less: 'Now it isn't,' he says, 'so excessively evil a thing as it's made out to be, and you aren't in this thing the first or the last. You have many companions. Let it be, old chap, you're not on your own. Many do much worse.' The third kind of flatterer is the worst, as I said, for he praises the evil person and his evil deed – like him who says to the knight who robs his poor, 'Ah sir, how rightly you act, for the serf needs to be plucked and peeled all the time, for he is like the willow, which sprouts out the better when it is often cut back.' *Laudatur peccator in desideriis anime sue et iniquus benedicitur. Augustinus: Adulantium lingue alligant hominem in peccatis.*[a] Thus these false flatterers blind those who listen to them, as I said before, and cover up their filth so that they cannot smell it. And that is their great misfortune: for if they smelled it they would be disgusted by it and run to confession, and spew it out there and shun it afterwards. *Clemens: Homicidarum tria esse genera dixit beatus Petrus et eorum parem penam esse uoluit: qui corporaliter occidit, et qui detrahit fratri, et qui inuidet.*[b]

Backbiters who bite others behind their backs are of two sorts, but the second is worse. The first comes quite openly and speaks evil of another and spews out his poison, as much as ever comes into his mouth, and vomits all out together what the poisonous heart sends up to the tongue. But the second comes on in a quite different way, a worse enemy than the other is, and under a cloak of friendship drops his head down, begins to sigh before he says anything, puts on a gloomy look and goes on with instances and excuses, so as to be better believed. When it does actually come out, it is yellow poison. 'Too bad,' she says, 'I'm very sorry that he (or she) has got such a reputation. I had a good go, but it didn't do any good. I knew about it early on, but it wouldn't have got any further because of me. But now because of

a The sinner is praised in the desire of his heart, and the evil man is blessed (Psalm 9.24). Augustine: The tongues of flatterers bind a man in his sins (*Expositions on the Psalms* 9.21).

b Clement: The blessed Peter said that there are three kinds of homicide and wanted them to have the same punishment: killing bodily, disparaging one's brother and envying (Pseudo-Clement, *Decretal Letters* 1).

others it has got about so much that I can't deny it. They say it's bad, and it's even worse. I'm sorry and sad that I have to say it, but the truth is that's how it is – and that's very sad, for in many other things he (or she) is much to be praised, but on this thing – I'm very sorry about it, no one can defend them.' This is the devil's snake of whom Solomon speaks. Our Lord, by his grace, keep your ears far from their poisonous tongues and never let you smell the foul pit which they uncover – as the flatterers cover and conceal it, as I said. To uncover it to the people themselves to whom it pertains, and conceal it from others, is a great virtue – not uncovering it to those who would smell it and hate the filth.

Now, my dear sisters, from all evil speech, which is of three kinds like this – idle, foul and poisonous – keep your ear far away. They say about anchoresses that each has to have an old woman to feed her ears: a jabberer who jabbers to her all the stories of the area, a magpie who cackles out all that she sees and hears, so that it is said in a proverb 'From mill and from market, from smithy and from anchor-house, people bring the news'.[40] Christ knows, this is a sad saying that the anchor-house, which should be the most solitary place of all, has to be linked with those three places in which there is most chatter. But Our Lord grant that all others were as free as you are of this sort of thing.

Now I have spoken separately about these three parts of the body, about the eye, about the mouth, about the ear. All this last section is about the ear – to the benefit of anchoresses, for it is not a likely thing that an anchoress should have a mouth of this kind, but it may be greatly feared that she sometimes bends her ear to such mouths. Sight, speech, listening have been spoken about separately in order. Let us now come back again and speak of them all jointly.

Zelatus sum Syon zelo magno: in propheta Zacharia.[a] Understand, anchoress, whose bride you are and how he is jealous about all your behaviour: *Ego sum Deus zelotes: in Exodo*[b] – 'I am,' he says of himself, 'the jealous God.' *Zelatus sum, et cetera* – 'I am jealous of you, Sion, my beloved, with a great jealousy.' It did not seem to him enough to have said that he is jealous about you, but he said as well, 'with a great jealousy'. *Auris zeli*

a I have been jealous for Sion with a great jealousy: in the prophet Zechariah (8.2).
b I am a jealous God: in Exodus (20.5).

audit omnia,[a] says Solomon the wise. *Vbi amor, ibi oculus*.[41][b] Now know this very well: his ear is always inclined towards you and he hears everything. His eye always sees you if you make any gesture, any look of love towards vices. *Zelatus sum Syon* – 'Sion', that is, mirror. He calls you his mirror, so much his that you are no one else's. Therefore he says *in Canticis: Ostende michi fatiem tuam*[c] – 'Show your face to me,' he says, 'and to none other. Look at me if you want to have bright sight with your heart's eyes; look within where I am, and do not seek me outside your heart. I am a wooer full of modesty and I do not want to embrace my beloved anywhere but in a secret place.' In this way does Our Lord speak to his bride. Let her not think it a great wonder, if she is not much on her own, that he should shun her – and so on her own that she puts every worldly throng and every worldly noise out of her heart, for it is God's room. Noise only comes into the heart from a thing that has been seen or heard, smelled or tasted, and felt outwardly. And know this to be true – that the more these senses are scattered outwards, the less they turn inwards. Always the more the recluse gazes outwards, the less light she has from Our Lord inwardly, and likewise with the other senses. *Qui exteriori oculo negligenter utitur, iusto Dei iudicio interiori cecatur*.[d] Look what St Gregory says: 'Whoever guards her outer eyes carelessly, through God's righteous judgement she is blinded in her inner', so that she cannot see God with her spiritual sight, nor recognize him through such sight and through the recognition love him above all things. For to the extent that one recognizes his great goodness and feels his sweet sweetness, so one loves him more or less.

Therefore, my dear sisters, be outwardly blind, as were the holy Jacob and Toby the good,[42] and God will, as he gave to them, give you light inwardly, to see him and recognize him and through the recognition to love him above all things. Then shall you see how all the world is nothing, how its comfort is false. Through that sight you shall see all the devil's tricks with which he beguiles wretches. You shall see in yourself what are still to be atoned for of your own sins. You shall

---

a The ear of jealousy heareth all things (Wisdom 1.10).

b Where one's love is, there is one's eye.

c In Canticles (2.14): Show me thy face.

d The person who employs his outer eye negligently is, by the just judgement of God, blinded in his inner [eye] (Gregory, *Morals on Job* 21.8, 13).

sometimes look at the torments of hell, so that you feel horror at them and flee from them the quicker. You shall see, spiritually, the joys of heaven, which will kindle your heart to hurry towards them. You shall, as in a mirror, see Our Lady with her maidens, all the host of angels, all the army of saints, and him above them all who gives joy to all of them and is the crown of them all. This sight, dear sisters, shall comfort you more than any worldly sight could. Holy men, who have made trial of it, know well that each earthly happiness is worthless in comparison to it. *Manna absconditum est, et cetera. Nomen nouum quod nemo scit nisi qui accipit*[a] – 'It is a secret linctus,' says St John the Evangelist in the Apocalypse, 'which no man knows who has not tasted it.' This taste and this knowing come of spiritual sight, of spiritual hearing, of spiritual speech, which they shall have who forgo for God's love worldly hearings, earthly speeches, fleshly sights. *Videamus enim quasi per speculum in enigmate.*[b] And after that sight which is now dim here, you shall have above the bright sight of God's face, from which all happiness comes in the joy of heaven, much beyond the others: for the righteous God has so ordained it that each one's reward there should correspond to the labour and the weariness which she here, for his love, humbly suffers. Therefore it is fitting that anchoresses should have these two morning-gifts[43] beyond others: swiftness and the light of clear sight – swiftness in return for their being now so bolted up, light of clear sight in return for their now here keeping themselves in darkness, and wishing not to see men or be seen by men. All those in heaven shall be as swift as man's thought is now, as the sun's ray is, which strikes from the east into the west, as the opening eye. But anchoresses locked up here shall be there, if any may, both lighter and swifter, and in such roomy shackles, as they say, play in heaven's broad pastures that the body shall be wherever the spirit wishes in a moment. This, then, is the one morning-gift which I said anchoresses should have above others. *Gregorius: Enim quod nesciunt ubi scientem omnia sciunt.*[c] All those in heaven see all things in God; and anchoresses shall, more

a It is hidden manna, etc. A new name, which no man knoweth but he that receiveth it (Apocalypse 2.17).
b We see now through a glass in a dark manner (1 Corinthians 13.12).
c Gregory: For what do they not know where they know the one who knows all? (see *Morals on Job* 2.3, 3 and *Dialogues* 4.33).

clearly for their blindfolding here, see and understand there God's secret mysteries and his dreadful judgements, who are not now concerned to know of outer things with ear or with eye.

Therefore, my dear sisters, if any man asks to see you, ask him what good may come of it, since I see many evils in it and no profit. If he is importunate, trust him the less. If any is so mad as to put his hand out towards the window curtain, quickly straight away shut the window right up and let him be. Likewise, as soon as anyone gets on to any wicked talk that has to do with foul love, fasten the window straight away, and do not answer him at all, but go away saying this verse so that he can hear it: *Declinate a me, maligni, et scrutabor mandata Dei mei; narrauerunt michi iniqui fabulationes, Domine, sed non ut lex tua,*[a] and go before your altar with *Miserere.*[44][b] Never rebuke such a man in another way. For in reply to the rebuke, he might answer in such a way and blow so gently that some spark might kindle. No wooing is so base as that in the guise of a lament – as if someone spoke thus: 'I would not, though I died, think of doing anything filthy with you', and swore deep vows: 'But even if I've sworn not to, I have to love you. Who's worse off than me? It stops me sleeping a lot. Now I'm very sorry that you know it. But now forgive me that I have told it you. Even if I go mad, you shall never more know how things stand with me.' She forgives it him because he speaks so nicely. Then she speaks about something else. But the eye is always on the wood-glade[45] – the heart is always on what was said before. Even after he has gone, she turns over words like this often in her thought, when she should be paying attention carefully to something else. Afterwards he looks for his moment to break his promise, swears he has to, and so the evil grows, getting worse the longer it goes on. For no enmity is so evil as false friendship. An enemy who seems to be a friend is the greatest of deceivers. Therefore, my dear sisters, do not give such a man an opening for speaking since, as Holy Writ says, his speech spreads like a cancer,[46] but instead of any sort of answer, go away from him just as I said above. You cannot in any way better save yourself and confound him.

a Depart from me, ye malignant, and I will search the commandments of my God (Psalm 118.115); the wicked have told me fables, Lord, but not as thy law (Psalm 118.85).

b Have mercy [on me, Lord] (Psalm 50).

Look, now, how appropriately the lady in *Canticis*, God's dear bride, by her saying teaches you how you should speak: *En dilectus meus loquitur michi: Surge, propera, amica mea, et cetera*[a] – 'Ah,' she says, 'listen: I hear my beloved speak. He calls me; I must go.' And go to your dear lover and complain in the ears of him who calls you lovingly to him with these words: *Surge, propera, amica mea, columba mea, formosa mea et veni. Ostende mihi fatiem tuam. Sonet vox tua in auribus meis*[b] – that is, 'Rise up, hurry from there and come to me, my beloved, my dove, my fair one, my bright bride.' *Ostende michi faciem tuam* – 'Show to me your beloved face and your lovely countenance. Turn away from others.' *Sonet vox tua in auribus meis* – 'Say who has done you harm, who has hurt my beloved. Sing in my ears. Because you only want to see my beauty, to speak only to me, your voice is sweet to me and your beauty bright.' *Vnde et subditur: Vox tua dulcis et facies tua decora.*[c] These are now two things that are loved very much – sweet speech and bright beauty. Whoever has them together, such Jesus Christ chooses as lover and as bride. If you wish to be such, show no man your beauty, and do not gladly allow your voice to be heard, but turn them both to Jesus Christ, to your precious husband, as he asks you in the words above, as you wish your speech to seem sweet to him and your beauty bright, and to have him as your beloved, who is a thousand times brighter than the sun.

Listen now carefully, my dear sisters, to quite another saying, different from this first one. Listen now how Jesus Christ speaks as in anger and as in fierce disdain and scorn to the anchoress who should be his lover and nevertheless seeks pleasure and comfort outwardly with eye or with tongue. *In Canticis: Si ignoras te, O pulchra inter mulieres, egredere et abi post uestigia gregum tuorum et pasce edos tuos iuxta tabernacula pastorum*[d] – these are the words: 'If you do not know yourself, beautiful

a Behold, my beloved speaketh to me: Arise, make haste, my love, etc. (Canticles 2. 10).
b Arise, make haste, my love, my dove, my beautiful one, and come (Canticles 2. 10). Show me thy face. Let thy voice sound in mine ears (Canticles 2.14).
c Following which there is also added: Thy voice is sweet and thy face comely (Canticles 2.14).
d In Canticles (1.7): If thou know not thyself, O fair among women, go forth, and follow after the steps of the flocks, and feed thy kids beside the herdsmen's tents.

among women, go out and follow the tracks of the herds and pasture your kids by the herdsmen's tents of boughs and leaves.' This is a cruel saying, a fierce saying as well, which Our Lord says as in anger and in scorn to peeping and want-to-hear and talkative anchoresses. It is wrapped up and hidden, but I will unfold it. 'If you do not know yourself,' says Our Lord – pay attention carefully now – that is, 'If you do not know whose wife you are, that you are queen of heaven if you are true to me as a wife ought to be. If you have forgotten this and care too little about it, go out,' he says. Where to? 'Out of this high state and this great honour and follow herds of goats,' he says. What are herds of goats? They are the flesh's desires which stink as goats do before Our Lord. 'If you have forgotten now your honourable rank as lady, go and follow these goats. Follow the flesh's desires.' Now after that comes 'And pasture your kids' – that is, as I said, 'Feed your eyes with gazing, your tongue with chattering, your ears with talking, your nose with smelling, your flesh with soft feeling.' These five senses he calls kids; for just as from a kid which has sweet flesh there comes a stinking nanny or a foul billy, exactly so from a young sweet looking, or from a sweet hearing, or from a soft feeling, there grows a stinking desire and a foul sin. Has any peeping anchoress, who is always poking her beak out like an untamed bird in a cage, ever had this happen to her? Has the cat of hell ever snatched at her and caught with his claws the head of her heart? Yes, truly, and pulled out all the body after with claws of hooked and sharp temptations and made her lose both God and man with ample shame and sin and deprived her at one stroke of earth and also of heaven. A sorry loss enough! An anchoress always poked her beak out like this to her destruction. *Egredere*, he says in anger. 'Go out, as did Dinah, Jacob's daughter, to her sorrow, to her destruction'[47] – that is to say: 'Leave me and my comfort, which is within your breast and go and seek outside the world's wretched comfort, which will always end in suffering and sorrow. Go to that and leave me since you prefer it so; for you shall in no way have these two comforts, mine and the world's, the joy of the Holy Ghost and the consolation of the flesh, together. Choose now one of these two, for you must leave the other.' *O pulchra inter mulieres.* 'If you do not know yourself, beautiful among women,' says Our Lord. 'Beautiful among women; yes, do now here what you should and you will certainly be beautiful elsewhere, not only among women, but among angels. You, my excellent wife,' says Our Lord, 'will you follow goats in the field?' – that is, the flesh's desires? The field is the extent of the will. 'Will you follow goats over the field in this way? You, who should in the bower of your heart ask me for kisses, like my beloved who says to me in the love-book *Osculetur me osculo oris sui*[a] – that is, 'May my beloved kiss me with the kiss of his mouth, sweetest of mouths.' This kiss, dear sisters, is a sweetness and a delight of the heart so immeasurably sweet that every worldly taste is bitter in comparison to it. But Our Lord does not kiss with this kiss any soul which loves anything except him and, for his sake, the things which help it to have him. And you, then, God's wife – who have been able to hear before this how sweetly your husband speaks and calls you to him so lovingly; after that how he changes tack and speaks very fiercely if you go out – keep in your room, do not feed kids outside your gate, but keep inside your hearing, your speech and your sight and shut their gates – the mouth, the eye and the ear – firmly. They are locked up behind a wall or a fence[48] for nothing, those who open these gates except to God's messenger and the livelihood of the soul. *Omni custodia custodi cor tuum*:[b] above all things, then, as Solomon teaches you – and I said a long way back at the beginning of this part – my dear sisters, guard your heart. The heart is well locked up if mouth and eye and ear are locked up sensibly; for they, as I said there, are the heart's wardens, and if the wardens go out, the home is badly protected. This is now three senses of which I have spoken. Let us now speak briefly of the other two. (However, speech is not the mouth's sense, but taste is: however, both are in the mouth.)

The nose's smell is the fourth of the five senses. Of this sense St Augustine says, *De odoribus non satago nimis: cum assunt non respuo; cum absunt non requiro*[c] – 'I do not bother much,' he says, 'about scents: whether they are near or far, in God's name, I do not care.' Our Lord, however, through Isaiah, threatens with the stench of hell those who

---

a Let him kiss me with the kiss of his mouth (Canticles 1.1).
b With all watchfulness keep thy heart (Proverbs 4.23).
c I am not much bothered by scents: when they are there I do not spurn them; when they are not there I do not seek them out (*Confessions* 10.32).

have pleasure here in fleshly scents. *Erit pro suaui odore fetor.*[a] On the other hand, they shall have heavenly scents, who here sometimes have a stench and a strong smell in their nose from the sweat caused by the iron they wear, or from the hairshirts, or from sweaty clothes, or from stuffy air and mouldy things in their house.

Be warned of this, my dear sisters – that sometimes the fiend makes a thing stink that you should use because he wants you to stay away from it. At other times the deceiver makes a sweet scent come from some hidden thing that you cannot see – such as the powder of hidden seeds – as though it were from heaven, so that you should think that God, because of your holy life, was sending you his comfort, and would have a good opinion of yourself and leap into pride. A scent that comes from God comforts the heart more than the nose. These and other deceptions with which he deceives many should be brought to nothing with holy water and with the sign of the holy cross. Whoever was to think how God himself was tormented in this sense would patiently suffer the torment of it.

On the hill of Calvary where Our Lord hung was the place of execution, where rotten bodies often lay above ground and stank very strongly. He, as he hung, was able to have their smell, with all his other suffering, directly in his nose.

He was tormented likewise in all his other senses: in his sight when he saw his precious mother's tears and St John the Evangelist's and the other Marys', and when he saw how his dear disciples all fled from him and left him alone. He wept himself three times with his fair eyes.[49] He endured in complete patience being blindfolded, when his eyes were in this shameful way blindfolded, to give the anchorite the clear sight of heaven. Though you, for his love and in memory of this, blindfold your eyes on earth to bear him fellowship, it is no great wonder.

They hit him on the mouth often enough when they struck his cheeks and spat on him in scorn – and an anchoress for one word is out of her wits. Since he patiently endured the Jews closing his precious mouth with their cruel fists, as they knocked him about, you too, for the love of him and for your own great benefit, should shut your

a There shall be stench instead of a sweet smell (Isaiah 3.24).

wittering mouth with your lips. Besides, he tasted gall on his tongue – to teach an anchoress that she should not complain any more about food or drink, however plain it may be. If she can eat it, let her eat it and thank God earnestly; if she cannot, let her be sorry that she has to ask for something more luxurious. But rather than her request raising any scandal, she should die a martyr in her distress. One ought to flee death as far as one may without sin, but one must sooner die than commit any capital sin; and is it not a great sin to make people say, 'This anchoress likes luxury; she asks a great deal'? But it is worse if people say she is a grumbler and rude, disdainful and difficult to please. Were she in the world, she would sometimes have to be pleased readily enough with less and with worse. It is very unreasonable to come into an anchor-house, into God's prison, willingly and wanting to, to a place of discomfort, to seek comfort in it and power and the standing of a lady beyond what she might readily enough have had in the world. Think, anchoress, what you were looking for when you forsook the world at your enclosure – to weep for your own sins and those of others and to lose all the joys of this life so as to embrace joyfully your joyous lover in the eternal life of heaven. O, says St Jerome, *quomodo obscuratum est aurum optimum, et cetera*[a] – 'O alas, alas, how has the gold become dark, how has the fairest colour turned and faded!' The Apostle speaks to such fiercely, as in anger: *Quis uos fascinauit, et cetera . . . vt cum spiritu ceperitis, carne consummamini*[b] – 'But what unblessed spirit has so bewitched you that you began in the spirit and will end in the flesh?' The spiritual life begun in the Holy Ghost has become utterly fleshly, laughing, light in conduct, one time light in words, another time vicious in words, luxurious and querulous – a grumbler's life, a complainer's, and even, which is worse, a curser's and a scolder's, bitter and poisonous with a swollen heart. It would not be suitable for such to be the lady of a castle; it is a mockery and unreasonable in an anointed anchoress, and a buried anchoress – for what is the anchor-house but her grave? – that she shall be more puffed up and thought more of a lady than the lady of a house. [She will be more highly thought of] if she gets angry at the guilt

a O, how is the finest gold become dim, etc. (Lamentations 4.1 – Jeremiah, not Jerome).

b Who hath bewitched you, etc., that whereas you began in the spirit you would now be made perfect by the flesh? (Galatians 3.1, 3).

of sin,[50] if she orders her words so equably that she does not seem over-excited and led on beyond what is reasonable, but speaks fervently and truly without haste or haughtiness in a quiet voice. *Filia fatua in deminoratione erit.*[a] This is Solomon's saying; may God never permit it to happen to any of you: 'A foolish daughter becomes like the moon in its waning.' She thrives like the fool – the longer, the worse. You, as you wish to wax and not go backwards, must be sure to row against the stream, push on with great labour and exert your spiritual arms sturdily. And so we[51] must all, for we are all in this stream, in the world's wild water which carries many away. As soon as ever we become weary and rest in sloth, our boat goes backwards, and we are the foolish daughter who is on the wane, the lukewarm person whom God spews up, as is written later,[52] who began in the spirit and ended in the flesh. No, no – but, as Job says,[53] 'a man who digs for treasure, the nearer he gets to it, the more eager and fresh his heart's gladness makes him for digging and delving deeper and deeper until he finds it'. Your heart is not on earth, and so you do not need to dig downwards but to lift the heart upwards, for that is the rowing up against this world's stream, and to drive against it to dig for the hoard of gold which is up in heaven. And what is the digging? Eager searching thought as to where it is and what it is and how it may be found. This is the digging, to be always eagerly about it, with single-minded desire, with the heat of a hungry heart, to wade up out of vices, to creep out of the flesh, to break out above it, to rise up in yourself with high thought towards heaven. It is so much the more necessary because your feeble tender flesh cannot endure hardship. Now then, to counter that give God your heart, in softness, in sweetness, in all kinds of meekness and softest humility. No groaning now and fretting, and then a loud voice, getting unthinkably angry, twisting the shoulders, throwing the head about so that God hates her and man despises her. No, no, mature words, mature behaviour and acts are appropriate for an anchoress. When words are humbly and truthfully spoken, not in an ill-bred or arrogant way, then they have the weight to be properly understood. Now this is all said so that, following Jesus Christ, who was struck in

a A foolish daughter shall be to his [i.e. her father's] loss (Ecclesiasticus 22.3. The author takes '*in deminoratione*' as 'on the wane').

..iouth and given gall to drink, you should guard yourselves against sin of the mouth and endure some torment in that sense, as he was tormented in it.

In his ear the heavenly Lord had all the reproach and the upbraiding, all the scorn and all the shame that an ear might hear; and he says about himself, to teach us, *Et factus sum sicut homo non audiens et non habens in ore suo redargutiones*[a] – 'I kept silent,' he says, 'as does a deaf and dumb man who has no answer, though people treat him badly or speak badly of him.' This is your lover's saying, and you, blessed anchoress, who are his bride, learn it from him eagerly so that you know it and can truly say it.

Now I have spoken of four of your senses and of God's comfort – how he through his senses comforts you as often as you in yours feel any misery. Now listen to the fifth, in which there is most need of comfort. For the pain is greatest in it – that is, in feeling – and the pleasure also, if things turn out that way.

The fifth sense is feeling. This one sense is in all the others and throughout the body, and therefore it needs to be guarded best. Our Lord knew it well, and therefore he wished to endure most in this sense precisely so as to comfort us if we endure suffering in it and to turn us from the pleasure which the desire of the flesh asks for, particularly in feeling, more than in the others.

Our Lord in this sense had pain not in one place but everywhere, not only throughout his body but even within his blessed soul. In it he felt the pang of sorry and sorrowful sorrow that made him sigh sore. This pang was threefold, such as if three spears struck him to his heart. The first was the weeping of his mother and the other Marys, who streamed with tears; the second that his dear disciples believed him no longer and did not think that he was God, because he did not help himself in his great pain, and all fled from him and left him like a stranger; the third was the great suffering and regret that he had within him for their being lost who put him to death – that he saw lost as far as they were concerned all the work he did on earth. These three pangs were in his soul. In his body each part, as St Augustine says, endured separate

---

a And I became as a man that heareth not and that hath no reproofs in his mouth (Psalm 37.15).

pains, and died all over his body as he had earlier all over his body sweated the sweat of death. And here St Bernard says that he wept not only with eyes but did so, as it were, with all the parts of his body: *Quasi, inquit, membris omnibus fleuisse uidetur*.[a] For so full of anguish was that sweat of distress which fell from his body at the thought of the agonizing death he was going to suffer that it seemed like red blood: *Factus est sudor eius quasi gutte sanguinis decurrentis in terram*.[b] And further, so freely and abundantly did that bloody sweat flow from his blessed body that the streams ran down to the earth. Such horror did his human flesh have at the thought of the terrible pain that it was going to endure – which was no strange surprise, for the more alive the flesh, so the sensation in it, and the hurt, is more intense. A small hurt in the eye is more painful than a large one in the heel, for the flesh is deader. Every man's flesh is dead in comparison to what God's flesh was, in that it was taken from the tender maiden and nothing was ever in it that deadened it, but it was always alive with the living Godhead which dwelt in it. Therefore in his flesh the pain was more intense than any man ever endured in his flesh, in that his flesh was more alive than all other fleshes. Here, look, is an illustration. A man is not bled for a sickness he has in the sick place but in the healthy, to heal the sick; but in all the world, which was in a fever, there was not found among all mankind one healthy place which might be bled, except only God's body, which was bled on the cross, not in the arm only, but in five places, to heal mankind of the sickness that the five senses had aroused. Thus, look, the healthy place and the living part drew the bad blood out from what was unhealthy and so healed what was sick. Through blood, in Holy Writ, sin is signified – the reasons for this are clearly shown later.[54] But take note of this, my dear sisters, that your precious husband, the love-deserving Lord, the healer from heaven, Jesus, God, God's Son, the ruler of all the world, when he was bled in this way – understand what his diet was that day. At that blood-letting, so baleful and so bitter, those he bled for did not bring him as a present wine or

a It seems as if, he says, he has wept with all the parts of his body (*Sermon Three on Palm Sunday* (4)).

b His sweat became as drops of blood, trickling down upon the ground (Luke 22. 44).

ale or water, even when he said *Sicio*[a] and complained, as he bled, of thirst on the cross, but brought bitter gall. Where was there ever such a poor pittance given to anyone being bled? And nevertheless he did not complain, but accepted it humbly to teach his people. But he did still more as an example for us – put his dear mouth to it and tasted it, though he could not make use of it. Who, then, is there after this – and most particularly an anchoress – who will complain if she does not have the food or drink her comfort requires? And, assuredly, whoever complains offers even now this hateful pittance to Our Lord, as the Jews did then, and is a friend of the Jews in offering him in his thirst a drink of sour gall. His thirst is nothing but yearning for our soul's health, and the complaining of a bitter and sour heart is sourer and more bitter to him now than was the gall then; and you, his dear bride, do not be the Jews' partner in pouring such drink for him, but bear him company and drink gladly with him all that seems sour or bitter to your flesh – that is, pain and misery and all discomforts – and he will repay you as his true friend with the linctus[55] of heaven.

Thus was Jesus Christ, the Almighty God, in all his five senses cruelly tormented, and especially in this last – that is, in feeling, for his flesh was all as alive as the tender eye is. And you should guard this sense – that is, the flesh's feeling – above all the others. God's hands were nailed on the cross. By the same nails I implore you, anchoresses (not you, for there is no need, but others, my dear sisters), keep your hands within your windows. Touching of hands or any contact between a man and an anchoress is a thing so unseemly and a deed so shameful and so naked a sin, so horrible to all the world and so great a scandal, that there is no need to speak or write against it, for without any writing at all the foulness is too apparent. God knows, I would much prefer to see you all, my dear sisters, dearest of women to me, hang on a gibbet so as to avoid sin, than see one of you give a single kiss to any man on earth in the way I mean. I am silent on anything further. Not only holding hands, but putting a hand out, unless out of necessity, is courting anger and attracting his wrath. For herself to look at her own white hands does harm to many an anchoress who keeps them too beautiful, like those who have nothing at all to do. They should each

a I thirst (John 19.28).

day scrape up the earth of their graves, in which they will rot.[56] God knows, the grave does a lot of good to many an anchoress, for as Solomon says, *Memorare nouissima tua et in eternum non peccabis.*[a] She who always has, as it were, before her eyes her death, of which the grave reminds her, if she thinks well about Judgement Day, on which the angels will tremble, and the eternal and terrible pains of hell, and above absolutely everything about Jesus Christ's passion – how he was tormented, as has been told in part, in all his five senses – she will not lightly follow the flesh's pleasure according to the will's desire, nor bring upon herself any capital sin with her five senses. This is enough now said about the five senses, which are like an outside guardian of the heart, in which is the soul's life – as we said above first of all that Solomon said, *Omni custodia custodi cor tuum, quoniam ex ipso uita procedit.*[b] Now, Christ be thanked, two parts have been got through. Let us go on now, with his help, to the third.

---

a Remember thy last end and thou shalt never sin (Ecclesiasticus 7.40).
b With all watchfulness keep thy heart, because life issueth out from it (Proverbs 4. 23).

PART THREE

Birds and Anchorites: the Inner Feelings

My dear sisters, just as you guard your senses well on the outside, so above all things see that you are on the inside soft and mild and humble, sweet and fragrant-hearted and patient in the face of injury caused by things that are said to you and of deeds that are wrongly done to you, lest you should lose all. Against bitter anchoresses David speaks this verse: *Similis factus sum pellicano solitudinis, et cetera*[a] – 'I am,' he says, 'like a pelican that lives on its own.' The pelican is a bird so passionate and so wrathful that it often kills its own chicks in anger, when they annoy it, and then soon afterwards it becomes very sorry and makes very great lamentation and strikes itself with its beak, with which it previously killed its chicks, and draws blood from its breast, and with the blood brings back to life its chicks which had been killed. This bird, the pelican, is the passionate anchoress. Her chicks are her good works, which she often kills with the beak of sharp wrath. But when she has done so, let her do as the pelican does: regret it very soon and with her own beak peck her breast – that is, with confession from her mouth, with which she sinned and killed her good works, draw the blood of sin out from her breast – that is, from the heart which the soul's life is in. And in this way will her chicks which had been killed come back to life – that is, her good works. Blood signifies sin. For just as a bloodstained man is fearful and horrible in men's eyes, so is the sinner before the eye of God. In addition, no one can examine blood well before it has cooled. So it is with sin. While the heart is boiling within with anger, there is no right judgement; or while desire is hot towards any sin, you cannot then judge well what it is or what will

a I am become like to a pelican of the wilderness, etc. (Psalm 101.7).

come of it. But let desire pass, and you will be pleased – let the heat cool, as someone who wants to examine blood does, and you will rightly judge the sin foul and loathsome which seemed attractive to you, and that so much evil would have come of it if you had done it while the heat lasted that you will judge yourself mad when you had thoughts of doing it. This is true of each sin (and is why blood signifies it), and especially of anger: *Impedit ira animum ne possit cernere uerum*[1][a] – 'Anger,' it says, 'while it lasts, so blinds the heart that it is unable to recognize the truth.' *Maga quedam est, transformans naturam humanam*[b] – anger is a shape-changer, like the ones in stories, since it takes from a man his reason and completely alters how he is and changes him from a man and gives him the nature of a beast. An angry woman is a she-wolf; a man a wolf, or a lion, or a unicorn. All the time anger is in a woman's heart, though she recite versicles, says her hours, *Aues*, *Pater nosters*, she is only howling. Like one who has been turned into a she-wolf in God's eyes, she only has a she-wolf's voice in his sensitive ears. *Ira furor breuis est.*[2][c] Wrath is a madness – isn't an angry man mad? How does he look, how does he speak, how is his heart going on inside? What's his behaviour all like outside? He doesn't recognize any man – how's he a man then? *Est enim homo animal mansuetum natura.*[d] Man is naturally mild. As soon as he loses mild-heartedness, he loses man's nature, and anger, the shape-changer, changes him into a beast, as I said earlier. And what if any anchoress, Jesus Christ's wife, is changed into a she-wolf? Isn't that a great sorrow? The only thing is quickly to throw off that rough pelt around the heart and with soft reconciliation make herself smooth and soft, as a woman's skin naturally is, for with that she-wolf's skin nothing that she does is pleasing to God.

Look, here are many remedies against anger, a great crowd of comforts and various helps. If people speak ill of you, think that you are earth: isn't earth trampled, isn't earth spat on? Even if people treated you in this way, they would be treating the earth right. If you bark back, you are dog-natured; if you sting back, you are snake-

---

a   Anger impedes the spirit so that it is not able to discern the truth (*Distichs of Cato* 2.4).

b   It is a sort of sorceress, transforming human nature.

c   Anger is a brief madness (Horace, *Epistles* 1.2, 62).

d   For man is an animal gentle by nature.

natured and not Christ's bride. Think – did he act like this? *Qui tanquam ouis ad occisionem ductus est et non aperuit os suum.*[a] After all the shameful torments that he endured during the long night before the Friday, he was taken in the morning to be hanged on the gibbet and have iron nails driven through his four limbs. But no more than a sheep, as the Holy Writ says, did he ever stir or speak.

Think again, in addition, what is a word but wind?[3] Too weakly is she fortified whom a puff of wind, a word, can fell and throw into sin. And who will not be amazed at an anchoress felled by the wind? Or again, once more, does she not show that she is dust and an unstable thing, who with the wind of a few words is immediately blown down? That same puff from his mouth, if you cast it beneath you, would bear you up towards the bliss of heaven; but, as it is, our great madness is a matter of great astonishment. Understand what I am saying: St Andrew was able to endure the hard cross lifting him towards heaven and lovingly embraced it.[4] Lawrence likewise endured the gridiron lifting him upwards with burning coals,[5] St Stephen the stones that were thrown at him;[6] and he received them gladly, and prayed for those who threw them at him on bended knees – and we are unable to endure the wind of a word bearing us towards heaven, but are enraged at those whom we should thank as the very ones who are doing us a great service, though it be against their will. *Impius uiuit pio uelit nolit.*[b] All that the wicked and evil person does for the sake of evil is all for the good of the good man – all is his gain and a preparation for bliss. Let him – and do it gladly – plait your crown. Think how the holy man in *Vitas Patrum*[7] kissed and blessed the hand of the other person who had harmed him and said so fervently, kissing it eagerly, 'Blessed for ever be this hand, for it has prepared for me the blisses of heaven.' And you should say likewise of the hand that does you ill, and of the mouth also that speaks any ill of you, 'Blessed be your mouth,' say, 'for you make of it a tool for preparing my crown. I am pleased for my good, and unhappy, though, for your evil, for you are doing me a benefit and harming yourself.' If any man or any woman has spoken ill of you or

a Who was led as a sheep to the slaughter and did not open his mouth (see Isaiah 53.7).
b The wicked person lives willy-nilly for the good person.

done you ill, you should speak like this. But, as it is, it is a matter of great astonishment, if we consider well how God's saints endured wounds in their bodies and we are enraged if a wind blows on us a bit – and the wind wounds nothing except only the air. For neither may the wind – that is, the words that are said – wound you in your flesh, or defile your soul, though it blows on you, unless you make it do so yourself. *Bernardus: Quid irritaris, quid inflammaris ad uerbi flatum, qui nec carnem uulnerat nec inquinat mentem.*[8a] You may well gather that there was there little fire of charity, which all flames up from Our Lord's love, little fire was there, if a puff could put it out; for where there is much fire, it grows with the wind.[9]

Against ill done or ill said look here, lastly, the best remedy. Listen to this illustration: a man who lay in prison and owed a great ransom and who was quite unable to get out, unless to be hanged, before he had paid the ransom in full – would he not be very grateful to a man who threw at him a purse of pennies with which to buy himself out and free himself from suffering? Even if he threw it very hard against his heart, all the hurt would be forgotten because of the gladness. In this same way we are all in prison here and owe God great debts for sin. Therefore we cry to him in the *Pater noster, Et dimitte nobis debita nostra*[b] – 'Lord,' we say, 'forgive us our debts, just as we forgive our debtors injury that is done us, either of word or of deed.' That is our ransom, with which we should redeem ourselves and clear our debts to Our Lord – that is, our sins – since without clearance no one is taken up out of this prison who is not immediately hanged, either in purgatory or in the torment of hell. And Our Lord himself says, *Dimittite et dimittetur uobis*[c] – 'Forgive and I forgive you,' as though he said, 'You are greatly in debt to me because of your sins, but if you want a good agreement, all that any man says ill of you or does ill to you I will accept against the debt that you owe me.' Now, then, though something said strike very hard on your breast and, as it seems to you at first, hurt your heart, think as the prisoner would whom the other

a Bernard: Why are you irritated, why are you inflamed at the breath of a word, which neither wounds the flesh nor defiles the mind? (*Declamations ... from the Sermons of St Bernard* 36.43).
b And forgive us our debts.
c Forgive and you shall be forgiven (Luke 6.37).

hurt badly with the purse and accept it gladly to clear yourself with it and think that he who sends it at you, though God may never thank him for having sent it, harms himself and profits you, if you are able to endure it. For as David says very well indeed, 'God puts in his treasury the wicked and the evil so as to hire with them, as one does with treasure, those who fight well.' *Ponens in thesauris abyssos. Glosa: Crudeles quibus donat milites suos.*[a]

Again, in addition, this bird, the pelican, has a second characteristic – that it is always thin,[10] and so, as I said, David likens himself to it, in the character of an anchorite, in an anchorite's voice: *Similis factus sum pellicano solitudinis*[b] – 'I am like a pelican that lives on its own.' And an anchoress ought to speak in this way and be like a pelican in so far as it is thin: *Judith, clausa in cubiculo, ieiunabat omnibus diebus uite sue, et cetera*[c] – Judith, shut in, as it tells in her book, led a very hard life, fasted and wore haircloth. Judith shut in signifies the anchoress shut in, who ought to lead a hard life, as did the lady Judith, according to her ability, not like a pig stalled in a sty to fatten and get large for the stroke of the axe.

There are two kinds of anchoress of which Our Lord speaks in the Gospel, false and true: *Vulpes foueas habent et uolucres celi nidos*[d] – that is, 'Foxes have their holes and birds of heaven their nests.' The foxes are false anchorites, as the fox is the falsest of beasts. 'These,' he says, 'have holes who dig holes into the earth with earthly vices and drag into their holes all that they can lay hold of and seize.' Thus hoarding anchoresses are likened by God in the Gospel to foxes.[11] The fox is a greedy beast and ravenous as well, and the false anchoress drags into her hole and eats, as the fox does, both geese and hens; she has, like the fox, an innocent look at times, but is nevertheless full of guile. They make themselves out to be other than they are, like the fox, which is a hypocrite. They think to beguile God as they dupe simple men – and beguile themselves most. They yelp as the fox does and boast of their

a Laying up the depths in storehouses (Psalm 32.7). Gloss: The cruel, whom he gives to his soldiers.
b I am become like to a pelican of the wilderness (Psalm 101.7).
c Judith, shut up in her chamber, fasted all the days of her life, etc. (Judith 8.5–6).
d The foxes have holes, and the birds of heaven nests (Matthew 8.20 and Luke 9.58).

goodness wherever they dare and are able. They chatter about trivial things and become so very worldly that in the end their name stinks like the fox as he goes about. For if they do evil, worse is said of them.

These went into the anchor-house as Saul did into the hole, not as the good David did. They both went into the hole, Saul and David, as it tells in *Regum*.[a] But Saul went into it to do his dirt in it, as is done by many. Some unfortunate anchoresses go into the hole of the anchor-house to befoul the place and do more secretly in it fleshly filthinesses than they might if they were out in the world. For who has more leisure to do her wickednesses than the false anchoress? Thus Saul went into the cave to defile the place; but David went into it only to hide himself from Saul, who hated him and was seeking him to slay him. The good anchoress does likewise, whom Saul – that is, the fiend – hates and hunts. She goes in to hide herself from his sharp claws: she hides herself in her hole both from worldly men and worldly sins, and therefore she is spiritually David, who is strong against the devil, and her face is lovely in Our Lord's eyes. For this is what this word 'David' means in the Hebrew language. The false anchoress is Saul, in accordance with what his name means. *Saul: Abutens, siue Abusio*[b] – for 'Saul' in Hebrew is 'misusing' in English, and the false anchoress misuses the name of an anchoress and all that an anchoress does. The good anchoress is Judith, as we said before, who is shut up, as she was, and just as she did fasts, keeps vigils, labours and wears harsh clothing. She is one of the birds of which Our Lord speaks after the foxes, which do not dig holes downwards with their desires, as do the foxes – that is, false anchoresses – but have, like birds of heaven, set their nests high up, that is, their rest. True anchoresses are called birds, for they leave the earth – that is, love of all worldly things – and through yearning in heart for heavenly things fly upwards towards heaven. And though they fly high in a high and holy life, they nevertheless hold their heads low in mild humility, as a flying bird bows its head, consider all that they do well worth nothing and say, as Our Lord taught all his own, *Cum omnia benefeceritis, dicite: Serui inutiles sumus*[c] – 'When you have done

a   Kings (1 Kings 24).
b   Saul: Abusing, or Abuse.
c   When you shall have done all things well, say: We are unprofitable servants (Luke 17.10).

everything well,' says Our Lord, 'say that you are useless servants.' Fly high and always hold your head low, nevertheless. The wings which bear them upwards, they are virtues which they must stir into good deeds as a bird when it wants to fly stirs its wings. Again, the true anchoresses, whom we are likening to birds (not we, though, but God), spread their wings and make crosses of themselves as a bird does when it flies – that is, in the thought of the heart and in the bitterness of the flesh bear God's cross.

Those birds fly well which have little flesh, as the pelican has, and many feathers. The ostrich, because of his abundant flesh, and other such birds, makes a show of flying and beats its wings, but its feet are always dragging to the earth. Likewise a fleshly anchoress who lives in the desires of the flesh and pursues her ease – the heaviness of her flesh and fleshly vices deprives her of her flight, and although she may make a show and a great noise with her wings (another's, not her own) – that is, pretend to be flying and to be a holy anchoress – whoever looks carefully laughs her to scorn, for her feet – that is, her desires – are always like the ostrich's, dragging to the earth. These are not like the thin bird, the pelican, and do not fly high up, but are earth-birds and nest on the earth. But God calls the good anchoresses birds of heaven, as I said before. *Vulpes foueas habent et uolucres celi nidos*[a] – foxes have their holes and birds of heaven have their nests. True anchoresses are indeed birds of heaven which fly up high and sit singing merrily on the green boughs – that is, direct their thoughts upwards at the bliss of heaven, which never fades but is always green – and sit in this greenness singing merrily – that is, take their rest in thoughts like these – and, like those that sing, have mirth in their hearts. A bird, however, sometimes comes down to the ground to seek its food, because of the flesh's need, but while it stays on the ground it never feels safe, but often turns around and always looks busily about. Likewise the good anchoress, fly she never so high, must sometimes come down to the ground of her body and eat, drink, sleep, work, speak and hear about what she needs to of earthly things. But then, as the bird does, she must look about her well, look around on every side, so that she does not go

a The foxes have holes, and the birds of heaven nests (Matthew 8.20 and Luke 9.58).

wrong anywhere in case she should be caught by one of the devil's snares or hurt in some way while she stays so low down.

'These birds have nests,' says Our Lord – *Volucres celi nidos*. A nest is hard on the outside, with pricking thorns; on the inside, yielding and soft. In this way shall the anchoress on the outside endure hardship in her flesh and pricking pains; so sensibly, though, shall she afflict her flesh, that she is able to say with the Psalmist, *Fortitudinem meam ad te custodiam*[a] – that is, 'I shall guard my strength, Lord, for your benefit.' Therefore let the flesh's suffering be according to each one's nature. Let the nest be hard outside, and soft and sweet the heart inside. Those who are bitter or hard of heart and soft towards their flesh, they make their nests in the opposite way, soft outside and thorny inside. These are the angry and easy-living anchoresses, bitter inside where there should be sweetness, easy-living outside where there should be hardship. These, in a nest like this, when they think carefully about it, are not going to get much rest, for they will bring their chicks out late from such a nest – that is, good deeds, which fly towards heaven. Job calls the anchor-house a nest and says, as if he were an anchorite, *In nidulo meo moriar*[b] – that is, 'I shall die in my nest, be as if dead in it, for that is an anchorite's duty, and dwell in it until death'; that is, 'I will never cease while my soul is in my body to suffer hardship outside, just as a nest is hard, and be soft inside.'

From dumb beasts learn wisdom and knowledge. The eagle puts in his nest a precious gemstone called an agate,[12] for no poisonous thing can come near the stone, nor, while it is in the nest, harm his chicks. This precious stone is Jesus Christ, true as stone and full of all powers, above all gemstones. He is the agate which the poison of sin never came near. Put him in your nest – that is, in your heart. Think what pain he suffered in his flesh on the outside, how sweet-hearted he was, how soft on the inside, and so shall you drive out every poison from your heart and bitterness from your body. For with thoughts like this, be it never so bitter, the pain which you endure for the love of him who suffered more for you shall seem sweet to you. This stone, as I said, expels poisonous things. If you have this stone within your breast,

a I will keep my strength for thee (Psalm 58.10).

b I shall die in my nest (Job 29.18).

where God's nest is, you need not fear the poisonous snake of hell. Your chicks – that is, your good works – are quite safe from his poison.

Whoever is not able to have and hold this gemstone in the nest of her heart, let her at least in the nest of her anchor-house have his likeness – that is, the crucifix – and look often at it, and kiss the places of the wounds in sweet remembrance of the real wounds which he, on the real cross, patiently endured. As far as she may, let her be Judith – that is, live a hard life – acknowledge often to God his great goodness towards her and her faults towards him, with which she repays him it badly. Let her cry to him earnestly for mercy and forgiveness for them and confess frequently. Then is she Judith, who killed Holofernes[13] – for 'Judith' in Hebrew is 'confession' in English, which kills spiritually the devil of hell. *Judith: Confessio.*[a] Therefore an anchoress says to each priest *Confiteor*[b] first of all and confesses often, so as to be Judith and slay Holofernes – that is, the devil's strength. For this name Holofernes means 'stinking in hell'. *Secundum nominis ethimologiam, Olofernus, olens in inferno; secundum interpretationem, infirmans uitulum saginatum.*[c] In the Hebrew language Holofernes is the fiend who makes feeble and weak the fat and over-wild calf – that is, the flesh, which goes wild as soon as ever it gets fat through ease and through abundance. *Incrassatus est dilectus et recalcitrauit*[d] – 'My beloved has grown fat,' says Our Lord, 'and strikes me with his heel.' As soon as the flesh has what it wants, it kicks out at once, like a fat and idle horse. The fiend has the strength to weaken this fat calf and incline it towards sin, for this is what this name 'Holofernes' means. But an anchoress must be Judith through a hard life and through true confession, and kill, as Judith did, the evil Holofernes, tame her flesh very well as soon as she feels that it is getting too wild with fasts, with vigils, with haircloth, with hard toil, with hard disciplines, wisely though, and warily. *Habete, inquit, sal in uobis. Item: In omni sacrifitio offeretis michi sal*[e] – that is, 'In each sacrifice,'

a Judith: Confession.
b I confess.
c According to the etymology of the name, Holofernes [means] 'stinking in hell'; according to the interpretation, 'weakening the fattened calf'.
d The beloved grew fat and kicked back (Deuteronomy 32.15).
e Have, he says, salt in you. Likewise: In all thy oblations thou shalt offer to me salt (Leviticus 2.13).

Our Lord says, 'always offer me salt. Fasting, vigil' and other such things as I mentioned just now 'are my sacrifices.' Salt signifies wisdom,[14] for salt gives flavour to food, and wisdom gives taste to all that we do well. Without the salt of wisdom all our deeds seem to God flavourless. In addition, without salt meat collects worms, stinks very foul and soon rots away. Just so, without wisdom flesh eats itself up like a worm and destroys itself, and perishes like a thing that rots away, and in the end kills itself. But to Our Lord a sacrifice like this stinks.

Though the flesh is our enemy, we are commanded to support it. We must often make it suffer as it very often deserves, but not destroy it completely, for however weak it may be, it is still coupled in such a way and so firmly linked to our precious soul, God's own form, that we might soon kill the one with the other. *Augustinus: Natura mentis humane que ad ymaginem Dei creata est et sine peccato est, solus Deus maior est.*[a] And this is one of the greatest wonders on earth, that the highest thing under God – that is, man's soul – as St Augustine testifies, has to be so firmly linked to the flesh, which is nothing but mud and foul earth, and because of that joining, love it so greatly, that to make it happy in its foul nature it departs from its high heavenly nature and to please itself angers its creator, who created it like himself, who is king and emperor of earth and of heaven. Wonder above wonders, and a shameful wonder, that so immeasurably low a thing – *fere nichil*,[b] 'nearly nothing,' says St Augustine – has to draw into sin so immeasurably high a thing as the soul is, which St Augustine calls *fere summum*[c] – that is, 'nearly the highest thing', except God.[15] But God did not want it to leap into pride, and did not wish it to climb and fall as Lucifer did, because he was without burden, and therefore tied a lump of heavy earth to it, as one does the hobble to a cow or to another beast that runs and roams about too much. This is what Job said: *Qui fecisti uentis – id est, spiritibus – pondus*[d] – 'Lord,' he says, 'you have made a load to load the soul with', that is, the heavy flesh which draws it downwards. But

a Augustine: Than the nature of the human mind, which was created in the image of God and is without sin, only God is greater (see *Against Maximus* 2.25).
b Almost nothing.
c Almost the highest thing.
d Who made a weight for the winds (Job 28.25) – that is, for spirits.

through the high estate of the soul the flesh shall become light, lighter than the wind is and brighter than the sun, if it follows it here and does not draw it too much into its low nature. Dear sisters, for love of him to whom the soul is like, do it honour. Do not allow the low flesh to master it too much. It is here in a strange land put in a prison, shut up in a death-cell, and it is not evident of what dignity it is, how high its nature is, nor what it shall seem hereafter in its own realm. The flesh is here at home – like earth that is in earth – and is therefore clever and quick, as they say the cur is brave on his own dung-hill. It has too much mastery, alas, over many. But the anchoress, as I have said, ought to be completely spiritual if she wants to fly well, like a bird that has little flesh and many feathers. Not only this, though; but besides taming her ill-disciplined flesh well, and strengthening and doing honour to the noble soul, besides this, she must further, by her example and by her holy prayers, give strength to others and hold them up so that they do not fall into the dung of sin. And therefore David at once, after he has likened the anchoress to a pelican, likens her to a night-bird that is under the eaves. *Similis factus sum pelicano solitudinis; factus sum sicut nicticorax*[16] *in domicilio.*[a]

The night-bird in the eves signifies recluses who live under the church's eaves, because they understand that they ought to be of so holy a life that all Holy Church – that is, Christian people – may lean and support itself upon them, and they may hold it up with their holiness of life and their blessed prayers. For this reason the anchoress is called an anchoress and anchored under the church like an anchor under a ship's side to hold the ship, so that waves and storms do not overturn it.[17] Just so all Holy Church, which is called a ship, must anchor on the anchoress, so that she may so hold it in order that the devil's blasts – that is, temptations – do not overturn it. Each anchoress has agreed to this, in virtue both of the name of anchoress and of her dwelling under the church to prop it up, should it be going to fall. If she breaks the agreement, let her consider to whom she is lying and how continually – for she never leaves her home. The anchoress's dwelling and her name proclaim this agreement all the time, even when she is sleeping.

a I am become like to a pelican of the wilderness: I am become like a night-raven in the house (Psalm 101.7).

In addition, the night-bird flies by night and gets its food in the dark. So must the anchoress fly with contemplation – that is, with high thought and with holy prayers – by night towards heaven and get by night her soul's food. By night ought the anchoress to be watchful and going busily about her spiritual profit; therefore there comes immediately after *Vigilaui et factus sum sicut passer solitarius in tecto. Vigilaui*[a] – 'I was watchful,' says David in the character of an anchorite, 'and like a sparrow alone under the roof.' *Vigilaui*: 'I was watchful', for that is an anchorite's duty, to keep vigil a great deal. *Ecclesiasticus: Vigilia honestatis tabefatiet carnes.*[b] Nothing subdues wild flesh or makes it tamer than much vigil. Vigil in Holy Writ is praised in many places. *Vigilate et orate ne intretis in temptationem*[c] – 'As you do not want to fall into temptation,' says Our Lord, 'stay awake and pray, and that will make you stand.' Afterwards he says, *Beatus quem inuenerit uigilantem*[d] – 'Blessed is that person whom, when Our Lord comes, he finds watching.' And he himself sometimes *pernoctauit in oratione*,[e] watched in prayer all night, and thus he taught us vigil – not only by his teaching, but by his deed.

Eight things particularly summon us always to be watching and working in some good deed: (i) this short life; (ii) this difficult path; (iii) our good, which is so meagre; (iv) our sins, which are so many; (v) death, of which we are certain and uncertain when; (vi) the stern judgement of Judgement Day – and so strict as well that each idle word will be brought forward and idle thoughts which were not atoned for here. *Dominus in Euuangelio: De omni uerbo otioso, et cetera. Item: Et capilli de capite non peribunt, id est, cogitatio non euadet inpunita. Anselmus: Quid faties in illa die quando exigetur a te omne tempus inpensum qualiter sit a te expensum, et usque ad minimam cogitationem?*[18][f] Look now what becomes

a I have watched and am become like a sparrow alone upon the house-top (Psalm 101.8). I have watched.

b Ecclesiasticus (31.1): The watch of honesty consumeth the flesh.

c Watch and pray, that you enter not into temptation (Mark 14.38).

d Blessed [is he] whom [the Lord] shall find watching (Luke 12.37).

e Passed the whole night in prayer (Luke 6.12).

f Our Lord in the Gospel: Every idle word that man shall speak [they shall render an account for it in the Day of Judgement] (Matthew 12.36). Likewise: Even the hairs of the head shall not perish (see Luke 21.18) – that is, no thought will escape unpunished. Anselm: What will you do on that day when an account will be demanded of you for all the time you have spent how you have spent it, even to the least thought? (*Meditation* 1).

of evil desires and sinful deeds. Then the seventh thing that reminds us to be watchful, that is, (vii) the sorrow of hell – on that, consider three things: the innumerable torments, the eternity of each one, the immeasurable bitterness. The eighth thing – (viii) how great is the reward in the bliss of heaven, world without end. Whoever watches well here a moment, whoever has these eight things often in her heart, she will shake off her sleep of evil sloth. In the quiet night, when nothing is seen or heard which hinders prayer, the heart is often so pure; for nothing is witness of what is done then except God's angel, who at such a time goes busily about urging us to good; for then nothing is lost as by day it often is. Listen now, dear sisters, how it is evil to display, and how good a thing it is to conceal, good deeds, and fly by night, like the night-bird, and to gather in darkness – that is, in privacy – and secretly the soul's food.

Oratio Hester placuit regi Assuero[a] – that is, 'Queen Esther's prayer was agreeable and pleasing to King Ahasuerus.' 'Esther' in Hebrew – that is, 'hidden' in English, and it is to be understood as saying that the prayer or other good deed that is done in secret is pleasing to Ahasuerus, that is, the king of heaven. For 'Ahasuerus' in Hebrew is 'blessed' in English, that is, Our Lord, who is blessed above all. David speaks to the anchoress who was wont to do well in secret and afterwards in some manner reveals and displays it: *Vt quid auertis manum tuam et dexteram tuam de medio sinu tuo, in finem?*[b] – that is, 'Why do you draw out your hand, and, further, your right hand, from the middle of your bosom?' *In finem* – 'in the end'. The right hand is a good work, the bosom is privacy; and it is as though he said, 'The right hand which you held, anchoress, in your bosom – that is, your good work which you had done privately, as a thing in the bosom is secret – why do you draw it out *in finem*, in the end?' – that is, 'so that your reward ends so soon, your reward which would be endless if your good deed were concealed – why do you disclose it and take so short a reward, a payment which is gone in a moment?' *Amen, dico uobis, receperunt mercedem suam.*[c] 'You

---

a The prayer of Esther was pleasing to King Ahasuerus (see Esther 5.4 etc.).

b Why dost thou turn away thy hand? And thy right hand out of the midst of thy bosom for ever? (Psalm 73.11).

c Amen, I say unto you, they have received their reward (Matthew 6.2).

have revealed your good,' says Our Lord, 'truly, you have received your reward.' St Gregory is amazed and says that men are mad who make such a bad bargain: *Magna uerecundia est grandia agere et laudibus inhiare. Vnde celum mereri potest nummum transitorii fauoris querit.*[a] 'It is great madness to do well and want the praise of it; to do that with which a person buys the kingdom of heaven and sell it for a puff of wind – a word of praise, of man's praising. 'Therefore, my dear sisters, keep your right hand within your bosom, lest an endless reward have a quick end. We read in Holy Writ[19] that the hand of Moses, God's prophet, as soon as he had drawn it out of his bosom, appeared to have the hospital-sickness[20] and seemed leprous, through which is signified that the good deed drawn forth is not only lost as it is revealed, but, further, seems horrible in the eye of God, as the hospital-evil is horrible in the eye of man. Look, some marvellously good words which the holy Job says: *Reposita est hec spes mea in sinu meo.*[b] 'In my bosom,' he says, 'is all my hope held' – as though he said, 'Whatever good I do, were it revealed and drawn forth from my bosom, all my hope would slip away. But because I conceal and hide it as in my bosom, I hope for reward.' Therefore, if anyone does any good, let her not draw it out, or boast about it at all, for with a little puff, with the wind of a word, it may all be blown away.

Our Lord in Joel complains much about those who waste and destroy all their good through desire of praise and says these words: *Decorticauit ficum meam, nudans spoliauit eam et proiecit; albi facti sunt rami eius.*[c] 'Alas,' says Our Lord, 'those who show their good have peeled my fig, torn all the bark off, stripped it stark naked and thrown it away, and the green boughs have dried out and turned into dry white sticks.' This saying is obscure, but take note now how I will make it clear. The fig is a kind of tree which bears sweet fruit which are called figs. The fig tree is peeled and the bark torn off when a good deed is revealed. The life is gone, the tree becomes dead when the bark is off; and it

a It is a great madness to do great things and to gape after praise. From that for which he is able to deserve heaven he seeks the small coin of transitory applause (*Morals in Job* 8.43, 70).

b This my hope is laid up in my bosom (Job 19.27).

c He hath peeled off the bark of my fig tree, he hath stripped it bare and cast it away; the branches thereof are made white (Joel 1.7).

neither bears fruit nor grows green with lovely leaves after that, but
the boughs dry and become white sticks, good for nothing but food for
the fire. The bough, when it becomes dead, it goes white on the outside
and dries up on the inside and drops its bark. Just so the good deed
that is going to become dead drops its bark away – that is, uncovers
itself. The bark that covers it is the tree's defence and keeps it strong
and alive. Just so the covering is the life of the good deed and keeps it
strong, but when the bark is off, then, as the bough dies, it goes white
on the outside through worldly praise and dries up on the inside and
loses the sweetness of God's grace, which made it green and delightful
for God to look at. For green above all colours comforts the eyes most.
When it is dried up like this, then it is good for nothing so much as the
fire of hell. For the first peeling, from which all this evil comes, is a
matter of pride alone. And is this not a great pity, that the fig, which
should with its sweet fruit – that is, good deeds – spiritually feed God,
the Lord of heaven, has to dry up without bark through being
uncovered, and become, without end, the food of hell-fire? And is she
not too wretched who with the price of heaven buys herself hell? Our
Lord in the Gospel himself likens the kingdom of heaven to a treasure
which, as he says, is hidden by whoever finds it – *quem qui inuenit homo
abscondit*.[a] Good deeds are the treasure which is likened to heaven, for
heaven is bought with it. And this treasure, unless it be the better
hidden and covered, is soon lost. For, as St Gregory says, *Depredari
desiderat qui thesaurum puplice portat in uia*[b] – 'He who carries treasure
openly on a road which is full of robbers and thieves *wants* to lose it
and be robbed.' This world is nothing other than a road to heaven or
to hell, and is all set about with hell's pilferers, who steal all the
treasure that they can see a man or a woman on this road opening up.
For that is as good as someone saying and shouting as he goes, 'I'm
carrying treasure, I'm carrying treasure – look here, red gold, plenty of
white silver and precious stones.' A soap-seller who only carries soap
and needles cries out loud what he is carrying. A rich mercer goes
along in total silence. Ask what happened to Hezekiah,[c] the good king,

a Which a man having found, hid it (Matthew 13.44).
b He who carries treasure openly on the road *wants* to be robbed (*Homilies on the
   Gospels* 11.1).
c See Isaiah 39.

because he showed the store-rooms for his spices, his great possessions, his precious treasure. Not for nothing is it written in the Holy Gospel of the three kings who came to offer Jesus Christ the three precious gifts: *Procidentes adorauerunt eum et apertis thesauris suis obtulerunt, et cetera,*[a] that what they wanted to offer him they kept hidden all the time until they came into his presence. Then first did they undo the presents they were carrying. Therefore, my dear sisters, by night, like the night-bird to which the anchorite is likened, be vigorously active. 'Night' is what I call 'privacy'; this night you may have each hour of the day, so that all the good that you ever do may be done as by night and by darkness, out of man's eye, out of man's ear. Thus at night be flying and seeking your soul's heavenly food. Then you will be not only *pellicanus solitudinis,*[b] but also *nicticorax in domicilio.*[c]

Vigilaui et factus sum sicut passer solitarius in tecto.[d] The anchoress is further likened here to the sparrow which is alone under the roof, like an anchoress. The sparrow is a twittering bird – it twitters and warbles all the time; but because many an anchoress has that same vice, David does not liken her to a sparrow who has a mate, but to a sparrow on its own. *Sicut passer solitarius* – 'I am,' he says of the anchoress, 'like a sparrow that is on its own.' For so ought an anchoress to warble and twitter her prayers on her own, being in the solitary place she is. And understand lovingly, my dear sisters, that I write of the solitary life to comfort anchoresses, and you above all.

How good it is to be alone is made clear both in the Old Law and in the New, for in both one finds that God shows his hidden mysteries and heavenly secrets to his dearest friends, not in the crowd of men, but where they were alone by themselves. And they themselves – as often as they wished to think clearly of God and offer pure prayers and be in their hearts spiritually raised towards heaven – always one finds that they fled the tumult of men, went off by themselves alone, and there God appeared to them and showed himself to them and granted

a Falling down they adored him, and when they had opened their treasures they offered him gifts, etc. (Matthew 2.11).
b Pelican of the wilderness (Psalm 101.7).
c Night-raven in the house (Psalm 101.7).
d I have watched and am become as a sparrow alone upon the house-top (Psalm 101.8).

them their prayers. Because I said that one finds this both in the Old Testament and also in the New, I shall offer illustrations from both.

Egressus est Ysaac in agrum ad meditandum, quod ei fuisse creditur consuetudinarium.[a] Isaac the patriarch, so as to think deeply, sought a solitary place, and went off by himself alone, as Genesis tells. And thus he met with the blessed Rebecca – that is, with God's grace: *Rebecca enim interpretatur multum dedit, et quicquid habet meriti preuentrix gratia donat.*[b]

In the same way, the blessed Jacob, when Our Lord showed him his precious face and gave him his blessing and changed his name for the better, had fled from men and was by himself all alone.[21] Never before in the crowd of men had he made such a gain. Through Moses and through Elijah, God's precious friends, it is clear and evident what strife there always is, and how fearful a life, among the throng, and how God shows his secrets to those who are on their own in private.[22] These things, dear sisters, will be told to you, for they would be too long to write here, and then you will understand all this clearly. *Set et Jeremias solus sedet*[c] – the blessed Jeremiah says he sits on his own, and he tells the reason why: *Quia comminatione tua replesti me*[d] – Our Lord had filled him with his threatening. God's threatening is misery and grief in body and in soul, world without end. The person who was, as he was, filled with his threatening, would have no empty place in the heart to receive fleshly laughter; therefore he prayed for a fountain of tears: *Quis dabit michi fontem lacrimarum?*[e] that it might never, no more than a spring, dry up, so as to weep for the people killed – that is, almost all the world, which has been spiritually killed with deadly sins: *Vt lugeant interfectos populi mei.*[f] And for this weeping – look now – he asks a solitary place: *Quis michi dabit diuersorium uiatorum in solitudine ut, et cetera?*[g] The holy prophet, to show definitely that whoever wishes to

---

a Isaac was gone forth to meditate in the field (Genesis 24.63), which is believed to have been customary with him.

b For Rebecca is interpreted 'she has given much and whatever merit she has, prevenient grace gives'.

c But Jeremiah also sits alone (see Jeremiah 15.17).

d Because thou hast filled me with thy threats (Jeremiah 15.17).

e Who will give me a fountain of tears? (Jeremiah 9.1).

f That they may weep for the slain of my people (Jeremiah 9.1).

g Who will give me in the wilderness a lodging-place of wayfaring men, so that [I might leave my people and go from them]? (Jeremiah 9.2).

weep for their own and others' sins, as an anchoress ought to do, and whoever wishes to find mercy and grace from the strict Judge, the one thing that most hinders him is sojourn – that is, dwelling – among men, and the thing that most furthers it is a solitary place for a man or woman to be alone. Jeremiah speaks again further of the solitary place: *Sedebit solitarius et tacebit*[a] – 'One shall sit,' he says, 'by oneself and be silent.' Of this silence he speaks a little before: *Bonum est prestolari cum silentio salutare Dei. Beatus qui portauerit iugum Domini ab adholescencia sua*[b] – 'It is good to wait in silence for God's grace and that one should bear God's yoke right from youth.' And then there comes after that: *Sedebit solitarius et tacebit, quia leuabit se supra se*[c] – 'Whoever wishes so to do must sit alone and keep silent, and so lift herself above herself' – that is, with a raised life rise towards heaven, above her nature. Beside this, the other good that may come of this solitary sitting of which Jeremiah speaks, and this blessed silence, comes immediately after: *Dabit percutienti se maxillam et saturabitur obprobriis*[d] – 'She who lives so,' he says, 'will offer her cheek to the striker and be filled up with shameful words.' Here in this saying are two blessed virtues, to be very carefully noted, which pertain to an anchoress. Patience in the first part; in the second, the humility of a mild and meek heart. For he is patient who bears patiently the injury that is done him. He is humble who can endure being spoken ill of. Those that I have mentioned here were from the Old Testament. Let us come now to the New.

St John the Baptist, of whom Our Lord said: *Inter natos mulierum non surrexit maior Iohanne baptista*[e] – that 'among the sons of women there never arose a higher', he teaches us openly by his own deed that a solitary place is both safe and beneficial; for though the angel Gabriel had foretold his birth – albeit he was filled with the Holy Ghost right away within his mother's womb, albeit he was born, by a miracle, of a

a He shall sit solitary and hold his peace (Lamentations 3.28).

b It is good to wait with silence for the salvation of God. Blessed is the man who has borne the yoke of the Lord from his youth (Lamentations 3.26–7).

c He shall sit solitary and hold his peace, for he shall lift himself above himself (Lamentations 3.28).

d He shall give his cheek to him that striketh him and he shall be filled with reproaches (Lamentations 3.30).

e Among those born of women there has not risen a greater than John the Baptist (Matthew 11.11).

barren woman and at his birth released his father's tongue into prophecy – for all this, he still did not dare to dwell among men, so much to be feared was the life he saw there, even if for nothing else but the talking alone. And therefore what did he do? Young in years, he fled away into the wilderness, so that he should not sully his clean life with talking – for so it is in his hymn:

> *Antra deserti teneris sub annis*
> *Ciuium turmas fugiens petisti*
> *Ne leui saltem maculare uitam*
> *Famine posses.*[23][a]

He had, as it seems, heard Isaiah, who lamented and said: *Ve michi qui homo pollutis labiis ego sum*[b] – 'Woe is me,' says the holy prophet, 'for I am a man of sullied lips.' And he tells the reason why: *Quia in medio populi polluta labia habentis ego habito*[c] – 'and that is because', he says, 'I dwell among men who sully their lips' with talk of all kind. Look how God's prophet says he was sullied by sojourn among men. So it is, to be sure: an ore, a metal, gold, silver, iron, steel, can never be so bright that it will not attract rust from another thing that is rusted in the event of them lying together long. Therefore St John fled the fellowship of filthy men, lest he should be made filthy. But further, to show us that one cannot flee the evil unless one flees the good, he fled his holy family, who had been chosen by Our Lord, and went to a solitary place and dwelt in the wilderness. And what did he gain there? He gained being the baptizer of Our God. Oh, the great honour that he should hold in baptism under his hands the Lord of heaven, who holds up the whole world by the might of himself alone! There the Holy Trinity – 'threeness'[24] in English – showed itself all to him: the Father in his voice, the Holy Ghost in the shape of a dove, the Son in his hands. In the solitary life he gained three distinctions: the privilege of a preacher, the merit of martyrdom, the reward of virginity. These three kinds of people have in heaven, with overflowing reward, crown upon crown.

a The caves of the desert in your tender years,/Fleeing the throngs of citizens, you sought,/So that at all events you should not be able to stain your life/With light speech.

b Woe is me, for I am a man of unclean lips (Isaiah 6.5).

Because I dwell in the midst of a people that hath unclean lips (Isaiah 6.5).

And the blessed John, being in a solitary place as he was, earned on his own all these three conditions.

Our dear Lady – did she not lead a solitary life? Did not the angel find her in a solitary place all by herself? She was not anywhere outside, but was securely shut up, for thus we find: *Ingressus angelus ad eam dixit: Aue Maria, gratia plena, Dominus tecum; beata tu in mulieribus*[a] – that is, 'The angel went in to her' – then she was within in a solitary place on her own. An angel has hardly ever appeared to someone in a crowd. In addition, because nowhere in Holy Writ is her speech written of, except four times, as is stated above, there is clear proof that she was a great deal on her own, seeing that she kept silence like this.

Why do I look for any other? – from God alone there would be example enough for all, who himself went off into a solitary place and fasted where he was alone in the wilderness, to show by that that among a crowd of people no one can do penance properly. 'There in the solitary place he hungered,' it says, as an encouragement to the anchoress who is distressed. There he permitted the fiend's tempting of him in various ways, but he overcame him, to show also that the fiend tempts much those who lead a solitary life, because of the hatred which he has for them, but he is overcome; for Our Lord himself stands by them there in the fight and emboldens them to resist stoutly and gives them of his strength. He, as Holy Writ says, whom no noise or crowd of people could hinder from his prayers or disturb his goodness, even so none the less, when he wanted to be at prayer fled not only other men, but even his holy precious Apostles, and went up alone on the hills, as an example to us that we should turn off by ourselves and climb with him on the hills, that is, think high and leave low down under us all earthly thoughts while we are at prayer. Paul and Antony, Hilarion and Benedict, Syncletica and Sarah, and many other such, men and women both, experienced certainly and perceived truly the profit of a solitary life, as ones who did with God all that they wished.[25] St Jerome more recently[26] says of himself, *Quotiens inter homines fui, minor homo recessi*[27][b] – 'As often as ever I was,' he says, 'among men, I came

---

a   The angel being come in said unto her: Hail Mary, full of grace, the Lord is with thee; blessed art thou among women (Luke 1.28).

b   As often as I was among men, I came away a lesser man.

away from them a lesser man than I was before.' Therefore the wise Ecclesiasticus says, *Ne oblecteris in turbis, assidua est enim commissio*[a] – that is, 'Let being among a crowd of people never seem good to you, for there is always sin there.' Did not the voice from heaven say to Arsenius, *Arseni fuge homines et saluaberis*[b] – 'Arsenius, flee men and you shall be saved' – *Arseni fuge, tace, quiesce*[c] – that is, 'Arsenius, flee, be silent and dwell steadfastly in a place away from men'?

Now you have heard, my dear sisters, illustrations from the Old Testament and the New showing why you ought to love the solitary life very much. After the illustrations, hear now reasons why one ought to flee the world – eight at least. I shall tell them briefly: pay attention all the better.

The first is safety. If a raging lion were running down the street, would not the sensible woman shut herself in quickly? And St Peter says that hell's lion ranges and roams about all the time to look for a way in so as to devour souls, and bids us be watchful and busy in holy prayers lest he should catch us: *Sobrii estote et uigilate in orationibus, quia aduersarius uester diabolus tanquam leo rugiens circuit querens quem deuoret.*[d] These are St Peter's words, which I gave before. Therefore anchoresses are wise who have shut themselves in well against the lion of hell in order to be the safer.

The second reason is: the person who was carrying a costly liquid, a precious fluid, such as balsam is, in a fragile container, linctus in a brittle glass, would she not go out of the crowd, unless she were a fool? *Habemus thesaurum istum in uasis fictilibus, dicit Apostolus.*[e] This brittle container – that is, woman's flesh – even though the balsam, the linctus is virginity that is in it (or after the loss of virginity, chaste cleanness) – this brittle container is as brittle as any glass, for should it once be broken, it will never be mended, mended or whole as it was before, any more than glass. But further, it takes less to break it than it does brittle

---

a   Take no pleasure in riotous assemblies, for their contention is continual (Ecclesiasticus 18.32).

b   Arsenius, flee men and you will be saved (*Lives of the Fathers* 3.190).

c   Arsenius, flee, be silent, become still (*Lives of the Fathers* 3.190).

d   Be sober and watch in prayers, because your adversary the devil, like a roaring lion, goeth about seeking whom he may devour (1 Peter 5.8).

e   We have this treasure in earthen vessels, says the Apostle (2 Corinthians 4.7).

glass. For glass does not break unless something touches it, and it, as regards loss of virginity, can lose its wholeness through a stinking desire – so far can that proceed and last so long. But this kind of break can be mended afterwards, made altogether as completely whole as it ever was, through the medicine of confession and repentance. Now the proof of this: St John the Evangelist – had he not brought home a bride?[28] Had he not intended then, if God had not prevented him, to abandon virginity? Afterwards, though, he was not in any way less whole a virgin, but was as a virgin entrusted with the keeping of a virgin: *Virginem uirgini commendauit.*[29] [a] Now, as I say, this precious linctus in the brittle container is virginity and cleanness in your brittle flesh, more brittle than any glass which, if you were in the world's crowd, you might with a little jostling lose completely, like the wretches in the world who jostle together and break their containers and spill their cleanness. Therefore Our Lord calls thus: *In mundo pressuram, in me autem pacem habebitis*[b] – 'Leave the world and come to me, for there you will be in the crowd – but rest and peace are in me.'

The third reason for fleeing from the world is the gaining of heaven. Heaven is very high. Whoever wishes to gain it and reach it, it is to her a little enough matter to cast all the world under her feet. Therefore all the saints made of the world a stool for their feet to reach heaven. *Apocalypsis: Vidi mulierem amictam sole et luna sub pedibus eius*[c] – these are St John the Evangelist's words in the Apocalypse: 'I saw a woman clothed with the sun and under her feet the moon.' The moon wanes and waxes and is never fixed, and signifies, therefore, worldly things which are, like the moon, always changing. This moon must the woman keep under her feet – that is, tread on and despise worldly things – who wishes to reach heaven and be clothed with the true sun.[30]

The fourth reason is proof of nobility and generosity. Noble people and those of gentle birth do not carry packs, nor do they travel bundled up with bundles or purses. It is for beggar-women to bear bags on their backs, townswomen to bear purses, not God's wife, who is a lady of

a He entrusted the Virgin to a virgin.
b In the world you shall have distress, but in me peace (John 16.33).
c Apocalypse (12.1): I saw a woman clothed with the sun and the moon under her feet.

heaven. Bundles and purses, bags and packs are worldly things, all earthly wealth and worldly possessions.

The fifth reason is that noble men and women are generous with what they leave. And who can be more generous than the man or woman who says with St Peter: *Ecce nos reliquimus omnia et secuti sumus te*[a] – 'Lord, so as to follow you we have left behind everything'? Is this not a generous leaving? Is this not a great legacy? My dear sisters, kings and emperors have their livelihood out of your generous leaving, which you have left. 'Lord, so as to follow you,' says St Peter, 'we have left everything', as though he said, 'We want to follow you in the great nobility of your generosity. You left to other men all riches and made of it all a thing left and a generous legacy. We want to follow you. We want to do likewise – leave all as you did; follow you on earth in that and in other things, so as to follow you also into the bliss of heaven and there still follow you everywhere wherever you go, as none may except virgins': *Hii secuntur Agnum quocumque ierit; utroque, scilicet, pede, id est, integritate cordis et corporis.*[b]

The sixth reason why you have fled the world, companionship, a large family, is so as to be in private with God. For he speaks thus through Hosea: *Ducam te in solitudinem et ibi loquar ad cor tuum*[c] – 'I shall lead you,' he says to his beloved, 'into a solitary place and there I shall lovingly speak to your heart, for the throng is hateful to me' – *Ego Dominus et ciuitatem non ingredior.*[d]

The seventh reason is so as to be the brighter and to see more brightly in heaven God's bright face, because you have fled the world and hide yourselves here because of it; but as well as that, so that you may be as swift as the sunbeam, because you have been shut in with Jesus Christ as in a sepulchre, confined as he was on the dear cross, as has been said above.[31]

The eighth reason is to have prayers full of life, and look carefully at why. The humble Queen Esther signifies the anchoress, for her name

a Behold, we have left all things and have followed thee (Matthew 19.27).
b These follow the Lamb whithersoever he goeth (Apocalypse 14.4) with, to be sure, both feet, that is, with wholeness of heart and of body.
c I will lead thee into a place of solitude and there I will speak to thy heart (Hosea 2.14).
d I am the Lord and I will not enter into the city (see Hosea 11.9).

means 'hidden' in the English language. As we read in her book,[32] she was above everything pleasing to King Ahasuerus, and through her prayer set free from death all her people, who had been condemned to death. This name 'Ahasuerus' is interpreted 'blessed', as I said earlier, and signifies God, blessed above all. He grants Queen Esther – that is, the true anchoress, who is a proper Esther, that is, properly hidden – he hears and grants her all her prayers and saves many people because of them. Many would be lost who are saved through the prayers of an anchoress, as they were through Esther's, when she is Esther and conducts herself as she, Mordecai's daughter, did. 'Mordecai' is interpreted *amare conterens inpudentem*[a] – 'bitterly trampling the shameless one'. The shameless one is the man who says or does anything improper in front of an anchoress. If, however, anyone does so, and she should bitterly break up his ill-disciplined speech or his foolish deed and trample them at once with expressions of contempt, then is she Esther, Mordecai's daughter, bitterly breaking the shameless one. She can never more bitterly or better break him than as is taught above[33] with *Narrauerunt michi*[b] or with this verse: *Declinate a me maligni et scrutabor mandata Dei mei*[c] – and going in at once to her altar and staying inside like Esther the hidden. Shimei in *Regum*[d] had deserved death, but she cried for mercy and Solomon forgave him it, though with an agreement that he should stay inside in Jerusalem where he lived, and hide himself in his house. If he went out anywhere, the agreement was such that he would again be convicted and condemned to death. He, however, broke the agreement in his misfortune. His servants escaped and ran away from him and he followed them and went out after them. What more do you want? He was soon denounced to King Solomon and, because of the breaking of the agreement, condemned to death. Understand this thoroughly, my dear sisters. Shimei signifies the anchoress turned to the outside, not Esther the hidden, for 'Shimei' means *audiens*,[e] that is, 'hearing' in our language; that is, the recluse

a Severely bruising the shameless one.
b [The wicked] have told me [fables] (Psalm 118.85).
c Depart from me, ye malignant, and I will search the commandments of my God (Psalm 118.115).
d Kings (3 Kings 2.36ff.).
e Hearing.

who has ass's ears – long to hear far, that is, listening for news. Shimei's place was Jerusalem, in which he had to hide himself if he wanted to live. This word 'Jerusalem' means 'sight of peace', and signifies the anchor-house, for in it she need see nothing except peace alone. Let her never be Shimei – that is, the recluse so very full of guilt towards the true Solomon – that is, Our Lord. Should she keep herself at home in Jerusalem, so that she knows nothing of the world's strife, Solomon gladly grants her his mercy; but if she meddles with outside things more than she need and her heart is on the outside, though a clod of earth – that is, her body – be within the four walls, she has gone, like Shimei, out of Jerusalem, just as he did after his servants. These servants are the five native senses, which should be at home and serve their lady. They then serve the anchoress their lady well when she employs them well about their soul's needs, when the eye is on the book or on some other good thing, the ear to God's word, the mouth at holy prayers. If she guards them badly and lets them, through heedlessness, escape her service, and follows them out with her heart – as it almost always happens that if the senses go out, the heart goes out after – she breaks Solomon's agreement with the unfortunate Shimei and is condemned to death.

Therefore, my dear sisters, do not be Shimei, but be Esther the hidden and you shall be raised up into the bliss of heaven, for the name of Esther means not only *abscondita*[a] – that is, not only 'hidden' – but as well as that *eleuata in populis*[b] – that is, 'raised high in the people' – and thus Esther, as her name says, was raised to a queen from a poor maiden. In this word 'Esther' are hiding and height linked together, and not only height but height above the people, to show definitely that those who hide themselves properly in their anchor-houses shall in heaven, above people of other kinds, be raised high in honour. Both Esther's name and her raising high prove what I say. In addition, understand you are in Jerusalem, you have fled to the church's sanctuary, for there is none of you who has not at some time been God's thief.[34] You are, as you know very well, lain in wait for outside, as are thieves who have taken refuge in church. Keep yourself securely inside;

a Hidden.
b Raised up among the peoples.

not your body alone, for that is of the least consequence, but your five senses, and your heart above absolutely everything, where the soul's life is.[35] For if it is trapped outside, it will simply be led away to the gallows, that is, the gibbet of hell. Be afraid of each man, just as the thief is, in case he draws you out – that is, deceives you with sin and lies in wait to get you into his clutches. Entreat God earnestly, like a thief who has taken refuge in church, to guard and protect you against all who lie in wait for you. Twitter your prayers all the time, as a lone sparrow does. For this lone word is said with regard to a lonely life and a lonely place, where one can be Esther, hidden away out of the world, and make each spiritual gain better than in the crowd. Therefore David likens the anchoress to the pelican, which leads a lonely life on its own, and to a lone sparrow.

The sparrow has a further characteristic which is advantageous for an anchoress, though people hate it – that is, the falling sickness, for there is a great need that an anchoress of high and holy life have the falling sickness; I do not mean the sickness which is given that name,[36] but illness of the body or trials of the flesh's temptations, through which it seems to her that she falls down from a height of holiness. She would turn wild otherwise or think too well of herself, and so come to nothing. The flesh would turn wild and become too ill-disciplined towards her lady if it were not beaten, and make the soul ill if illness did not tame it with sickness or with sin.[37]

If the body or the soul were neither of them ill, as seldom happens, pride would waken, which is the illness most of all to be feared. If God tries an anchoress with any sickness on the outside, or the fiend does on the inside with spiritual vices, such as pride, anger, envy, or with the desires of the flesh, she has the falling sickness, which they say is a sickness of sparrows. God wishes, therefore, that she should be always humble and, in holding herself low, fall to the earth so that she does not fall into pride.

Now we come, dear sisters, to the fourth part, which I said would be about many temptations – for there are outer and inner, and many kinds of each. I promised to teach you remedies against them and cures, and how whoever has them may gather from this part comfort and encouragement against them all. That I, through the teaching of the Holy Ghost, may keep my promise – let him grant it me through your prayers.

PART FOUR

Fleshly and Spiritual Temptations and Comforts and Remedies for Them

Let no one of a high life think that she will not be tempted. The good who have climbed high are tempted more than the weak; and that is only right, for the higher the hill the more the wind is on it – the higher the hill of holy and high life, the stronger and more frequent are the fiend's blasts, the winds of temptations, on it. If there is any anchoress who feels no temptations, she should be very much afraid on this score in case she is being too much and too strongly tempted, for St Gregory speaks thus: *Tunc maxime inpugnaris cum te inpugnari non sentis.*[a] Some circumstances are much to be feared when a man is sick: the one is when he does not feel his own sickness, and therefore does not seek a doctor or medical help and does not ask anyone's advice and dies suddenly before it is the least expected. This is the anchoress who does not know what temptation is. To such speaks the angel in the Apocalypse: *Dicis quia diues sum et nullius egeo et nescis quia miser es et nudus et pauper et cecus*[b] – 'You say you need no medicine, but you are blind-hearted and do not see how you are poor and naked of holiness, and a spiritual wretch.' The second circumstance to be feared in a sick man is quite different from this; that is when he feels so much agony that he cannot bear having his hurt touched, or himself healed. This is an anchoress who feels her temptations so strongly and is so terribly afraid, that no spiritual comfort may gladden her and make her understand that through them she can be and shall be saved the more readily. Does it not tell in the Gospel that the Holy Ghost led Our Lord

a You are then most assaulted when you do not feel you are being assaulted (see Jerome, *Letter to Heliodorus* 4).
b Thou sayest, 'I am rich and have need of nothing', and knowest not that thou art wretched and naked and poor and blind (Apocalypse 3.17).

himself into a solitary place to lead a solitary life, so as to be tempted by the enemy from hell? *Ductus est Iesus in desertum a spiritu ut temptaretur a diabolo.*[a] But his temptation – he who could not sin was only on the outside.

Understand then first of all, dear sisters, that there are two kinds of temptations, two kinds of trials,[1] outer and inner, and both are of many sorts. An outer temptation is one from which comes pleasure or displeasure, outside or inside. Displeasure outside, such as sickness, distress, shame, misfortune and each bodily hardship which troubles the flesh; inside, heart-sickness, wrath and anger also at being in pain. Pleasure outside, health of the body, food, drink, enough clothing and each comfort of the flesh to do with such things. Pleasure inside, such as some false happiness, either from men's praise or if one is more liked than someone else, more flattered, or has more kindnesses done or more respect paid to one. This part of this temptation which is called outer is more deceptive than the other part. Both are one temptation and each, the inside and the outside, both parts of it. But it is called outer because it is always either in a thing outside or from a thing outside, and the outer thing is the temptation. This temptation some-times comes from God, sometimes from man. From God, such as in a friend's death, sickness either of friends or your own, poverty, misfor-tune and other such; health and comfort also. From man, such as various injuries, either of word or of deed, towards you or yours; also praise or good deeds. These also come from God, but not as the others do, without any intermediary. But with them all he tries a man as to how he fears and loves him. Inner temptations are various vices, or the desire to do them, or deceptive thoughts which, however, seem good. These inner temptations come from the devil, from the world and from our flesh sometimes. For the outer temptations there is need of patience – that is, long-suffering.[2] For the inner, there is need of wisdom and spiritual strength. We must now speak of the outer and those who have it – how they may, with God's grace, find a remedy, that is, strength against it to comfort themselves.

Beatus uir qui suffert temptationem, quoniam cum probatus fuerit accipiet

a Jesus was led by the spirit into the desert to be tempted by the devil (Matthew 4. 1).

coronam uite quam repromisit Deus diligentibus se[a] – 'Blessed and happy is she who has patience under temptation, for when she has been proved,' it says, 'she will be crowned with the crown of life which God has promised to his dear chosen ones.' 'When she is proved,' it says; it is well said, for so God proves his dear chosen ones as the goldsmith does the gold in the fire. The false gold perishes in it, the good comes out brighter.[3]

Sickness is a hot fire to endure, but nothing cleanses gold as it does the soul. Sickness that God sends, not that someone gets through their own stupidity, does these six things: (i) washes away the sins that have been committed before; (ii) guards against those that were on the way; (iii) proves patience; (iv) keeps one in humility; (v) increases the reward; (vi) makes the patient person equal to a martyr. Sickness is thus the soul's healing, medicine for its wounds, a shield to prevent it getting others, as God sees it would, if sickness did not prevent it. Sickness makes a man understand what he is, know himself, and, like a good master, beats so as to teach well how powerful God is, how worthless the world's bliss is. Sickness is your goldsmith, who gilds your crown in the bliss of heaven. The greater the sickness, the busier the goldsmith, and the longer it lasts, the more he brightens it. To be a martyr's equal through a temporary suffering – what greater grace is there for those who had deserved the torments of hell, world without end? Would he not be reckoned the stupidest of all men who avoided a blow for a spear's wound instead? A needle's pricking for a beheading? A beating for a hanging on hell's gibbet – always for eternity? God knows, dear sisters, all the suffering in this world is equivalent to the least of all hell's torments; it is all just a ball game, it is all not as much as a little drop of dew compared to the wide sea and all the world's waters. The person who can escape that fearful suffering, the terrible torments, through sickness which passes, through any evil there is here, may call herself happy.

In addition, learn many kinds of comfort in the face of the outer temptation which comes from man's evil, for this of which I have

---

a Blessed is the man that endureth temptation, for when he hath been proved, he shall receive the crown of life which God hath promised to them that love him (James 1.12).

spoken is of God's sending. Whoever speaks ill of you or does you ill, take note and understand that he is your file, such as metal workers have, and files away all your rust and roughness of sin; for he devours himself, alas, as does the file, but he makes your soul smooth and bright.

Or again, think whoever harms you or causes you any suffering – shame, anger, vexation – he is God's stick; for he speaks thus through St John's mouth in the Apocalypse: *Ego quos amo, arguo et castigo.*[a] He beats no one except the person he loves and considers his daughter – any more than you would beat a strange child, though it were very much at fault. But let him not congratulate himself on being God's stick, for as the father, when he has beaten his child enough and has disciplined it well, throws the stick into the fire because it is no use any more, so the father of heaven, when with a wicked man or a wicked woman he has beaten his dear child for its good, he throws the stick – that is, the wicked person – into the fire of hell. Therefore he says elsewhere: *Michi uindictam; ego retribuam*[b] – that is, 'Mine is the vengeance; I shall repay' – as though he said, 'Do not you avenge yourselves, and do not complain or curse when a person offends against you, but think at once that he is your father's stick and that he will repay him his stick's service.' And is that child not ill-disciplined who scratches at and bites on the stick? The well-behaved child, when it is beaten, if the father orders it, it kisses the stick;[4] and do likewise yourselves, my dear sisters, for so your father orders – that you should kiss, not with your mouth, but with the love of your heart, those with whom he beats you: *Diligite inimicos uestros. Benefacite hiis qui oderunt uos, et orate pro persequentibus et calumpniantibus uos.*[c] This is God's command – which is much dearer to him than your eating coarse bread or wearing hard haircloth. 'Love your enemy,' he says, 'and do good, if you can, to those that fight you. If you cannot in any other way, pray earnestly for those who do you any harm, or speak ill of you.' And the Apostle teaches, 'Never repay evil for evil, but always do good in return for evil',[5] as Our Lord himself did, and all his holy saints. If you thus keep God's command,

a   Such as I love, I rebuke and chastise (Apocalypse 3.19).
b   Revenge is mine; I will repay (Romans 12.19; see Deuteronomy 32.35).
c   Love your enemies. Do good to them that hate you, and pray for them that persecute and calumniate you (Luke 6.27–8).

then you are his good child and kiss the stick which he has thrashed you with. Now sometimes someone says, 'I shall love his soul (or hers) well, his body not at all.' But this should not be said. The soul and the body are but one person, and one judgement faces them both. Will you part in two what God has joined into one? He forbids it and says: *Quod Deus coniunxit homo non separet*[a] – 'Let no one be so mad as to part what God has linked.'

Again, think like this. A child, if it stumbles on something or gets hurt, one hits the thing it got hurt on and the child is well pleased, forgets all its hurt and stops its tears. Therefore comfort yourselves: *Letabitur iustus cum uiderit uindictam.*[b] God will on Judgement Day act as though he said, 'Daughter, did this person hurt you, did he make you stumble in anger or in heart-sickness, in shame or in any vexation? Look, daughter, look,' he says, 'how he shall pay for it.' And there you shall see him bashed with the devil's mallets, so that he is sorry he is alive. You will be well pleased at that, for your will and God's will will be so linked that you will want all that ever he wants and he all that you want.

Above all other thoughts, in all your suffering, always think intensely about God's torments – that the world's ruler would for his servants suffer such ignominies, scornings, buffets, spitting, blindfolding, crowning with thorns, which sat on his head in such a way that the bloody streams ran down and flowed down to the ground; his sweet body bound naked to the hard pillar and so beaten that the precious blood ran on every side; the poisonous drink that was given to him when he was thirsty on the cross; their heads staring up at him when they cried so loud in mockery, 'Look, here is he who healed others, look how he now heals and helps himself.'[6] Turn back to where I speak of how he was tormented in all his five senses,[7] and compare all your suffering, sickness and other things, injury in word or in deed and all that man may endure, with what he endured, and you will easily see how little it comes to, especially if you think that he was completely innocent and that he suffered all this not on his own account, for he never did any wrong. If you endure suffering, you have deserved worse, and all that you endure is on your own account.

a What God hath joined together, let not man put asunder (Matthew 19.6).
b The just shall rejoice when he shall see the revenge (Psalm 57.11).

Go then more gladly along the difficult and laborious path towards the great feast of heaven, where your glad friend is waiting for your coming, than stupid worldly men go along the green path towards the gibbet and the death of hell. It is better to go sick to heaven than healthy to hell, to mirth in distress than to suffering in comfort. *Salomon: Via impiorum complantata est lapidibus – id est, duris afflictionibus.*[a] Nevertheless, assuredly wretched worldly men buy hell more dearly than you do heaven. Know one thing for a truth: one thing wrongly said that you endure, one day's weariness, a single hour's sickness, if someone bargained with you for one of these on Judgement Day – that is, for the reward that arises from it – you would not sell it for all the world in gold. For this shall be your song before Our Lord: *Letati sumus pro diebus quibus nos humiliasti, annis quibus uidimus mala*[b] – that is, 'We rejoice for the days when you brought us low through other people's evil deeds, and we rejoice now, Lord, for those years in which we were sick and saw sickness and sorrow.' Each worldly woe is God's envoy. A noble's messenger must be nobly received and well entertained, especially if he is intimate with his lord; and who was more intimate with the king of heaven while he dwelt here than this envoy – that is, the world's misery, which never left him until his life's end? What does this messenger tell you? He comforts you in this way: 'God, loving me as he did, sent me to his dear friends. Though my coming and my dwelling seem poisonous, they are health-giving.' Would not that thing be frightful, the shadow of which you could not feel without pain? What would you say about the terrible thing from which it came? Know for a truth that all the suffering of this world is only a shadow of the suffering of hell. 'I am the shadow,' says this messenger – that is, the world's misery. 'Of necessity, you must either receive me or the frightful suffering of which I am the shadow. Whoever receives me gladly and gives me good entertainment, my lord sends her word that she is free from the thing of which I am the shadow.' Thus speaks God's messenger. Therefore St James says, *Omne gaudium existimate,*

---

a   Solomon: The way of sinners is set about with stones (Ecclesiasticus 21.11) – that is, with hard afflictions.

b   We have rejoiced for the days in which thou hast humbled us, for the years in which we have seen evils (Psalm 89.15).

fratres, cum in temptationes uarias incideritis[a] – 'Consider it all bliss to fall into various of these temptations' which are called outer. And St Paul: *Omnis disciplina in presenti uidetur esse non gaudii set meroris; postmodum uero fructum, et cetera*[b] – 'All these temptations that we are now beaten with seem dejection, not joy, but they turn afterwards to delight and eternal bliss.'

The inner temptation is twofold, just as the outer is, for the outer is [displeasure] in adversity and in prosperity pleasure that belongs to sin.[8] I say this because there is some pleasure, and some displeasure, that deserves a great reward, such as pleasure in God's love and displeasure at sin. Now, as I say, the inner temptation is twofold, fleshly and spiritual: fleshly, as of lechery, of gluttony, of sloth; spiritual, as of pride, of envy and of anger – also of covetousness. Thus the inner temptations are the seven capital sins and their foul offspring.[9] Temptation of the flesh may be likened to a foot wound; spiritual temptation, of which one has greater fear, may, because of the danger, be called a breast wound. But fleshly temptations seem greater to us because they are easy to feel. The others, though we may have them, we often do not know it, and they are nevertheless great and frightful in God's eye, and are, therefore, much the more to be feared. For the others, which are clearly felt, ask for a doctor and medicine. The spiritual hurts do not seem painful and are not treated with confession or with penitence, and draw on to eternal death before it is the least suspected.

Holy men and women are often very much tempted with all sorts of temptations – and for their welfare, for through the fight against them they obtain the blessed crown of champions. Look, however, how they complain in Jeremiah: *Persecutores nostri uelociores aquilis celi; super montes persecuti sunt nos, in deserto insidiati sunt nobis*[c] – that is, 'Our enemies, swifter than eagles upon the hills, they climbed after us and there fought with us and still they spied on us in the wilderness so as to kill us.' Our enemies are three: the fiend, the world, our own flesh, as I said earlier.[10]

a Count it all joy, brothers, when you shall fall into divers temptations (James 1.2).
b All chastisement for the present seemeth not to bring with it joy but sorrow; but afterwards [it will yield to them that are exercised by it the most peaceable] fruit [of justice] (Hebrews 12.11).
c Our persecutors were swifter than the eagles of the air; they pursued us upon the mountains, they lay in wait for us in the wilderness (Lamentations 4.19).

Sometimes it is not easy for someone to know which of these three is attacking him, for they each help the others, though the fiend particularly urges to poisonousness, such as pride, disdain, envy and anger and their poisonous offspring, which will be named afterwards.[11] The flesh incites particularly towards sweetness, ease and softness. The world bids a man covet the world's wealth and honour and other such gewgaws which delude foolish men into loving a shadow. These enemies, it says, follow us on the hills and lie in wait in the wilderness to see how they can harm us. A hill, that is, a high life, where the devil's assaults are often strongest. The wilderness is the solitary life of the anchoress's dwelling, for just as in the wilderness there are all the wild beasts, and they will not endure men coming near but flee when they hear them, so should anchorites, above all other women, be wild in this way, and then they will be desirable, above other women, to Our Lord and seem sweetest to him, for of all meats the meat of wild animals is the most desirable and sweet.

Through this wilderness Our Lord's people went, as Exodus tells, towards the blessed land of Jerusalem, which he had promised them. And you, my dear sisters, go by the same path towards the high Jerusalem, the kingdom which he has promised his chosen. Go very carefully, however, for in this wilderness are many evil beasts: the lion of pride, the snake of poisonous envy, the unicorn of anger, the bear of dead sloth, the fox of covetousness, the sow of gluttony, the scorpion with the tail of stinging lechery – that is, lust.[12] Here now have been listed in order the seven capital sins.

The lion of pride has very many cubs, and I shall name some of them. *Vana Gloria*[a] – that is, whoever thinks well of anything that she does or says or has – beauty or intelligence, knowing important people, or greater reputation than someone else, or family or power or her wishes being seen to more. And what is beauty worth in this case? A gold ring in a sow's nose. Knowing important people, as a religious? It often creates misery. All is *Uana Gloria*, which thinks well of anything and would have it spoken about, and is well pleased if she is praised and displeased if she is not valued as she would wish. A second is *Indignatio*,[b] that is, the person who has contemptuous ideas about

a Vainglory.
b Indignation.

anything she sees or hears about another person and despises correction or the teaching of any inferior. The third cub is *Ypocresis*,[a] who makes herself out to be better than she is. The fourth is *Presumtio*,[b] who takes upon herself more than she can achieve, or interferes with a thing that is not her concern, or who is overconfident of God's grace, or of herself – too bold towards any man, who is fleshly, as she is, and can be tempted. The fifth cub is called Disobedience, who not only does not obey, but complains about doing a thing, or waits too long – the child which does not obey its parents, the subordinate his prelate, the parishioner his priest, the maid her lady – every inferior his superior. The sixth is Loquacity. This cub is fed by the person who speaks a great deal, boasts, judges others, lies sometimes, jeers, reproaches, scolds, flatters, raises laughter. The seventh is Blasphemy. This cub's nurse is the person who swears great oaths or curses bitterly, or speaks ill of God or of his saints, because of something he suffers, sees or hears. The eighth is Impatience. This cub is fed by the person who is not patient in the face of all injuries and all evils. The ninth is Contumacy, and this is fed by whoever is obstinate in a thing she[13] has undertaken to do, be it good or bad, so that no wiser advice can bring her off her false scent. The tenth is *Contentio*,[c] that is, struggling to overcome, so that the other should be seen to be thrown down underneath and have surrendered, and herself be victor in the debate and swaggering like a champion who has won the field. In this vice are reproach and censure of all the evil that she can think of about the other person – and the more bitterly it bites, the better it pleases her, though it might be something put right long ago. In among this are sometimes not only bitter words but foul-stinking ones, shameless and shameful, with on occasion great swearing, many proud words with cursings and lies. Here belongs comparison of themselves, of their family, what they said or did. This is found among nuns – and they go with mouths like this afterwards, before confession has washed them, to worship God with songs of praise, or say their private prayers. But, cursed things, do they not know that their songs and their prayers to

a Hypocrisy.
b Presumption.
c Contention.

94

God stink fouler to him and to all his saints than any rotten dog? The eleventh cub is fed with airs and graces,[14] with expressions and gestures, such as carrying the head high, arching the neck, looking sideways, watching with contempt, blinking the eyes, pursing up the mouth, making derisive gestures with hand or with head, throwing one leg over the other, sitting or walking stiffly as if she were staked up, giving men love-looks, speaking like an innocent and putting on a lisp. Here belong excessive decoration of the veil, of the head-cloth, of every other piece of clothing, either in colouring or pleating, girdles and wearing girdles in the style of a young lady, daubing with ointments, foul flauntings, dyeing the hair, painting the face, plucking the eyebrows or arching them up with wet fingers. There are many other things that come from wealth, from prosperity, from good family, from fine clothes, from intelligence, from beauty, from strength. Pride grows from a high life and from holy virtues. The lion of pride has many more cubs than I have named, but study these very closely, for I am passing quickly over them, and am only naming them, but wherever I go on more rapidly, linger there longest yourselves, for there I am making one word carry ten or twelve. Whoever has any of these vices which I have named here, or any like them, she certainly has pride, however her habit is shaped or coloured. She is the mate of the lion of which I have spoken, and feeds her raging cubs within her breast.

The snake of poisonous envy has seven[15] young. *Ingratitudo*:[a] this offspring is bred by whoever does not acknowledge good deeds, but values them little or forgets them completely. I mean not only the good deeds which man does him, but those which God does him, or has done him (either him or her) more than she comprehends, if she[16] considered the matter well. Too little attention is given to this vice, and it is the one most hateful of all to God and most contrary to his grace. The second offspring is *Rancor siue Odium*[b] – that is, hatred or swollen heart. He who breeds this in the breast, to God all that ever he does is poisonous. The third offspring is Regret at Another's Good; the fourth, Gladness at his Harm; the fifth, Accusation; the sixth, Backbiting; the seventh, Reproaching, or Deriding. The eighth is *Suspitio*[c]

a Ingratitude.
b Rancour or Hatred.
c Suspicion.

lack of trust in a man or a woman without certain evidence, thinking, 'She is making this pretence; she is saying (or doing) this to make me angry, mock me or harm me' – and that when the other one is never thinking of it. To this belongs false judgement, which God strictly forbids, such as to think or to say, 'Yes, she doesn't like me – she accused me of this – look, now they're speaking about me, the two of them (or the three, or more who are sitting together). She's this and she's that and she did it to do harm.' In thoughts like this we are often deceived, for often what seems evil is good; and therefore every day men judge falsely.[17] To this pertain malicious new inventions and hateful lies produced by spite and envy. The ninth offspring is the Sowing of Hostility, of Anger and of Discord. She who sows this devil's seed is cursed by God. The tenth is Malicious Keeping of Silence – the devil's silence, the one for envy not being willing to speak about the other – and this kind is also the offspring of anger, for their progeny are often mixed together. Where any of these was, there was the offspring of the poisonous snake of envy – or the mother original.

The unicorn of anger which bears on its nose the horn with which he gores all that he reaches has six foals.[18] The first is Contention, or Strife. The second is Rage; look at the eyes and the face when raging anger is rising, look at her bearing, look at her behaviour, listen to how the mouth goes, and you may well judge her out of her wits. The third is Shameful Reproaching. The fourth is Cursing. The fifth is Striking. The sixth is Desire that Evil should Happen to Someone, either to the person himself or to his friend, or to his property. The seventh foal is Doing Wrong out of Anger, or Omitting to Do Good – forgoing food or drink, avenging herself with tears if she cannot do it otherwise and splitting her head in wrath with cursing, or in any way harming herself, in either soul or body. This is homicide and murder of herself.

The bear of heavy sloth has these cubs. *Torpor*[a] is the first, that is, a lukewarm heart – lack of desire for anything – which should flame up all aflame with the love of Our Lord. The second is *Pusillanimitas*,[b] that is, a heart too poor and too cowardly as well to undertake any high thing in the hope of God's help and in trust in his grace, not in its own

a Torpor.
b Pusillanimity.

strength. The third is *Cordis Grauitas*:[a] whoever does good and does it, nevertheless, with a dead and a heavy heart has this. The fourth is Idleness: whoever stops completely.[19] The fifth is Grumbling at Heart. The sixth is a Dead Sorrow for the loss of any worldly thing, or for any unpleasantness, except sin alone. The seventh is Heedlessness, either in saying or in doing or in contemplating before or in thinking afterwards or in taking bad care of anything she has for looking after. The eighth is Lack of Hope; this last bear cub is the most frightful of all, for it chews up and devours God's mild mercy and his great forgivingness and his immeasurable grace.

The fox of covetousness has these cubs: Treachery and Guile, Theft, Rapine, Fining and Extortion, False Witness or Oath, Secret Simony, Interest Charges, Usury,[20] Meanness, Reluctance in Giving or Lending – this is a clenched heart, a vice most hateful to God, who gave us all of himself – Murder sometimes. This vice is likened to a fox for many reasons. I shall mention two. There is much guile in the fox, and so there is in covetousness of worldly gain. A second: the fox rips the throats of a whole flock, though it can only swallow in its greed one of it. Likewise a covetous person covets what many thousands might get by on, but though his heart burst, he can only use on himself one man's share. All that a man or a woman desires more than that with which they are able to lead their life properly, in accordance with what they are, all is covetousness and the root of mortal sin. This is right religion – that each after his estate should borrow of this wretched world as little as they possibly can of meat, of clothing, of property, of all its things. Note that I say 'each after his estate', for that remark is carrying a load. You can, as you know, find great significance in many a remark, think about it long and by that one remark understand many that relate to it. For if I should write everything, when would I come to an end?

The sow of greediness has pigs named thus: 'Too Early', one is called, the second 'Too Luxuriously', the third 'Too Greedily'; the fourth is called 'Too Much', the fifth 'Too Often'. These pigs are farrowed more in drink than in food. I speak briefly of them, for I am not afraid, my dear sisters, of your feeding them.

a Heaviness of Heart.

The scorpion of lechery, that is, of lust, has offspring of such a kind that it is not fitting to mention the names of some of them in a well-disciplined mouth, for the name alone might hurt any well-disciplined ear and sully pure hearts. Those, however, one may properly mention whose names are well known and which are, more is the pity, all too familiar to many: Fornication, Adultery, Loss of Virginity and Incest, which exists between kindred in the flesh and in the spirit.[21] It is divided into many parts: foul desire for that filthiness with the consent of reason, helping others towards it, being aware of and witness to it, hunting after it with wooing, with romping or with any wrestling, with a giddy girl's laughter, with whore's eyes, any flighty behaviour, with gifts, with enticing words, or with love-talk, kisses, indecent touching (which can be a capital sin), loving the time or the place for getting into such situations, and other occasions which must be avoided, if one does not want to fall and muddy oneself in the great filthiness. As St Augustine says: *Omissis occasionibus que solent aditum aperire peccatis, potest consciencia esse incolumis*[a] – that is, 'Whoever wants to keep their conscience healthy and beautiful, she must flee the occasions which have been wont often to open the entrance and let in sin.' I do not dare name the unnatural offspring of this devil's scorpion with the poisonous tail. But sorry may she be who, without a companion, or with one, has fed an offspring of her lust in such a way of which I cannot speak for shame – and dare not for fear that someone should learn more evil than they know and be tempted by it. But let her think about her own accursed invention in her lust – for however that is quenched with the pleasure of the flesh, when she is awake and willing, except only in marriage, it ends in mortal sin.[22] In youth outrageous things are done. Let her who feels herself guilty vomit it out completely in confession as she did it, or she will be condemned by the quenching of that foul fire to the eternal fire of hell. Let her who breeds up in her bosom the scorpion's offspring shake it out with confession, and with penance kill it. You who know nothing of such things need not wonder or think what I mean. But give thanks to God that you have not indulged in such uncleanness, and have pity for those who have fallen into it.

a If the occasions which are wont to open the entrance to sins are passed over, the conscience can be safe.

It is evident enough why I have likened pride to a lion, envy to a snake, and all the rest of these, except this last – that is, why lust is likened to a scorpion. But look, here is the reason for it, clear and evident. The scorpion is a kind of snake which has a face, so they say, somewhat like a woman's and is a snake behind. It makes a fair show and fawns with its head – and stings with its tail. This is lechery, this is the devil's beast which he leads to market and to every gathering and puts up for sale and deceives many, because they only look at the fair face, or the fair head. That head is the beginning of the sin of lust and the pleasure, while it lasts, which seems very sweet. The tail is the end of it – that is, painful regret – and stings here with the poison of bitter repentance and penance. And she may call herself happy who finds the tail such, for that poison goes away, but if she does not feel pain, the tail and the poisonous end are the eternal torment of hell. And is not someone a foolish trader who, when he wants to buy a horse or an ox, will not look at anything except the head alone? Therefore when the devil puts this beast on offer – offers to sell it and asks your soul for it – he always hides the tail and puts the head on show. But go yourself right round and put the end on show as well – how the tail stings – and quickly flee from it before you are poisoned.

Thus, my dear sisters, in the wilderness in which you are going with God's people towards the land of Jerusalem – that is, the kingdom of heaven – there are these sorts of beasts, these sorts of snakes, and I do not know any sin which may not be traced to one of those seven, or to their progeny. Wavering faith, against God's teaching, is it not disobedience, a species of pride? Here belong enchantments, false charms, belief in dreams, in sneezing and in all kinds of witchcraft. Taking communion while in any capital sin, or any other sacrament, is it not the species of pride which I called *Presumptio*, if what the sin is is known? If it is not known, then it is heedlessness, coming under inertia, which I called sloth.[23] The person who does not warn another of his evil or his profit, is it not sluggish heedlessness or poisonous envy? Tithing wrongly, withholding something promised, found or lent, or using it wrongly, is it not a species of covetousness and a kind of theft? To withhold another's pay beyond the due time – is it not flagrant rapine for anyone who can pay it, coming under covetousness? If one takes worse care of anything lent or entrusted to one's safekeeping than the person who owns it expects, is it not either treachery or heedlessness, coming from sloth? So is a stupid command or a foolishly given promise, being long unconfirmed, making confession falsely or waiting too long, not teaching one's godchild the *Pater noster* or *Credo*. These and all such things are traceable to sloth, which is the fourth mother of the seven sins. The person who drank a drink or did anything because of which no child should be conceived on her, or one which had been conceived should die – is this not flagrant murder, stirred up by lust? No one could reckon up all sins separately by their individual names. But in those which I have mentioned all the others are contained. And there is, I think, no one who cannot understand his particular sin under one of those groups that are written here. Of these seven beasts and their progeny in the wilderness of the solitary life we have spoken to this point, who try to destroy all the wayfarers. The lion of pride kills all the proud, all those who are high- and haughty-hearted. The poisonous snake, the envious and those with malicious thoughts. The angry, the unicorn. Likewise with the others in order. To God they are killed, but they live to the fiend and are all under his control and serve in his court, each in the job that is appropriate to him.

The proud are his trumpeters; they draw wind in with worldly praise and afterwards puff it out with idle boasting, as the trumpeters do; they make a noise and a loud din[24] to show their pride. But if they thought carefully about God's trumpeters, about the angels' trumpets, which will, on the four sides of the world, before the terrible Judgement, blow fearfully, 'Arise you dead, arise, come to God's Judgement to be judged', where no proud trumpeter shall be saved – if they thought carefully about this, they would soon enough trumpet more softly in the devil's service. Of these trumpeters Jeremiah says: *Onager solitarius in desiderio anime sue attraxit uentum amoris sui.*[a] Of the drawing in of wind for the love of praise he says as I said.

There are some jesters who are not able to provide any other entertainment except the making of faces, twisting the mouth awry, squinting with their eyes. This is the job the unfortunate envious perform in the devil's court, to make their envious lord laugh. If

a A lone wild ass in the desire of his heart snuffed up the wind of his love (Jeremiah 2. 24).

anyone says or does well, they are quite unable to look at it with the right eye of a good heart, but they wink on that side and look on the left to see if there is anything to blame, or squint at it hideously with both eyes. When they hear good they turn the flaps of their ears down, but the left is always wide open for evil. A person twists the mouth then, when he turns good into evil, and, if it is somewhat evil, through more censure twists it into something worse. These are foretellers – their own prophets. They foreshow in advance how the horrible devils will later terrify them with their grimacing, and they shall themselves grimace and sneer and make sour faces because of the great agony in the torment of hell. But they have the less to complain about because they are learning in advance their job of making grim faces.

The angry person juggles in front of the fiend with knives and is his knife-thrower and does tricks with swords. He supports them by the sharp point on his tongue. Sword and knife both are the sharp and cutting words which he throws out from himself and juggles at others, and he foreshows how the devils will do tricks with him with their sharp hooks, juggle him and fling him about like a bit of old leather from one to another and with the swords of hell pierce him right through – that is, sharp and horrible and cutting torments.

The slothful person lies and sleeps in the devil's bosom as his darling, and the devil lays his lips down to his ear and lisps to him all he wishes, for so it certainly is with whoever is idle in doing good – the fiend talks earnestly to him and the idle person lovingly receives his teaching. Idle and heedless is the sleep of this devil's child. But he will have a frightful awakening on Judgement Day, at the fearful sound of the angels' trumpets, and will wake eternally in the misery of hell: *Surgite, aiunt, mortui, et uenite ad Iudicium Saluatoris.*[25a]

The covetous person is his ashbum.[26] He plays about with the ashes and sets himself busily to heap together many great heaps. He blows on them and blinds himself, he pokes about and makes arithmetical figures in them, as these accountants do who have a lot to count. This is all the fool's joy and the fiend looks at this joke and laughs fit to burst. Every wise man well understands that both gold and silver and every earthly possession are only earth and ashes, which blind everyone who blows

a Arise, they say, you dead, and come to the Judgement of the Saviour.

on them – that is, who becomes swollen in pride of heart because of them. And all that he piles up and gathers together and holds back – of anything that is only ashes – more than is necessary shall in hell become for him toads and snakes; and, as Isaiah says, both the blanket and the sheet of him who would not feed and clothe the needy with them shall be of worms: *Subter te sternetur tinea et operimentum tuum uermis.*[a]

The greedy glutton is the fiend's manciple.[27] But he always stays in the cellar or in the kitchen. His heart is in the dishes, his thought completely in the bowls, his life in the barrel, his soul in the pot. He comes before his lord besmirched and beslobbered, a dish in his one hand, a cup in the other. He speaks his words wrong, staggers about like a drunken man who is going to fall, looks at his great belly – and the devil laughs. These God threatens thus through Isaiah: *Serui mei comedent et uos esurietis, et cetera*[b] – 'My men will eat and you will always hunger and you will be fiends' food, world without end.' *Quantum glorificauit se in deliciis fuit, tantum date illi tormentum et luctum – in Apocalipsi: Contra unum poculum quod miscuit miscete ei duo*[c] – 'Give the soak molten brass to drink, pour it into his wide throat so that he dies inside – for one give him two.' This is God's judgement against the greedy and drunk in the Apocalypse.

The lechers in the devil's court have their own proper name. For in these great courts those people are called lechers who have so abandoned shame that they have no shame at all, but seek how they can do the most wickedness.[28] The lecher in the devil's court befouls himself foully and all his fellows, stinks of that filth and pleases his lord with that stinking smell better than he would with any sweet perfume. How he stinks to God the angel in *Vitas Patrum* showed when he held his nose when the proud lecher came riding by, and not because of the rotten body which he helped the hermit to bury.[29] Of all the others, then, these have the foulest job in the fiend's court who thus defile themselves. And he will defile them, torment them with eternal stench in the pit of hell.

a Under thee shall the moth be strewed and worms shall be thy covering (Isaiah 14. 11).

b My servants shall eat and you shall be hungry, etc. (Isaiah 65.13).

c As much as she hath glorified herself and lived in delicacies, so much torment and sorrow give ye to her. In Apocalypse: In the cup wherein she hath mingled, mingle ye double unto her (Apocalypse 18.7, 6).

Now you have heard one part, my dear sisters – about those which are called the seven mother sins and about their offspring, and what jobs those men do in the fiend's court who have married those seven hags, and why they are very much to be hated and avoided. You are very far from them, Our Lord be thanked. But that foul smell of the last vice – that is, lechery – stinks so far and wide, because the fiend sows it and blows it everywhere, that I am somewhat afraid that it may on occasion leap into your heart's nose. Stench goes upwards, and you have climbed high where the wind of severe temptations is strong.[30] May Our Lord give you strength to resist well.

Some think that they will be most severely tempted in the first year that they start the life of an anchoress, or the second after that, and, when after several years they feel them severely, are much surprised and afraid that God has quite cast them away. No, it is not so. In the first years it is only ball games for many people in orders. But take note how things go through an illustration.[31] When a wise man has just brought a wife home he takes note very quietly of her behaviour; though he should see in her what displeases him, he lets it be for the moment, is pleasant towards her, and is after every way of getting her to love him deeply in her heart. When he understands for sure that her love is truly fixed on him, then he can safely punish her openly for her vices, which he earlier put up with as if he did not know them. He makes himself very stern, gives her nasty looks,[32] to try further if he can unfasten her love for him. Lastly, when he understands that she is thoroughly well-disciplined, and does not love him the less for anything he does to her, but more and more, if she can, from day to day, then he shows her that he loves her sweetly and does all that she wishes, as one whom he knows well. Then is all that grief turned to gladness. If Jesus Christ your husband acts in this way towards you, my dear sisters, it should never seem surprising to you. In the beginning there is only being charming to draw in love. But as soon as ever he understands that he is on intimate terms, he will put up with you less. After the testing, in the end, then is the great joy. In exactly this way, when he wanted to lead his people out of servitude, out of Pharaoh's power, out of Egypt, he did for them all that they wanted, many fine miracles: drew back the Red Sea and made a free passage through it for them, and where they went dry-foot drowned Pharaoh and all their enemies. In the desert,

later, when he had led them far into the wilderness, he let them endure
misery enough – hunger, thirst and great labour, and many great wars.
In the end he gave them rest and all prosperity and joy, all their heart's
desire, and ease and comfort of the flesh: *Terram fluentem lacte et melle.*[a]
Thus Our Lord at first spares the young and the feeble and draws them
out of this world sweetly and pleasurably.[33] As soon as he sees them
become hard, he lets war awake and teaches them to fight and to
endure misery. In the end, after long toil, he gives them sweet rest – I
mean in this world, before they come to heaven. And it then seems so
good, the rest after the toil – the great comfort after the great
discomfort seems so sweet!

Now there are in the Psalter, under the two temptations I spoke of
earlier – that is, the outer and the inner, which give birth to all the
others – four parts divided thus: slight and hidden temptation, slight
and open temptation, severe and hidden temptation, severe and open
temptation, as may be understood in *Non timebis a timore nocturno, a
sagitta uolante in die, a negotio perambulante in tenebris, ab incursu et demonio
meridiano.*[b] About slight and hidden temptation Job says these words:
Lapides excauant aque, et alluuione paulatim terra consumitur[c] – 'Little drops
pierce the flint when they fall on it often' – and slight hidden temptations[34] which one is not aware of make a true heart false. Of the slight
open ones, about which he also says, *Lucebit post eum semita,*[d] one does
not have so much fear. Of strong temptation which is, though, hidden,
Job also complains when he says, *Insidiati sunt michi et preualuerunt, et non
erat qui adiuuaret*[e] – that is, 'My enemies lie in wait for me with treachery
and with treason and they have prevailed upon me, and there was no
one who might help me.' *Ysaias: Veniet malum super te et nescies ortum
eius*[f] – 'Woe shall come upon you and you shall not know from where.'

a A land flowing with milk and honey (Leviticus 20.24).
b Thou shalt not be afraid of the terror of the night, of the arrow that flieth in the
  day, of the business that walketh about in the dark, of invasion, or of the noonday
  devil (Psalm 90.5–6).
c Waters wear away the stones, and with inundation the ground by little and little is
  washed away (Job 14.19).
d A path shall shine after him (Job 41.23).
e They have lain in wait against me and they have prevailed, and there was none to
  help (Job 30.13).
f Isaiah (47.11): Evil shall come upon thee and thou shalt not know the rising thereof.

Of the fourth temptation, the holy Job makes his complaint of his enemies and says: *Quasi rupto muro et aperta ianua irruerunt super me*[a] – that is, 'They burst in upon me, as though the wall were broken down and the gates open.' The first and the third temptations of these four are mostly all under the inner. The second and the fourth fall under the outer and are mostly all fleshly – and easy, therefore, to feel. The other two are spiritual, to spiritual vices, and are often concealed and hidden when they distress most and are therefore much more to be feared. Many who do not think it breed in their breast some lion cub, some snake young, which devours the soul, of whom Hosea says: *Alieni comederunt robur eius et ipse nesciuit*[b] – that is, 'Enemies devour the strength of his soul and he does not know it.' But one has most dread of when the deceiver of hell urges to a thing that seems very good indeed and is, though, the soul's killer and the way to deadly sin. He does so whenever he cannot make his strength known with open evil. 'No,' he says, 'I cannot make this one sin through greediness, but I shall, like the wrestler, twist her in the direction to which she most leans and throw her on that side and fling her down suddenly, before she the least suspects it' – and urges her towards so much abstinence that she is the weaker in God's service, and to lead so hard a life and so to torment the body that the soul perishes. He looks at another whom he can in no way make have malicious thoughts, so full of love and pity is her heart. 'I shall make her,' he says, 'too completely full of pity. I shall do so much to her that she will love possessions and think less about God and lose her reputation.' And then he puts a thought like this in her soft heart: 'St Mary – isn't that man (or that woman) in distress and no one will do anything for them? They would for me if I asked them, and in this way I could help them and give them alms.' He leads her on to gather and give all, at first to the poor, later to other friends – lastly to hold feasts and become completely worldly, degenerating from an anchoress into a housewife in a hall. God knows, this sort of feast makes whores of some. She thinks she is doing right, as stupid and foolish people give her to understand: they flatter her for her

a They have rushed in upon me, as when a wall is broken and a gate opened (Job 30.14).

b Strangers have devoured his strength and he knew it not (Hosea 7.9).

generosity, praise and extol the alms-giving that she does – how widely she is known! And she thinks well of this and leaps into pride. Soon enough someone is saying that she is treasure-gathering, so that both her house and herself may get robbed. Pity above pity! Thus the traitor of hell makes himself out to be a true counsellor. Don't ever believe him. David calls him *demonium meridianum*[a] – 'bright shining devil'. And St Paul *angelum lucis*[b] – that is, 'angel of light' – for such he often makes himself out to be and as such shows himself to many. Account no vision that you see, either in a dream or waking, as anything but delusion, for it is only his guile. He has often deceived wise men of holy and high life, like the one he came to in the likeness of a woman in the wilderness – said she had gone astray, a poor thing looking for shelter.[35] And the other holy man whom he made believe he was an angel, and of his father that he was the devil, and made him kill his father – so often before that had he told him the truth all the time, so as to deceive him wretchedly in the end.[36] Also the holy man whom he made come home so as to share out his father's money among the needy and the poor and stay so long that he committed deadly sin with a woman and so fell into despair and died in capital sin.[37] Listen to such stories from people who speak to you – how you must guard yourself against the devil's tricks so that he does not deceive you. He has sometimes made one of you believe that it would be flattery if she spoke politely and if she humbly complained of her need, if she thanked someone for his good deed – and it was contempt more likely to quench charity than righteousness. He goes about making someone flee the comfort of men so much that she falls into a deadly sorrow – that is, inertia – or into deep thought, so that she goes mad. Another hates sin so much that she has contempt for another who falls, when she should be weeping for her and be terribly afraid of such happening to herself, and be saying like the holy man who sighed and wept and said, when they told him of the fall of one of his brothers, *Ille hodie, ego cras*[c] – 'Alas, severely was he tempted before he fell like that: as he fell today, I may,' he said, 'likewise fall tomorrow.'[38]

a   Noonday devil (Psalm 90.6).
b   Angel of light (2 Corinthians 11.14).
c   He today, I tomorrow (see *Lives of the Fathers* 7.16).

Now, my dear sisters, I have named for you many temptations under the seven sins – not, though, the thousandth part of those with which one is tempted. No one, I think, could name them individually. But in those that have been mentioned they are all contained: there are few in this world – or none at all – who are not sometimes tempted by one of them. He has so many boxes full of his medicines, the evil doctor of hell, that to one who refuses one, he offers another straight away – and a third and a fourth and so on all the time until he comes across one that is in the end accepted, and he then pours that one out for him frequently. Think here of the number of his phials. Now hear, as I promised, many kinds of comfort against all temptations, and – with God's grace – after that, the remedies.

Whoever is established in a high life may be sure of temptation. And this is the first consolation: for the higher a tower is, the stronger the winds it has. You are a tower yourselves, my dear sisters, but do not fear while you are so truly and firmly cemented with the cement of constant love, each of you to the others. For the devil's blast need not be feared unless the cement fail, that is to say, unless the love between you deteriorate because of the fiend. As soon as anyone uncements herself, she is quickly swept off, unless the others hold her; she is quickly pitched down, as the loose stone is from the top of the tower, into the deep ditch of some filthy sin.

Now a second encouragement. It ought to console you a great deal when you are tempted. The tower is not attacked – nor the castle or the city – when they have been won. Likewise the warrior of hell does not attack with temptation anyone whom he has in his control, but those whom he does not have. Therefore, dear sisters, whoever is not attacked may be very much afraid in case she has been won.

The third comfort is that Our Lord himself in the *Pater noster* teaches us to pray: *Et ne nos inducas in temptationem*[a] – that is, 'Lord, Father, do not allow the fiend to lead us wholly into temptation.' Look, take note. He does not want us to pray that we should not be tempted, for that is our purgatory, our cleansing fire, but that we be not wholly brought into it with the consent of the heart and reason's agreement.

The fourth solace is assurance of God's help in the fighting back, as

a And lead us not into temptation (Matthew 6.13).

St Paul testifies: *Fidelis est Deus, qui non sinit nos temptari ultra quam pati possumus, set, et cetera*[a] – 'God,' he says, 'is faithful, and he will never permit the devil to tempt us above what he sees clearly that we are able to endure.' But, in the temptation, he has set the fiend a limit, as though he said, 'Tempt her so far, but you shall not go any further' – and so far he gives her strength to resist: the fiend cannot go a jot further.

And this is the fifth solace, that he can do nothing to us except by God's leave. That was clearly shown, as the Gospel tells, when the devils which Our Lord cast out of a man entreated him and said, *Si eicitis nos hinc, mittite nos in porcos*[b] – 'If you drive us hence, put us into these pigs here' (a herd of which was going about there). And he granted it them. Look how they were not able to torment foul pigs without his leave. And the pigs immediately ran in a rush to the sea to drown themselves. St Mary! he stank so to the pigs that they preferred to drown themselves rather than carry him – and an unhappy sinner, God's likeness, carries him in his breast and never gives heed! All that he did to Job – all the time he got leave for it from Our Lord. See that you know the story in the Dialogue – how the holy man used to say to the devil's snake: *Si licenciam accepisti, ego non prohibeo*[c] – 'If you have leave, go on, sting if you can' – and offered his cheek. But it had none then, except to frighten him, if faith failed him; and when God gives him leave to tempt his dear children, why is it, except for their great benefit, even if it may give them great pain?

The sixth comfort is that Our Lord, when he allows us to be tempted, is playing with us like a mother with her little darling – runs away from him and hides, and lets him stay on his own and look anxiously about, call, 'Mummy, Mummy',[39] and cry for a while and then with arms spread leaps out laughing, cuddles and kisses him and wipes his eyes. So Our Lord lets us be on our own sometimes and withdraws his grace, his comfort and his encouragement, so that we find no sweetness in anything that we do well or savour at heart; and

---

a God is faithful, who will not suffer you to be tempted above that which you are able, but, etc. (1 Corinthians 10.13).

b If thou cast us out hence, send us into the swine (Matthew 8.31).

c If you have received permission, I do not prohibit you (Gregory, *Dialogues* 3.16).

nevertheless at that moment Our Lord does not love us any the less, but he does it out of great love. And that David understood well when he said, *Non me derelinquas usquequaque*[a] 'Do not, Lord,' he said, 'leave me altogether.' Look how he wanted him to leave him, but not altogether. And note six reasons why God, for our good, sometimes withdraws himself. One is so that we do not become proud. A second, so that we know our own feebleness, our great lack of strength and our weakness. And this is a very great good, as St Gregory says: *Magna perfectio est sue inperfectionis cognitio*[b] – that is, 'A great goodness it is to know well one's wretchedness and weakness.' *Ecclesiasticus: Intemptatus qualia scit*[c] – 'What does he know,' says Solomon, 'who is untempted?' And St Augustine bears witness to St Gregory with these words: *Melior est animus cui propria est infirmitas nota, quam qui scrutatur celorum fastigia et terrarum fundamenta*[d] – 'Better is he who tracks down and seeks out thoroughly his own feebleness than he who measures how high the heaven is and how deep the earth.' When two are bearing a burden and one of them lets go of it, the one who supports it can then feel how much it weighs. Just so, dear sisters, while God bears your temptation with you, you do not know at all how heavy it is, and therefore on occasion he leaves you on your own so that you may understand your own feebleness and call for his help and cry loud for him if he is too long. Support it well in the meantime, however grievously it afflicts you. Whoever is certain of help coming to him soon and nevertheless gives up his castle to his enemies is much to be blamed. Think here of the story of how the holy man in his temptation saw in the west ranged against him so great an army of devils, and lost, out of great fear, the strength of his faith until the other said to him. 'Look,' he said, 'in the east: *Plures nobiscum sunt quam cum illis*'[e] – 'We have more than they to help on our side.'[40] For the third thing is that you should never be completely assured, for assurance breeds heedlessness and presumption,

---

a Do not thou utterly forsake me! (Psalm 118.8).

b The recognition of one's imperfection is great perfection.

c Ecclesiasticus (34.11): He that hath not been tried, what manner of things doth he know?

d The soul to which its own weakness is known is better than that which searches the heights of the skies and the depth of the lands (see *The Trinity* 4.1).

e There are more with us than with them (*Lives of the Fathers* 5.18).

and both these breed disobedience. The fourth reason why Our Lord
hides himself is so that you should seek him more eagerly, and call and
weep for him, as the little baby does for his mother. After that the fifth
is that you should take his return the more gladly. The sixth that you
should, afterwards, watch him more wisely when you have caught him,
and hold him more firmly, and say with his beloved: *Tenui eum nec
dimittam*.[a] These six reasons are under the sixth consolation which you
may have, my dear sisters, in the face of temptation.

The seventh comfort is that all the holy saints were fiercely tempted.
Take first of all one of the highest. To St Peter Our Lord said: *Ecce
Sathan expetiuit uos ut cribraret sicut triticum, et cetera*[b] – 'Look,' he said,
'Satan is working hard to sieve you out of my chosen. But I have made
entreaty for you that your faith should not altogether fail.' St Paul had,
as he himself tells, a pricking of the flesh: *Datus est michi stimulus carnis
mee*,[c] and prayed Our Lord earnestly that he should put it from him,
and he would not, but said: *Sufficit tibi gratia mea: virtus in infirmitate
perficitur*[d] – that is 'My grace will guard you so that you are not
overcome.' To be strong in lack of strength – that is great power. All
the others have been crowned through the fight with temptation. St
Sarah[41] – was she not fully thirteen years tempted in her flesh? But
because she knew that in the great anguish the great reward arose, she
would never once entreat Our Lord to deliver her altogether from it,
but this was her prayer: *Domine, da michi uirtutem resistendi*[e] – 'Lord,
give me strength to resist.' After thirteen years the accursed spirit who
had tempted her came, black as a Moor, and began to cry, 'Sarah, you
have overcome me,' and she answered him: 'You lie,' she said, 'foul
thing – not I, but Jesus Christ, my Lord, has.' Look – the deceiver!
how he would make her at the last leap into pride; but she was well
aware of that and ascribed all the victory to God's strength. St
Benedict, St Antony and the others – you know well how they were

a I held him and I will not let him go (Canticles 3.4).
b Behold, Satan hath desired to have you that he may sift you as wheat, etc. (Luke
   22.31).
c There was given me a sting of my flesh (2 Corinthians 12.7).
d My grace is sufficient for thee: power is made perfect in infirmity (2 Corinthians
   12.9).
e Lord, give me the power of resisting (see *Lives of the Fathers* 5.5, 10).

tempted, and through the temptations proved as true champions, and so by right deserved the warrior's crown.[42]

And this is the eighth encouragement, that, as the goldsmith purifies the gold in the fire, so does God the soul in the fire of temptation.

The ninth comfort is that if the fiend causes you much grief with temptation, you cause him a hundred times more when you resist – for three reasons in particular. The first is that he loses, as Origen says, his strength to tempt with that kind of sin for evermore thereafter.[43] The second is that he further increases his torment; the third eats his heart with bitter anger and vexation, that he quite unwillingly, in the temptation which you stand against, increases your reward and, instead of the torment that he thought to draw you towards, plaits your crown of bliss – and not one or two, but as many times as you overcome him, so many crowns, that is to say, so many honours of different kinds of happiness. For so St Bernard says: *Quotiens uincis, totiens coronaberis.*[a] The story in *Vitas Patrum*[b] testifies to the same thing – about the disciple who sat before his master, and his master fell asleep while he taught him and slept until midnight, when he awoke. 'Are you,' he said, 'still here? Go and sleep straight away.' The holy man, his master, fell asleep again quickly, he having kept many vigils before this, and saw a very beautiful place and a throne set out, and on it seven crowns; and there came a voice and said, 'This seat and these crowns has your disciple deserved this night.' And the holy man awoke and called him to him. 'Tell me,' he said, 'how did you get on while you sat before me as I slept?' 'I thought,' he said, 'often that I would wake you, and, because you were sleeping sweetly, I could not for pity. And then I thought I would go away to sleep, because I wanted to, and would not without leave.' 'How often,' said his master, 'did you overcome your thought like this?' 'Seven times,' he said. Then his master understood clearly what the seven crowns were: seven kinds of joy which his disciple had on each occasion deserved, because he opposed the fiend and overcame himself.

In just this way, dear sisters, in wrestling with temptation arises the

a As many times as you conquer, so many times will you be crowned (see *Sermons for Quadragesima* 5.3).

b *Lives of the Fathers* (5.7, 43)

gain. *Nemo coronabitur nisi qui legitime certauerit*[a] – 'No one will be crowned,' says St Paul, 'except whoever strenuously and faithfully fights against the world, against themselves, against the fiend of hell.' They fight faithfully who, however much they are attacked by these three enemies – especially the flesh – whatever the desire may be, the more violent it is, struggle more firmly against it and deny the granting of it with a constant heart, however much it may goad them. They who do thus are Jesus Christ's companions. For they do as he did hanging on the cross: *Cum gustasset acetum, noluit bibere*[b] – that is, 'He tasted the bitter drink and drew back at once, and would not drink though he was thirsty.' She who does likewise is with God on his cross, though she thirst with desire and the devil offer her his linctus to drink; understand and think, though, that there is gall in it and, though it be a torment, it is better to endure thirst than to be poisoned. Let desire pass and you will afterwards be pleased. While the itching lasts it seems good to scratch, but afterwards one feels it smart painfully. Alas, and many a one is, because of great heat, so very thirsty indeed that while she drinks that drink, however bitter it may be, she never notices it, but gulps it down greedily with no concern at all. When it is all gone she spits and shakes her head, starts to screw up her face and grimace – but it is too late, then. Spew it out at once to the priest in confession, for leave it inside and it will breed death. Therefore, my dear sisters, be on your guard in advance, and, after the consolations that I have written down here against all temptations, seek these remedies.

Against all temptations, and especially against fleshly ones, the remedies and cures, under God's grace, are holy meditations, fervent and persistent, and anguished prayers, bold faith, reading, fasts, vigils and bodily labours, consolation from others in speaking to them at that moment when temptation is strong. Humility, generosity of heart and all virtues are weapons in this fight – and constancy of love above all the others. He who throws away his weapons *wants* to be wounded.

Holy meditations are embraced in a verse which has been previously taught you,[44] my dear sisters:

a No one shall be crowned unless he strive lawfully (2 Timothy 2.5).
b When he had tasted the vinegar, he would not drink (Matthew 27.34).

Mors tua, mors Christi, nota culpa, gaudia celi,
Iudicii terror figantur mente fideli.[a]

That is:

> Think of your sins with sorrow often,
> Think of hell's misery, of joys in heaven,
> Think of your death, of God's death on the cross,
> Call to mind the fierce judgement of Judgement Day oft,
> Think how false is the world, what is its meed,
> Think what you owe God for his good deeds.

Each one of these sayings would need a long time to be unfolded well. But if *I* hurry on, *you* should delay the longer. I will make one remark. After your sins, whenever you think of hell's misery and of heaven's joys, understand that God wants in some fashion to show them to men in this world through worldly sufferings and worldly joys, and puts them on show as shadows.[45] For they are no more like the joy of heaven or the misery of hell than a shadow is to the thing of which it is the shadow. You are above the sea of this world, on the bridge of heaven. Look out that you are not like the nervous horse which shies because of a shadow and falls down into the water from the high bridge. They are too childish who run away from a picture that seems to them frightful and fearful to look at. Misery and joy in this world – it is all only painting, all only shadow.

Not only holy meditations – as on Our Lord and on all his deeds and on all his words, on the dear Lady and on all holy saints – but other thoughts have on occasion helped in persistent temptations; four kinds particularly to those who are persistently assailed by temptations of the flesh – full of fear, full of wonder, full of joy and full of sorrow, voluntarily without compulsion raised in the heart. For instance, thinking what you would do if you saw standing openly before you, with his mouth gaping wide at you, the devil of hell, as he does hiddenly in the temptation; if someone cried 'Fire! fire!' – that the church was burning; if you heard burglars breaking down your walls; these and other such thoughts full of fear. Full of wonder and full of joy, as if you saw Jesus

---

a Let your death, the death of Christ, known guilt, the joys of heaven,/The terror of judgement, be fixed in [your] faithful mind.

Christ and heard him ask you what was dearest to you after your salvation and that of your dearest friends, of things in this life, and he offered you your choice provided you resisted; if you saw quite distinctly all heaven's inhabitants and hell's inhabitants look at you alone in the temptation; if someone came and told you that the man who is dearest to you,[46] by some miracle, such as a voice from heaven, had been chosen as Pope; and all other such. Full of wonder and full of sorrow, as if you heard tell that the man who is dearest to you had been suddenly drowned, killed or murdered, that your sisters had been burnt to death in their house. Thoughts like this often, in fleshly souls, expel fleshly temptations sooner than some of the others before. Fervent and persistent and anxious[47] prayers – the devil of hell is very afraid of them, for besides drawing down assistance against him, and God's hand from heaven, they do him two injuries, bind him and burn him. Look, here is the proof of both. Publius, a holy man, was at his prayers and the fiend came flying in the air and was going right on towards the western part of the world at the command of Julian the Emperor, and was bound tight by the holy man's prayers, which overtook him as they flew up towards heaven, so that he could not move hither or thither for ten whole days.[48] Do you not also have the story of Ruffin the Devil, Belial's brother, in your English book about St Margaret?[49] One reads of that other one that he cried loud to St Bartholomew, who was much at his prayers, *Incendunt me orationes tue*[a] – 'Bartholomew, woe is me, your prayers are burning me up.' Whoever may, through God's gift, have tears at her prayers, she may do with God all that ever she desires.[50] For thus we read: *Oratio lenit, lacrima cogit; haec ungit, illa pungit*[b] – 'Blessed prayer softens and pleases Our Lord, but tears compel him. Prayers anoint him with soft coaxing, but tears prick him and never give him peace before he grants them all that they ask.' When towns or castles are attacked, those inside pour out scalding water and thus guard the walls. And do likewise yourselves, as often as the fiend attacks your castle and the soul's city: with fervent prayers throw out on him scalding tears, so that David may say of you, *Contribulasti capita draconum in aquis*[c] – 'You have scalded the dragon's head with boiling

a Your prayers are burning me (Pseudo-Bede, *Homilies* 2.90).
b Prayer softens, a tear compels; the former oils, the latter stings.
c Thou didst crush the heads of the dragons in the waters (Psalm 73.13).

water', that is, with hot tears. Where this water is, to be sure, the fiend flees in case he is scalded. Or again: a castle which has a ditch round it and water in the ditch – the castle is quite without concern in the face of its enemies. The castle is each good man that the devil wars against, but if you have a deep ditch of deep humility, and wet tears for it, you are a strong castle. The warrior of hell can long attack you and waste his time. Again, they say – and it's true – that a great wind is laid with a little rain, and the sun afterwards shines the brighter. Likewise a great temptation – that is, the fiend's blast – subsides with the gentle rain of a few tears and the true sun shines afterwards more brightly on the soul. Thus tears with fervent prayers are good. And, if you understand, I have mentioned their four great effects, for which they are to be loved. In all your needs quickly send these messengers at once to heaven, for, as Solomon says, *Oratio humiliantis se penetrat nubes, et cetera*[a] – that is, 'The prayer of a humble person pierces the clouds.' And on this St Augustine says, *Magna est uirtus pure consciente que ad Deum intrat et mandata peragit ubi caro peruenire nequit*[b] – 'Oh, great is the power of a bright, clean prayer which flies up and comes in before Almighty God and does the errand' – so well that God has written in the book of life all that she[51] says, as St Bernard testifies,[52] and keeps her with him and sends down his angel to do all that she asks. I will not here say any more about prayer.

Bold faith puts the devil to flight straight away. To that St James testifies: *Resistite diabolo et fugiet a uobis*[c] – 'Resist the fiend and he will take flight.' Resist – in what power? St Peter teaches: *Cui resistite, fortes in fide*[d] – 'Stand against him with strong faith'; be confident of God's help and know how weak he is who has no power over us except from ourselves. He can only put on show some of his fake stock[53] and coax or threaten so that people buy it. Whichever he does, scorn him; laugh the old ape loudly to shame through true faith and he considers himself disgraced and takes to flight quickly. *Sancti per fidem uicerunt*

---

a The prayer of him that humbleth himself shall pierce the clouds, etc. (Ecclesiasticus 35.21).
b Great is the virtue of a pure conscience which enters into God and executes commissions where flesh cannot come.
c Resist the devil and he will flee from you (James 4.7).
d Whom resist ye, strong in faith (1 Peter 5.9).

regna[a] – that is, 'All the holy saints overcame through faith the devil's rule, which is only sin, for he rules over nothing but sin alone.' Now pay close attention to how all the seven deadly sins may be put to flight through true faith. First, now, on pride.

Who considers himself great, as the proud man does, when he considers how small the great Lord made himself within a poor maiden's breast?

Who is envious, who considers with the eyes of faith how Jesus, God – not for his own good, but for the good of others – did and said and endured all that he endured? The envious man would not care to have anyone sharing in his good things – and God Almighty, even after everything else, went down to hell to look for companions and to share with them the good things that he had. Look, now, how different the envious are from Our Lord. The anchoress who refused the loan of a book to another would have the eye of her faith far away from this.

Who nurses anger who considers that God came down to earth to make a threefold peace: between man and man, between God and man, between man and angel? And after his resurrection, when he came and showed himself, this was his greeting to his dear disciples: *Pax uobis*[b] – 'Peace be among you.' Now pay attention carefully. When a dear friend goes away from another, the last words that he says should be best retained. Our Lord's last words when he ascended up to heaven and left his dear friends in a strange land were of sweet love and of peace. *Pacem relinquo uobis, pacem meam do uobis*[c] – that is, 'I set peace among you, I leave peace with you.' This was his love token, which he left and gave them at his departure – *In hoc cognoscetis quod discipuli mei sitis, si dilectionem adinuicem habueritis.*[d] Look carefully now, what mark he set on his chosen, out of his precious love, when he ascended to heaven: *In hoc cognoscetis quod, et cetera* – 'By this you shall know,' he said, 'that you are my disciples – if sweet love and peace is between you at all times.' May God know it – and he does know it – I would prefer you all to have the hospital-sickness[54] than that you were envious or cruel-hearted. For

a Saints by faith conquered kingdoms (see Hebrews 11.33).
b Peace be to you (John 20.19).
c Peace I leave with you, my peace I give unto you (John 14.27).
d By this you shall know that you are my disciples, if you have love for one another (John 13.35).

Jesus is all love and in love he rests and has his dwelling: *In pace factus est locus eius; ibi confregit potencias arcum, scutum, gladium et bellum*[a] – that is, 'In peace is God's place, and wherever peace is and love, there he brings to nothing all the devil's power.' 'There he breaks his bow' it says – that is, hidden temptations which he shoots from afar – 'and his sword as well' – that is, sharp temptations which cut from close at hand.

Now take careful note, through many illustrations, how good united-ness in love is and unity of heart. For there is nothing under the sun that I would rather – or as much – that you had. Don't you know that where men fight in these strong armies, those who hold firmly together can never be routed in any way? It is just so in the spiritual fight against the devil. His whole intent is to separate hearts, to take away the love that holds people together. For when love subsides, then they are parted, and the devil gets himself in between and kills on either side. Dumb animals are clever in this way – that when they are attacked by a wolf or by a lion they crowd together, all the flock tightly, and make shields of themselves for one another, and are safe while doing so. If any unfortunate beast goes out, it soon has its throat torn out. A third illustration: where a single person goes alone along a slippery path, he slides about and soon falls; where many go together, and each holds the other's hand, if anyone starts to slide about, the next person pulls him up before he falls right over. If they get tired, each one holds himself up on the next. Temptation is sliding about; by tiredness are signified the vices under sloth which have been mentioned above. It is this that St Gregory is speaking of: *Cum nos nobis per orationis opem coniungimus, per lubricum incedentes, quasi adinuicem manus teneamus, vt tanto quisque amplius roboretur quanto alteri innititur.*[b] Just as in a strong wind and in swift waters which people have to wade across, when there are many each holds the next, and the person who gets separated is swept away and perishes every time, too well we know

---

a His place is in peace; there hath he broken the powers of bows, the shield, the sword and the battle (Psalm 75.3–4).

b When we join ourselves together through the power of prayer, it is as if, walking a slippery path, we are holding one another's hands, so that each person is strengthened more fully to the extent that they lean on someone else (*Letters* 1.25).

how the path of this world is slippery, how the wind and the stream of temptation are strong. There is a great need for each to hold the next person's hand with busy prayers and with love. For as Solomon says, *Ve soli, quia cum ceciderit, non habet subleuantem*[a] – 'Woe every time to the man on his own, for when he falls, he does not have anyone to raise him.' No one is on his own who has God as a companion – and that is everyone who has true love in his heart. The seventh illustration, if you count right, is this. Dust and grit, as you see, because it is separated and none of it holds on to the next bit, a little puff of wind gets rid of it completely. Where it is stuck together in a clod, it lies completely unmoved. A handful of sticks are difficult to break while they are together; each stick separated breaks easily. A tree which is going to fall, put another underneath it and it stands firm; separate them and both fall. Now you have nine. In this way find illustrations in outside things of how good unity of love is and agreement, which holds the good together so that none can be destroyed. And, certainly, proper faith wants to have this. Consider carefully and understand Jesus Christ's precious words and deeds, which were all in love and in sweetness. Above everything I would like anchoresses to learn the teaching of this lesson well. For many, more's the pity, are Samson's foxes, who had their faces turned each away from the others and were tied together by their tails, as *Iudicum*[b] tells, and at each one's tail a burning brand. I spoke about the foxes a long way back, but not in this way. Take good heed what this means. One happily turns one's face towards a thing that one loves and away from a thing that one hates. They then have their faces turned away from one another, when no one loves the others, but they are together at the tails and bear the devil's brands, the burning of lust. In another way, tail signifies end. At their end they shall be bound together as were Samson's foxes by the tails and brands set at them – that is, the fire of hell.

All this is said, my dear sisters, so that your dear faces should be at all times turned together with loving expressions and sweet looks; so that you should always be cemented together in the unity of one heart

a Woe to him that is alone, for, when he falleth, he hath none to lift him up (Ecclesiastes 4.10).
b Judges (15.4).

and one will, as it is written of Our Lord's disciples: *Multitudinis credentium erat cor unum et anima una. Pax uobis.*[a] This was God's greeting to his dear disciples: 'Peace be among you.' You are the anchoresses of England, so many together – twenty now or more;[55] God increase you in good – among whom is most peace, most unity and singleness and agreement in a united life according to one rule, so that you all pull one way, all turned in one direction and no one away from the others, as report has it. Therefore you go on well and succeed on your way, for everyone goes along with the others in one manner of living, as though you were a community of London or of Oxford, of Shrewsbury or of Chester, where all are one with a common manner without singularity – that is, individual difference – a base thing in religion, for it shatters unity and the common manner which ought to exist in an order. Now this, then, that you are all as if one community, is your high fame. This is pleasing to God. This is now recently widely known, so that your community begins to spread towards the end of England.[56] You are, as it were, the motherhouse of which they are begotten. You are like a spring. If the spring grows muddy, the streams grow muddy also. Ah, alas, if you grow muddy, I shall never abide it. If there is any among you who takes a singular way and does not follow the community, but turns aside from the flock, which is as if in a cloister that Jesus is high prior over, turns aside like a restive sheep and wanders off on her own into a bramble thicket, into a wolf's mouth, on the way to the throat of hell – if any such is among you, God turn her back into the flock, direct her into the community and grant that you who are in it may so hold yourselves in it that God, the high prior, may at the end take you from there up into the cloister of heaven. While you keep yourselves together as one, the fiend may frighten you if he has leave, but not harm you at all. That he knows full well and therefore day and night works at uncementing you through anger or vicious envy, and sends a man or a woman to tell the one some distressing story about the other, which sister should not say about sister. Let none of you – I forbid you – believe the devil's messenger, but see that each of you recognizes when he is speaking with the evil man's tongue, and say

a   The multitude of believers had but one heart and one soul (Acts 4.32). Peace be to you (John 20.19).

straight away, 'Our director has written to us, as a command to keep, that we are to tell him all that each hears of the others, and therefore see that you tell me nothing that I cannot tell him who can put things right and knows how to do it in such a way that you and I shall both, if we are telling the truth, not be blamed.' Let each none the less warn the other through a very trustworthy messenger, sweetly and lovingly as her dear sister, about the thing she is doing wrong, if she knows it to be true, and make whoever takes what she has to say repeat it in front of her often before she goes, as she will say it, so that she doesn't say it differently, or patch any more on to it, for a little patch can disfigure completely a big single piece. She who gets this love-cure from her sister should thank her earnestly and say with the Psalmist: *Corripiet me iustus in misericordia et increpabit me; oleum autem peccatoris non inpinguet caput meum,*[a] and after that with Solomon: *Meliora sunt uulnera corripientis quam oscula blandientis*[b] – 'If she did not love me, she would not warn me out of pity. Her wounds are dearer to me than flattering kisses.' Always respond like this and if it is otherwise than the other supposes, let her send word of it back, lovingly and gently, and let the other believe it straight away; for I also want this – that each of you should love the others as her self. If the fiend blows any anger between you, or swollen heart (which Jesus Christ forbid), let no one be so foolish, before it has quite settled down, as to take God's flesh and his blood, or even so much as to look at them once, or to look towards him in foul anger, who came down to man on earth from heaven to make a threefold peace, as has been said above.[57] Let each then send word to the other that she has, as though she were in her presence, made to her her *Venie.*[c] And she who first draws forth the love of her sister in this way and obtains peace and takes on herself the guilt, though the other may be more at fault, she shall be my precious and dear daughter. For she is God's daughter – he himself says it: *Beati pacifici, quoniam filii Dei uocabuntur.*[d] Thus pride and envy and anger are put to flight everywhere

a The just man shall correct me in mercy and shall reprove me; but let not the oil of the sinner fatten my head (Psalm 140.5).
b Better are the wounds of a rebuker than the kisses of a flatterer (see Proverbs 27.6).
c Pardons.
d Blessed are the peacemakers, for they shall be called the children of God (Matthew 5.9).

where true love is and firm faith in God's merciful deeds and loving words. Let us go on now to the others in order.

Who can be, for shame, sleepy and sluggish and slothful who considers how very busy Our Lord was on earth? – *Pertransiit bene-faciendo et sanando omnes.*[a] After all the rest, consider how at the end of his life he toiled on the hard cross. Others have rest, get away from the light in their rooms, hide away when they are being let blood from a vein in the arm. And he, on Mount Calvary, went up still higher on the cross. And no man ever toiled as hard and as painfully as he did that day when in five places he bled streams from most broad and deep wounds, beside the great veins that bled on his head under the sharp crown of thorns, and beside the pitiful gashes of the violent scourging over all his lovely body, not only on the legs. Against slothful people and sleepers stands very plainly his early resurrection[58] from death to life.

Against covetousness is his great poverty which grew on him all the time, the longer, the greater. For when he was first born, he who made the earth, he did not find on the earth space enough for his little body to be laid upon. So cramped was the place that his mother and Joseph could hardly sit in it and so they laid him on a manger high up, wrapped in rags, as the Gospel says: *Pannis eum inuoluit.*[b] This is how finely he was clothed, the heavenly creator who clothes the sun! After this the poor virgin of heaven nursed him and fed him with her little milk – what a virgin ought to have. This was great poverty, but greater came after. For at least he still then had the food that was appropriate to him, and instead of an inn his cradle gave him lodging. Afterwards, as he complained, he did not have a place where he could hide his head: *Filius hominis non habet ubi caput suum reclinet.*[c] This is how poor he was as to an inn. As to food, he was so needful that, when he had preached all day in Jerusalem on Palm Sunday and night was coming on, he looked about, it says in the Gospel, to see if anyone would invite him to food or to lodging, but there was no one, and so he went out of the great city into Bethany, to the house of Mary and Martha, where he went on occasion with his disciples. They broke off ears of corn by the

a He went about doing good and healing everyone (Acts 10.38).
b She wrapped him up in swaddling clothes (Luke 2.7).
c The Son of man hath not where to lay his head (Matthew 8.20).

side of the road and kneaded the kernels between their hands and ate them, because of their hunger, and were strongly rebuked for that. But the greatest poverty of all came after this again; for he was stripped stark naked on the cross. When he complained of thirst, he could not have water, yet the greatest wonder is that of all the broad earth he might not have a speck to die on. The cross had a foot, or a little more - and that was for his torment. When the world's ruler wished to be as poor as this, he lacks faith who loves and covets too much the world's wealth and prosperity.

Against gluttony is his poor pittance [59] which he had on the cross. Two kinds of people need to eat well, those labouring and those who are let blood. The day that he was both at hard labour and let blood, as I have just said, his pittance on the cross was only a sponge of gall. Look now – who will grumble, if they think about this well, about a poor meal of tasteless food, of a poor pittance? You must not make a complaint about any man or woman, or lament any want, except to some trusty friend who can put it right and benefit them or you; and that should be said in private, as under the seal of confession, so that you are not blamed. If you are in want of anything and some friend asks you earnestly if you are in any want, if you expect good of him, answer in this way: 'May the Lord God repay you: I fear I have more than I deserve, and endure less want than is necessary for me.' If he asks more pressingly, thank him earnestly and say: 'I dare not lie about myself; I *am* in want – as is proper. What anchoress comes into an anchor-house to have her ease? But now you want to know about it anyhow – may Our Lord reward you – this now is one thing that I need; and thus our rule commands that we show to good friends our distress, as other of God's poor do theirs, with mild humility.' And we must not at all refuse the grace of God's sending, but thank him earnestly lest he become angry with us and withdraw his generous hand and afterwards with too much want abate our pride. And is it not very unreasonable, when God offers his hand, to say, putting it back, 'I don't care for it, have it yourself. I want to try and see if I can live without this.' I have heard of such who because of this had a bad end.

Against lechery is his being born of a pure virgin and all his pure life that he led on earth – and all those who followed him. Thus, look, the articles – which are, as one might say, the joints – of our faith, in respect of God's manhood, if anyone considers them closely, fight against the fiend who tempts us with these deadly sins. Therefore St Peter says: *Christo in carne passo et uos eadem cogitatione armemini*[a] – 'Arm yourselves,' he says, 'with thought about Jesus Christ, who was tormented in our flesh.' And St Paul: *Recogitate qualem aput semet ipsum sustinuit contradic-tionem ut non fatigetis*[b] – 'Think, think,'[60] says St Paul, 'when you grow weary in the fight against the devil, how Our Lord denied his fleshly will, and deny yours.' *Nondum enim usque ad sanguinem restitistis*[c] – 'You have not yet resisted to the shedding of your blood', [as he did with his for you – against himself, in so far as he was a man of our nature. And you still have that blood,][61] that blessed body which came of the virgin and died on the cross night and day beside you – there is only a wall between – and each day he comes forth and shows himself fleshly and bodily, in the mass – changed, though, to the appearance of something else, under the form of bread.[62] For in his own our eyes could not endure the bright vision. But in this way he shows himself to you, as though he said, 'Look, here I am, what do you want? Tell me what you would like. What do you need? Complain of your need.' If the fiend's army – that is, his temptations – is attacking you hard, answer him and say: *Metati sumus castra iuxta lapidem adiutorii. Porro Philistiim venerunt in Afech*[d] – 'Yes, Lord, it is wonderful. We are encamped here beside you, who are the stone of help, tower of true aid, castle of strength, and the devil's army is more furious against us than against any other.' This I take from *Regum*, for there it tells in just this way that Israel, God's people, came and encamped by the stone of help, and the Philistines came into Afech. The Philistines are devils. 'Afech' in Hebrew means 'new fury'. So it is to be sure, when someone encamps by Our Lord, then first the devil begins to grow furious – but there it tells that Israel soon turned its back and four thousand were killed in the flight. Do not turn your back, my dear sisters, but resist the fiend's army head-on,

a Christ therefore having suffered in the flesh, be you also armed with the same thought (1 Peter 4.1).
b Think diligently what opposition within himself he endured, that you be not wearied (Hebrews 12.3).
c For you have not yet resisted unto blood (Hebrews 12.4).
d We are encamped beside the stone of help. And the Philistines came to Aphec (see 1 Kings 4.1).

as is said above, with strong faith, and with the good Jehoshaphat, quickly send prayer as a messenger for help to the prince of heaven.[63] *In Paralipomenon: In nobis quidem non est tanta fortitudo ut possimus huic multitudini resistere, que irruit super nos. Set cum ignoremus quid agere debeamus, hoc solum habemus residui – ut oculos nostros dirigamus ad te. Sequitur: Hec dicit Dominus uobis: Nolite timere, et ne paueatis hanc multitudinem. Non enim est uestra pugna set Dei. Tantummodo confidenter state, et uidebitis auxilium Domini super uos. Credite in Domino Deo uestro, et securi eritis.*[a] This is the English: 'In us there is not, precious Lord, enough strength to withstand the devil's army, which is so strong against us. But when we are so harassed and so strongly beset that we are entirely unable to think what to do for ourselves, this one thing we can do: raise our eyes up to the merciful Lord. You send us aid, you drive off our foes – for we look to you.' Thus, with the good Jehoshaphat, when God comes before you and asks what you want – and at every time when you have need – show it sweetly like this to his sweet ear. If he does not hear you soon, cry louder and more insistently and threaten that you will yield up the castle unless he sends you help the sooner and hurries the more. But do you know how he answered Jehoshaphat the Good? Thus, in this way: *Nolite timere, et cetera.*[b] Thus he answers you when you call for help: 'Do not be afraid, do not fear them at all, though they be strong and many: the fight is mine, not yours. Simply stand assured and you shall see my succour. Only have firm faith in me and you will be quite safe.' Look, now, what a help bold faith is. For all that help which God promises, the strength to stand well, all is in it alone. Bold faith makes one stand upright, and to the devil nothing is more hateful. Therefore this is what he says in Isaiah: *Incuruare ut transeamus*[c] – 'Bend down,' he says, 'so that I can get over you.' She bends who bends her heart to his temptations, for while she stands

a In Paralipomenon (2 Chronicles 20): As for us, we have not strength enough to be able to resist this multitude, which cometh violently upon us. But as we know not what to do, we can only turn our eyes to thee (12). There follows: Thus saith the Lord to you: Fear ye not, and be not dismayed at this multitude. For the battle is not yours, but God's (15). Only stand with confidence, and you shall see the help of the Lord over you (17). Believe in the Lord your God, and you shall be secure (20).

b Fear ye not, etc.

c Bow down, that we may go over (Isaiah 51.23).

upright, he can neither straddle nor ride her. Look how the traitor says, *Incuruare ut transeamus* – 'Bend, let me leap up, I do not want to ride you long, but shall pass over.' 'He lies,' says St Bernard, 'do not believe the traitor.' *Non uult transire, set residere*[a] – 'He does not want to pass over, but wants to sit absolutely tight.' There was a person who believed him – thought he would soon get down, as he had always promised. 'Do this,' he says, 'once, and confess it tomorrow. Bend your heart and let me up; shake me down with confession, if I want to ride you long after all.' Someone, as I said, believed him and bent down for him and he leapt up and rode her both day and night fully twenty years – that is, she committed a sin in the course of that night because of his pricking and thought she would confess in the morning and did it again and again and fell in this way into an evil habit, so that she lay and rotted in it all that time I said, and if there had not been a miracle which blew down the devil who sat on her so tight, she would have tumbled with him – horse and load both – down to the bottom of hell. Therefore, my dear sisters, keep yourselves straight upright in true faith. Boldly trust that all the devil's strength melts through the grace of that holy sacrament which is highest above the others, which you see as often as the priest celebrates Mass – the Virgin's child, Jesus, God, God's Son who comes down at certain times[64] in bodily fashion to your inn and within you humbly takes his lodging. God knows, they are too weak- and wicked-hearted who, with such a guest, do not fight boldly. You must have faith that all Holy Church does, reads or sings and all her sacraments strengthen you spiritually, but none as much as this, for it brings to nothing all the devil's wiles – not only his violence and acts of force, but his cunning cheats, his tricksy witchcrafts and all his frauds, such as lying dreams, false showings, fearful scarings, treacherous and deceptive counsels, even though it were for God's sake and good to do – for that is his evil trick, as I said before, which holy men fear most, by which he has beguiled many holy men: when he cannot bring people to an open evil, he incites to a thing that seems good. 'You should,' he says, 'be gentler and let your censure be, not trouble your heart and stir it to anger.' This he says so that you should not censure your maid for her fault or discipline her well and that he may

a   He does not want to pass over, but to stay sitting there.

bring you into heedlessness instead of humility. Afterwards exactly the opposite: 'Do not allow any fault to be forgiven her,' he says. 'If you want her to fear you, keep her strictly. Righteousness,' he says, 'must of necessity be stern', and thus he paints cruelty with the colour of righteousness. One can be too righteous altogether. *Noli esse iustus nimis. In Ecclesiaste.*[a] Wise art is better than brute force. When you have been keeping vigil for a long time and should go to sleep, '*Now*,' he says, 'it is virtue to keep vigil when it makes you suffer. Say another nocturn.'[65] Why does he act like this? So that you should sleep afterwards when the time came to keep vigil. Afterwards exactly the opposite: if you are well able to keep vigil, he lays on you a heaviness or puts in your thought, 'Being sensible is the best of things, and I shall go to sleep now and get up presently and do more quickly than now what I should now be doing', and in this way you are often readily enough not doing it at either time. Of this matter I spoke a great deal above. In temptations like this no one is so wise and so wary, unless God warns him, as not to be often beguiled. But this high sacrament, taken in bold faith, above everything else uncovers his tricks and breaks up his acts of violence. Indeed, dear sisters, when you feel him near, as long as you have bold faith, you will simply laugh him loudly to scorn that he is so much of an old fool that he comes to increase his torment and plait crowns for you. As soon as he sees you firm and bold in God's grace his might melts and he flees soon. But if he can perceive that your faith is failing, so that it seems to you that you might be utterly led away if you were to be strongly tempted at that time – with that you grow weak and his power increases.

We read in *Regum* that Ishbosheth[66] lay and slept and had set a woman as gatekeeper who winnowed wheat; and Rechab's sons, Remmon and Baana, came and found the woman ceased from her winnowing and fallen asleep, and went in and killed the unfortunate Isboseth, who guarded himself so badly. The signification of this it is very necessary to understand. 'Ishbosheth' in Hebrew is 'a man bewildered' in English – and is he not certainly bewildered and out of his mind who, amidst his enemies, lays himself down to sleep? The gatekeeper is the understanding, which ought to winnow wheat, separate the awns and the chaff

a Be not over just. In Ecclesiastes (7.17).

from the pure grains – that is, through busy alertness divide good from evil, put the wheat in the granary and blow away all the time the devil's chaff, which is only good for hell-smoke. But the bewildered Ishbosheth – see how confusedly he acted – set a woman as gatekeeper, which is a feeble protection. Alas, that many do the same. Woman is reason – that is, the understanding – when it grows weak, and should be manly, stalwart and brave in true faith. This gatekeeper lies down to sleep as soon as one begins to consent to sin, to allow desire to go inside and the pleasure to increase. When Rechab's sons – that is, hell's children – find so sleepy and so soft a gatekeeper, they go in and kill Ishbosheth – that is, the bewildered spirit – which in a sleepy negligence neglects itself. This is not to be forgotten – that, as Holy Writ says, they stabbed him through the groin. Here St Gregory says: *In inguine ferire est uitam mentis carnis delectatione perforare*[a] – 'The fiend stabs through the groin when the pleasure of lechery pierces the heart.' And this is only in the sleep of heedlessness and of sloth, as St Gregory testifies: *Antiquus hostis, mox ut mentem otiosam inuenerit, ad eam sub quibusdam occasionibus locuturus uenit, et quedam ei de gestis preteritis ad memoriam reducit. Et infra: Putruerunt et deteriorate sunt cicatrices mee. Cicatrix quidem est figura uulneris, set sanati. Cicatrix ergo ad putredinem redit quando peccati uulnus, quod per penitentiam sanatum est, in delectationem sui animum concutit.*[b] This is the English: When the old enemy sees our understanding sleepy, he comes along to her at once and probes her with speech. 'Do you recall,' he says, 'how he (or she) spoke of the lust of the flesh?' And in this way the old deceiver speaks to her heart words which she previously heard foully spoken, or a sight that she saw, or her own filthinesses that she once did. All this he sets out before her heart's eyes, so as to befoul her with the thought of old sins, when he cannot with new, and so he often brings again into the bemused soul, through pleasure, those sins which

---

a To strike in the groin is to pierce the life of the spirit with the pleasure of the flesh (*Morals on Job* 1.35, 49).

b The old enemy, as soon as he finds the mind at leisure, taking certain opportunities comes to it to speak and brings back to its memory certain things it did in the past. And below: My scars are putrified and become worse (Psalm 37.6). For a scar is the mark of a wound, but a healed one. Therefore a scar returns to putridity when the wound of sin, which has been healed through penance, agitates the soul into delight in it (*Letters* 9.2, 52).

through pitiful suffering had been atoned for long ago, so that she may weep and make a sorry complaint with the Psalmist: *Putruerunt, et cetera*[a] – 'Alas, my wounds, which were well healed, collect new pus and begin to fester again.' A healed wound begins then to fester, when sin which had been atoned for comes again with pleasure into the memory and kills the unwary soul. *Gregorius: Ysboset inopinate morti nequaquam succumberet nisi ad ingressum mentis mulierem – id est, mollem custodiam – deputasset.*[b] All this misfortune came about because of the sleep of the gatekeeper who was not wary and watchful and not manly but womanly, easy to overthrow. Whether it be man or woman, all their strength, then, is according to their faith and according to their trusting in God's help, which is near, unless faith fail, as I said before above.[67] They make the devil weak, make him flee straight away. Therefore be at all times as bold as a lion against him in true faith, especially in the temptation in which Ishbosheth died – that is, lust. Look how you can know that he is cowardly and wicked when he strikes in that direction. Is he not a cowardly champion who thrusts at the feet, who goes for his opponent so low? Desire of the flesh is a foot-wound, as was said a long way back.[68] And this is the reason. As our feet carry us, so our desires often carry us to the thing that we desire. Now, then, though your enemy hurt you in the feet – that is to say, tempts[69] you with the desires of the flesh – do not fear too greatly on account of so low a wound unless it swell too much, through the consent of reason, with too much pleasure up towards the heart. But then drink the antidote and drive the swelling back again from the heart – that is to say, think about the poisonous torment which God drank on the cross, and the swelling will go down. Pride and envy and wrath, anguish of heart for worldly things, misery from longing, covetousness of possessions, these are the heart's wounds – and all that flows from them – and give a death-blow at once unless they are treated. When the fiend strikes in that direction, then, indeed, one should be afraid, but not on account of foot-wounds.

Pride's remedy is humility; envy's, neighbourly love; anger's, patience;

a   They are putrified, etc. (Psalm 37.6).
b   Gregory: Ishbosheth would in no way have succumbed unexpectedly to death if he had not appointed a woman – that is, a slack guard – at the entrance of his mind (*Morals in Job* 1.35, 49).

inertia's, reading, various kinds of work, spiritual consolation; covetousness's, contempt for earthly things; avarice's, a generous heart. Now
about the first, first of all. If you want to be humble, think all the time
what you are lacking in holiness and in spiritual virtues; think what you
have of yourself. You are of two parts, of body and of soul. In each
there are two things which may make you very meek if you consider
them well. In the body there is filth and weakness. Does there not come
out of a vessel the sort of thing that is in it? Does the smell of spices or
of sweet balsam come from your flesh's vessel? What! Do dry twigs
bear grapes? Briars rose-blooms? What fruit does your flesh bear at all
its openings? In the middle of the glory of your face, which is your
most beautiful part, between the mouth's taste and the nose's smell, do
you not bear two toilet holes, as it were? Are you not come of foul
slime, are you not a vat of filth, will you not be worm's food?
Philosophus: Sperma es fluidum, vas stercorum, esca uermium.[70][a] Now a fly
can harm you and make you flinch – you can be proud all right! Look
at holy men in the past, how they fasted, how they kept vigil, in what
suffering and in what labour they lived, and thus you may recognize
your own weakness. But do you know what makes the feeble eyes of a
man who has climbed high swim? When he looks down. Likewise,
whoever looks at those who are of a low life, this makes him think that
he is of a high life. But always look up towards heavenly men who have
climbed so high and then you will see how low you stand. *Augustinus:
Sicut incentiuum est elationis respectus inferioris, sic cautela est humilitatis,
consideratio superioris.*[b] To fast a week on bread and water, to keep vigil
three nights in a row – how would that weaken your fleshly strength?
In this way consider these two things in your body, filth and weakness.
In the soul there are two others, sin and ignorance – that is, lack of
wisdom and lack of awareness;[71] for often what you think is good is
evil and soul-murder. Look at your shameful sins with wet eyes. Still
fear your weak nature, which is easily thrown, and say with the holy
man, who began to weep and said, when he was told that one of his
companions had fallen into filth of the flesh with a woman, *Ille hodie, ego*

a The Philosopher: You are liquid sperm, a vat of dung, food of the worms.
b Augustine: As the sight of an inferior is an incentive to pride, so consideration of
   a superior is a warning to humility.

cras[a] – that is, 'He today, I tomorrow' – as though he said, 'I am of as weak a nature as he was, and just the same may happen to me unless God keep me.'[72] Thus, look, the holy man had no wondering contempt for the other's fall, and wept for his misfortune and feared a similar one might happen to him. In this way make yourselves humble and meek. *Bernardus: Superbia est appetitus proprie excellencie; humilitas contemptus eiusdem*[73][b] – that is, 'Just as pride is desire of honour, exactly so, in contrast, humility is rejecting of honour' and love of little praise and of lowness. This virtue is the mother of all virtues and begets them all. The person who sets about gathering virtues without her carries dust in the wind, as St Gregory says: *Qui sine humilitate uirtutes congregat, quasi qui in uento puluerem portat.*[c] This alone will be saved; this alone will avoid the traps of the devil of hell, as Our Lord showed to St Antony, who saw all the world full of the devil's snare-laying. 'Ah, Lord,' he said, 'who can guard himself against these so as not to be caught by one of them?' 'Only the patient,' said Our Lord.[74] So delicate a thing is humility, and so elegantly slim and lithe, that no snare can hold her – and look, a great wonder: though she makes herself so slim and so meek, she is the strongest of things, so that from her comes every spiritual strength. St Cassiodorus testifies to it: *Omnis fortitudo ex humilitate.*[75][d] But Solomon tells the reason why: *Vbi humilitas, ibi sapientia*[e] – 'Where there is humility, there,' he says, 'is Jesus Christ – that is, his Father's wisdom and his Father's strength.' It is then no wonder, though there be strength where he is through his indwelling grace. Through the strength of humility, he threw the monster of hell. The cunning wrestler takes note what move the opponent with whom he is wrestling does not know, for with that move he can throw him unawares. Just so Our Lord did, and saw how many the terrible wrestler of hell swung up on his hip and threw with the haunch-move into lust which rules in the loins, heaved many high up and turned

a He today, I tomorrow (*Lives of the Fathers* 7.16).
b Bernard: Pride is the desire for one's own pre-eminence; humility, contempt of the same (*The Degrees of Humility and Pride* 4.14).
c The person who gathers virtues and does not include humility is like one who carries dust in the wind (*Homilies on the Gospels* 7.4).
d All fortitude comes from humility.
e Where humility is, there also is wisdom (Proverbs 11.2).

around with them and flung them through pride down into the bottom
of hell. Our Lord who saw all this thought, 'I shall make a move on
you that you never knew and can never know, the move of humility –
that is, the falling move', and fell from heaven to earth and stretched
himself on the earth in such a way that the fiend thought he was
entirely earthly and was misled by this move – and is still each day by
men and women who know it. In addition, as Job says, he can still
only, for pride, look high. *Omne sublime uident oculi eius.*[a] Holy men who
keep themselves little and of a low life are out of his sight. The wild
boar cannot bow down to strike. Whoever falls down and in meek
humility stretches himself on the earth has no worries about his tusks.[76]
This is not contrary to what I have said before,[77] that one must always
stand against the devil, for the standing is the true trust of brave faith
in God's strength. This falling is humble knowledge of your own
weakness and of your lack of strength. And no one can stand in this
way unless they fall thus – that is, always think themselves of little
account and unworthy and insignificant, and look at their black and not
his white, for white makes the eyes swim. Humility can never be fully
praised, for that was the lesson that Our Lord most insistently taught
his chosen, both by word and by deed: *Discite a me, quia mitis sum et
humilis corde.*[b] Into it he pours his graces, not just drop by drop but in
flowing springs, as the Psalmist says: *Qui emittis fontes in conuallibus*[c] –
'In the valleys you make,' he says, 'springs well up.' The heart swollen
and lifted up like a hill retains none of the moisture of grace. A bladder
swollen with air does not plunge into these sanctifying waters. But
the pricking of a needle lets out all the air. An insignificant pain
or ache makes one understand how little pride is worth, how foolish
arrogance is.

Envy's remedy, I said, was neighbourly love; good wishes and good
will where the power of action is lacking. So much strength do love
and good will have that they make others' good our good as well as his
who does it. Only love his good, be pleased and glad about it – thus
you turn it to yourself and make it your own. St Gregory testifies to it:

---

a His eyes behold every high thing (Job 41.25).
b Learn of me, because I am meek and humble of heart (Matthew 11.29).
c Who sendest forth springs in the vales (Psalm 103.10).

Aliena bona si diligis, tua facis.[a] If you have envy of another's good, you poison yourself with linctus and wound yourself with medicine. Your medicine it is, if you love it, against the soul's hurt, and all the good that another person does is your strength against the fiend if you really wish it. Truly I believe temptations of the flesh shall never then master you, any more than spiritual ones, if you are sweet-hearted, humble and mild and love all men and women so fervently, and especially anchoresses, your dear sisters, that you are sorry for their evil and glad of their good, as of your own. Wish that all who love you love them as they do you and give them comfort as they do you. If you have a knife or a piece of cloth, food or drink, scroll or book – the holy man's consolation – or any other thing that would help them, wish that you should lack it yourself provided that they had it. If there is anyone who does not have her heart trained like this, with sorrowful sighs both by day and by night let her cry on Our Lord and never give him peace until he, through his grace, has changed her into such.

The remedy for anger, I said, is patience, which has three steps, high, higher and highest of all and nearest to the high heaven. The step is high if you suffer because of your guilt; higher if you are without guilt; highest of all if you suffer for your good deeds. 'No,' says some bewildered thing, 'if I were guilty of it, I would never complain.' Have you who say so taken leave of yourself? Do you prefer to be Judas's companion rather than Jesus Christ's partner? Both were hanged, but Judas for his guilt – Jesus without guilt, for his great goodness, was hanged on the cross. Which one's partner do you want to be? With which do you want to suffer? Much is written about this above,[78] how he is your file who says ill of or does ill to you. *Lime* is the French for 'file'.[79] Is it not accursed metal which becomes darker and rougher the more it is filed, and rusts the quicker the more it is scoured hard? Gold, silver, steel, iron – it is all metal.

Gold and silver get cleansed of their dross in the fire. If you gather dross in it, that is against nature. The chalice which was melted in it and boiled up hard and afterwards, through so much beating and polishing fashioned so very finely into God's cup – would it curse the purifying fire and the hands of its maker? *Argentum reprobatum uocate eos.*[b]

a If you love others' good acts, you make them yours (*Pastoral Rule* 3.10).
b Call them reprobate silver (Jeremiah 6.30).

All this world is God's smithy for smithying his chosen. Do you want God to have no fire in his smithy, no bellows or hammers? The fire is shame and pain. Your bellows are those who speak ill of you, your hammers those that harm you. Think about this illustration: when a day is set for doing justice, does he not show disrespect for the judge who before the appointed day breaks the truce and avenges himself on the other, on his own initiative? *Augustinus: Quid gloriatur impius si de ipso flagellum fatiat Pater meus?*[a] And who does not know that Judgement Day is the day set for doing justice to all men? Keep the truce in the meantime, whatever injury is done you. The righteous judge has set a day to determine justice between you. Do not show him disrespect in despising the vengeance of his judgement and taking your own. There are two things that God has held back for himself; they are worship and vengeance, as Holy Writ testifies: *Gloriam meam alteri non dabo. Item: Michi vindictam; ego retribuam.*[b] Whoever takes on himself either of these robs and steals from God. What! Are you so angry with a man or a woman that to avenge yourself you want to steal from God by force?

Inertia's remedy is spiritual gladness and the consolation of glad hope, through reading, through holy thinking, or from people's mouths. Often, dear sisters, you must pray less in order to read more. Reading is good prayer. Reading teaches how and what to pray, and prayer obtains it afterwards. During reading, when the heart is pleased, a devotion arises which is worth many prayers. Therefore St Jerome says: *Ieronimus:*[80] *Semper in manu tua sacra sit lectio; tenenti tibi librum sompnus subripiat, et cadentem faciem pagina sancta suscipiat*[c] – 'Let holy reading be at all times in your hands. Let sleep come upon you as you look at it, and let the holy page support your drooping face.'[81] You must read earnestly and long like this. Everything, however, can be overdone: moderation is always best.

a Augustine: Why does the impious man glory if my Father makes a whip of him? (*Expositions on the Psalms* 36.2, 4 (on Psalm 36, verse 17)).

b I will not give my glory to another (Isaiah 42.8). Likewise: Revenge is mine; I will repay (Romans 12.19; see Deuteronomy 32.35).

c Jerome: Let there be holy reading always in your hand; let sleep steal away your book from you as you hold it, and let the holy page receive your drooping head (*Letter* 22).

Against covetousness – I would that the others avoided gathering as you do. Too much generosity often breeds it. You must be generous-hearted. Anchoresses generous in other ways have sometimes been too generous of themselves.

Lust comes of greediness and of the ease of the flesh, for as St Gregory says, 'Food and drink more than is proper breeds a brood of three: light words, light deeds and lechery's desires.' May Our Lord be thanked who has healed you of greediness entirely, but lechery will never be altogether quite extinguished in the temptation of the flesh. But understand this well, that there are three degrees in it, as St Bernard testifies. The first is cogitation, the second affection, the third consent. Cogitations are fleeting thoughts which do not last, and these, as St Bernard says, do not hurt the soul, but nevertheless they speckle her with their black spots in such a way that she is not worthy of being embraced or kissed by Jesus her beloved, who is entirely beautiful, before she is washed. Such filthiness as this comes easily and goes away easily with *Venies*,[a] with *Confiteor*,[b] with all good deeds. Affection is when the thought goes inward and pleasure comes up and the desire grows. Then, as before there was a spot on the white skin, a wound grows and goes in deep towards the soul, as the desire and the pleasure in it go on further and further. Then there is a need to cry, *Sana me, Domine*[c] – 'Ah Lord, heal me, for I am wounded.' *Ruben, primogenitus meus, ne crescas*[d] – 'Ruben, you red thought, you bloody pleasure, do not ever grow.' Consent is reason's granting, when the pleasure in the desire has gone so very far that there would be no resisting if there were leisure to accomplish the deed. This is when the heart draws towards her evil desire as a thing that is dazed and begins, as it were, to shut her eyes, to let the fiend be, and lays herself down, bends for him as he commands and cries, 'I yield, I yield', as one feebly fainting. Then he is courageous who before was a cur; then he leaps at her who before stood far off, and bites God's dear wife with the bite of death – the bite of death indeed, for his teeth are poisonous like those of a mad dog. David in the Psalter

a Pardons.
b I confess.
c Heal me, Lord (Psalm 6.3).
d Ruben, my first born, grow thou not (Genesis 49.3–4).

calls him a dog: *Erue a framea, Deus, animam meam et de manu canis unicam meam.*[a]

Therefore, my dear sister, as soon as ever you perceive that this dog of hell is coming sneaking up with his bloody flies of stinking thoughts, do not lie still or sit either, to see what he will do and how far he will go, and do not say sleepily, 'Hey, boy, out you go! What do you want in here now?' This attracts him inside. But take up the crucifix at once, with the naming of it in your mouth, with the sign in your hand, with the thought in your heart, and order him out fiercely, the foul cur-hound, and beat him viciously with violent blows on the back from the holy crucifix – that is, spring up, stir yourself, lift your eyes and hands on high towards heaven, cry for help: *Deus, in adiutorium meum intende. Domine, ad adiuuandum. Veni Creator Spiritus. Exurgat Deus et dissipentur inimici eius. Deus, in nomine tuo saluum me fac. Domine, quid multiplicati sunt. Ad te, Domine, leuaui animam meam. Ad te leuaui oculos meos. Leuaui oculos meos in montes.*[b] If help does not come to you soon, cry louder with a hot heart: *Vsquequo, Domine, obliuisceris me in finem? Vsquequo auerteris faciem tuam a me?* [c] – and so all the psalm through; *Pater noster, Credo, Aue Maria,* with imploring prayers in your own language.[82] Kneel down smartly on the ground and lift up the crucifix and swing it to the four corners against the hell-dog – that is, simply bless yourself all about with the blessed sign of the cross. Spit in his beard in contempt and in scorn, who flits around you like this and flatters you with a dog's fawning. When he for so low a price, for the enjoyment of a desire for a moment, bargains for your soul, God's dear purchase, which he bought with his blood and with his precious death on the precious cross, always consider the price that he paid for her and judge her value accordingly, and hold her the dearer, and never sell so cheaply to his foe and yours, God's precious

a Deliver, God, my soul from the sword and my only one from the hand of the dog (Psalm 21.21).

b God, come to my assistance. Lord, [make haste] to help me (Psalm 69.1). Come, Creator Spirit. Let God arise, and let his enemies be scattered (Psalm 67.2). Save me, God, by thy name (Psalm 53.3). Why, Lord, are they multiplied [that afflict me] (Psalm 3.2). To thee, Lord, have I lifted up my soul (Psalm 24.1). To thee I have lifted up my eyes (Psalm 122.1). I have lifted up my eyes to the mountains (Psalm 120.1).

c How long, Lord, wilt thou forget me unto the end? How long dost thou turn away thy face from me? (Psalm 12.1).

bride who cost him so dear. To make a devil's whore of her is pity beyond pity. Too utterly wicked is she who can by lifting up her three fingers overcome her foe and does not please to do it for sloth. Therefore lift up your three fingers in firm and bold faith, and with the holy crucifix, which is the most hateful cudgel to him, lay on the dog-devil, name Jesus often, call on the help of his passion, implore him by his torment, by his precious blood, by his death on the cross. Flee to his wounds. He loved us much who let such holes be made in him to hide us in. Creep into them with your thought – are they not quite open? – and with his precious blood bloody your heart. *Ingredere in petram, abscondere fossa humo*[a] – 'Go into the rock,' says the prophet, 'and hide yourself in the dug earth' – that is, in the wounds of Our Lord's flesh, which was, as it were, dug with the blunt nails, as he said long before in the Psalter: *Foderunt manus meas et pedes meos*[b] – 'They dug both my hands and my feet.' He did not say 'pierced', for, according to the literal meaning here, as our scholars say, the nails were blunt in such a way that they dug his flesh and broke the bone more than pierced it, to torment him more grievously. He himself calls you towards these wounds: *Columba mea in foraminibus petre, in cauernis macerie*[c] – 'My dove,' he says, 'come, hide yourself in the holes in my limbs, in the hole in my side.' He showed great love to his beloved dove in making such a hiding place. Look now that you, whom he calls a dove, have a dove's nature, which is without gall, and come boldly to him and make a shield of his passion and say with Jeremiah, *Dabis scutum cordis, laborem tuum*[d] – that is, 'You shall give me, Lord, a shield against the fiend, your laborious torment.' That it was laborious he showed clearly enough when he sweated, like a sweat of blood, drops that ran to the ground. A shield has to be held up above the head in combat, or against the breast, not dragged behind. Exactly so, if you want the cross to shield you and God's grievous passion to cause the devil's weapons to fail, do not drag it after you, but lift it high up above the head of your heart, before the eyes of your breast.[83] Hold it up in the face of the fiend; show it clearly to him – the sight of it alone puts him

a Enter thou into the rock and hide thee in the pit (Isaiah 2.10).

b They have dug my hands and my feet (Psalm 21.17).

c My dove in the clefts of the rock, in the hollow places of the wall (Canticles 2.14).

d Thou shalt give [them] a buckler of heart, thy labour (Lamentations 3.65).

to flight, for he is both ashamed at it and scared out of his wits, after that time that Our Lord with it brought so low to the earth his cunning covertness and his proud strength. If you, through your heedlessness, defend yourself weakly at first and give entry too far to the fiend in the beginning, so that you cannot drive him back again because of your great weakness, but are brought so very far that you cannot hold this shield over your heart or withdraw her[84] under it out of the devil's arrows, take out at the last St Benedict's medicine, though it need not be so exceedingly strong as his was, who, from his rolling about, ran with blood and gore all over his back and side and stomach.[85] But at least give yourself, when it is strongest on you, a smart discipline.[86] Drive that sweet pleasure into smarting, as he did; if you do not do thus, but guard yourself sleepily, he will advance too far on you before you have the least suspicion, and bring you from foul thought into the pleasure of foul desire, and so he brings you all the way to the consent of reason, which is deadly sin, without the deed; and so also is the pleasure of that stinking desire without consent to action – so long may it last. *Numquam enim iudicanda est delectatio esse morosa, dum ratio reluctatur et negat assensum.*[a] It then lasts too long, when the reason no longer fights against it.[87] Therefore, dear sister, trample the snake's head – that is, the beginning of his temptation. *Beatus qui tenebit et allidet paruulos suos ad petram*[b] – 'Blessed is she,' says David, 'who holds herself back at first and breaks on the rock the first stirrings when the flesh rises up, while they are young.' Our Lord is called a rock because of his faithfulness. *Et in Canticis: Capite nobis uulpes paruulas que detruunt uineas*[c] – 'Take and catch for us at once, beloved, the young foxes,' Our Lord says, 'which destroy the vineyards', that is, the first prickings, which destroy our souls, which have to have a great deal of labour to bear grapes. The devil is bear-natured and has an ass's nature, for he is strong behind and weak at the head, that is, in the beginning. Never give him entry, but tap him on the skull, for he is cowardly like a bear about it, and in this way hurry him off and chase him away in such

---

a For the pleasure must never be judged too lingering while reason struggles against it and refuses assent.

b Blessed be he that shall take and dash thy little ones against the rock (Psalm 136.9).

c And in Canticles (2.15): Catch us the little foxes that destroy the vines.

shame as soon as you perceive him, that he is afraid of the place in which you live, for he is the proudest of things and to him shame is most hateful.

Just so, dear sister, as soon as ever you feel that your heart is inclining at all beyond measure with love to anything, straight away beware of the snake's poison and trample his head. The old woman who set fire to her whole dwelling with a straw said very truly that much comes of little. And take note now how things go. The spark that flies up does not immediately set the house all alight, but lies and collects more fire and feeds it up and grows from less to more, until the whole house blazes up, before it is the least suspected. And the devil blows on it from when it first kindles, and increases the blast of his bellows all the time as it grows. Understand this of yourself: a sight that you see, or a single word that you should not hear, if it stirs you at all, extinguish it with the water of tears and with Jesus Christ's blood while it is only a spark, before it grows and so kindles you that you cannot extinguish it. For so it often happens – and it is the just decree of God – that she who doesn't when she can, shan't when she wants.[88] *Ecclesiasticus: A scintilla una augetur ignis.*[a]

There are many kinds of temptation in this fourth part, various solaces and all sorts of remedies. Our Lord give you grace that they may help you. Of all the others, confession, then, is the most beneficial. The fifth part will be about it, as I promised above.[89] And take note how each part flows into the next, as I said there.

a   Ecclesiasticus (11.34): Of one spark there grows a fire.

PART FIVE
Confession

Take note of two things about confession at the beginning. The first, what its power is; the second, what it must be like. Now these are like two limbs, and each is divided, the first into six, the second into sixteen parts. This now is about the first.

Confession has many powers, but I do not want to speak of them all, only six: three against the devil and three over ourselves. Confession puts the devil to shame, hacks off his head and routs his army. Confession washes us of all our filthinesses, gives us back all our losses, makes us God's children. Each has its three parts: let us now demonstrate them all. The first three are all shown in Judith's deeds. Judith – that is, confession, as was said before – killed Holofernes – that is, the fiend of hell. Turn back to where we spoke of the nature of birds which are compared to anchoresses.[1] She hacked off his head and afterwards came and showed it to the city priests. The fiend is then put to shame when all his wickednesses are shown. His head is hacked off and he is killed within the man as soon as ever he is truly sorry for his sins and in his heart intends to confess, but he is not yet put to shame while his head is covered, as Judith did at first, before it is shown – that is, before the mouth, in confession, sets forth the capital sin; not the sin only, but all the beginning of it and the preliminaries which brought in the sin – that is, the devil's head, which must be trampled at once, as I said before. Then his army flees at once – as did Holofernes's – his wiles and his tricks with which he assails us. They all take to flight and the city which they had besieged is set free – that is to say, the sinner is delivered. Judas Maccabeus – who stood against him? Likewise in *Iudicum*, when the people asked after Joshua's death who should be their commander and lead them in battle: *Quis erit dux noster?*[a] Our Lord answered them, 'Judah shall go before you and I shall deliver into his hands your foe's land.' Look now very carefully what is being said here. 'Joshua' means 'health' and 'Judah' 'confession', like 'Judith'. Joshua is then dead when the soul's health is lost through any deadly sin. The sinful self is the land of the Evil One, who is our deadly foe. But this land Our Lord promised to give into Judah's hands, for which reason he goes in front. Confession, look, is the standard-bearer, and bears the banner in front of all God's army – that is, the virtues. Confession takes away his land from the fiend – that is, the sinful man

and entirely routs Canaan, the fiend of hell's army. Judas did it bodily, and confession, which it signifies, does the same spiritually. Here now are three things that it does for ourselves (that is, these now following). Confession washes us of all our filthinesses, for it is written thus: *Omnia in confessione lauantur – glosa super: Confitebimur tibi, Deus, confitebimur.*[b] And that was signified when Judith washed herself and took off her widow's clothing, which was a sign of sorrow – and sorrow only arises because of sin. *Lauit corpus suum et exuit se uestimentis sue uiduitatis.*[c] Next, confession brings again all the good that we had lost and gives it all back together. *Joel: Reddam uobis annos quos comedit locusta, brucus, rubigo et erugo.*[d] This was signified in Judith's clothing herself in festival clothes and adorning herself on the outside, as confession does us on the inside, with all the beautiful adornments which signify bliss. And Our Lord says through Zechariah: *Erunt sicut fuerunt antequam proieceram eos*[e] – that is, 'Confession shall make the man just as he was before he sinned, as clean and as fair and as rich in all good that pertains to the soul.' The third thing that confession does for ourselves is the fruit of these other two and completes them both – that is, makes us God's children. This is signified by the fact that Judah in Genesis won Benjamin from Jacob. Benjamin is as much as to say 'son

a Who shall be our leader? (see Judges 1.1).

b Everything is washed in confession a gloss on: We will confess to thee, O God, we will confess (Psalm 74.1).

c She washed her body and put away the garments of her widowhood (Judith 10. 3, 2).

d Joel (2.25): I will restore to you the years that the locust and the bruchus and the mildew and the palmer-worm have eaten.

e They shall be as they were when I had cast them off (Zechariah 10.6).

of the right side'; Judah, that is, confession, just as Judith is,[2] for they both mean one thing in the Hebrew language. This spiritual Judah obtains from Jacob his father – that is, Our Lord – the status of the son of the right hand and the enjoyment, without end, of the inheritance of heaven. Now we have said what confession's power is, what effects it has, and mentioned six. Let us now look carefully at what confession, which is of such strength, must be like; and to show it better, let us divide this limb into sixteen parts.

Confession must be accusatory, bitter with sorrow, complete, naked, made often, speedy, humble, full of shame, [full of fear,][3] full of hope, wise, true and willing, one's own and steadfast, thought about long before. Here are now, as it were, sixteen parts which are linked to confession, and let us say some words about each separately.

Confession must be accusatory. One must accuse oneself in confession, not defend oneself and say, 'I did it at another's prompting'; 'I was forced into it'; 'the fiend made me do it'. Thus Adam and Eve defended themselves – Adam at Eve's prompting, and Eve at the snake's. The fiend cannot force anyone into any sin, though he may urge to it, but he is very pleased when anyone says that he made him sin – as though he had strength, who has none at all, except from ourselves. But one ought to say, 'My own wickedness did it and, willingly and wanting to, I submitted to the devil.' If you blame your sin on anything except yourself, you are not confessing; if you say that your weakness could not do otherwise, you deflect your sin on to God himself, who made you such that by your account you could not resist. Let us then accuse ourselves, for look what St Paul says: *Si nos ipsos diiudicaremus, non utique iudicaremur*[a] – that is, 'If we accuse ourselves properly here and give ourselves judgement here, we shall be free of accusation at the great Judgement', of which St Anselm speaks these dreadful words: *Hinc erunt accusancia peccata, illinc terrens iusticia; supra iratus iudex, subtus patens horridum chaos inferni; intus urens consciencia, foris ardens mundus. Peccator sic deprehensus in quam partem se premet?*[4][b] On the

a If we would judge ourselves, we should not be judged (1 Corinthians 11.31).
b On this side there will be accusing sins, on that side frightful justice; above, the angry judge, below, the horrible chaos of hell lying open; within, burning conscience; outside, the world on fire. In which direction will the sinner caught like this turn? (*Meditation* 1).

one side on Judgement Day our black sins will vigorously accuse us of
the murder of our soul. On the other side stands righteousness, with
whom there is no pity, dreadful and frightful and horrible to behold.
Above us the angry judge, for he is as hard there as he is soft here, as
stern then as he is mild now; a lamb here, a lion there, as the prophet
testifies: *Leo rugiet, quis non timebit?*[a] – 'The lion will roar,' he says. 'Who
is able not to be frightened?' (Here we call him lamb as often as we sing
Agnus Dei, qui tollis peccata mundi.)[b] Now, as I said, shall we see above us
that same angry judge who is also a witness and knows all our offences;
beneath us, yawning, the wide throat of hell; within ourselves, our own
conscience – that is, our inner judgement[5] – blackening itself with the
fire of sin; outside us, all the world flaming with black flames up into
the skies. The sorry sinner thus surrounded, how shall it stand with
him? To which of these four may he turn? He can only hear that hard
saying, that woeful saying, that horrible saying, terrible beyond everything, *Ite, maledicti, in ignem eternum, qui paratus est diabolo et angelis suis*[c] –
'Go, you accursed, out of the sight of my eyes into the eternal fire that
was prepared for the fiend and for his angels. You evaded the sentence
on men, to which I sentenced man, which was to live in toil and pain
on earth, and you shall now therefore have the devil's sentence – burn
with him eternally in the fire of hell.' With this shall the lost let out a
cry at which both heaven and earth are going to tremble horribly.
Therefore St Augustine lovingly teaches us: *Ascendat homo tribunal
mentis sue, si illud quod oportet eum exiberi ante tribunal Christi. Assit
accusatrix cogitatio, testis consciencia, carnifex timor*[d] – that is, let a man
think about Judgement Day and judge himself here in this way; let
reason sit as judge on the judgement seat. After that let his memory
come forward, accuse him and indict him of various sins: 'Good friend,
this you did there, and this there, and this there and in this way.' Let
his conscience acknowledge this and bear witness to it: 'It is true, it is

a The lion shall roar: Who will not fear? (Amos 3.8).
b Lamb of God, who takest away the sins of the world.
c Depart, you cursed, into everlasting fire, which was prepared for the devil and
   his angels (Matthew 25.41).
d A man should ascend the tribunal of his own mind, if he thinks about the fact that
   he has to be presented before the tribunal of Christ. Thought should be present as
   accuser, conscience as witness, fear as executioner (*Sermons* 351.4, 7).

true – this and much more.' After that let fear come forward at the command of the judge, who sternly orders, 'Take and bind him tight, for he is deserving of death. Bind each part of the body with which he has sinned in such a way that he cannot sin with them anymore.' Fear has bound him when for fear he dares not stir in pursuit of sin. Still the judge – that is, reason – is not satisfied, though he be in bonds and restrain himself from sin, unless he pays for the sin which he has done, and calls forward pain and sorrow and orders sorrow to thrash the heart on the inside with hurtful repentance, so that it feels pain, and torment the flesh on the outside with fasts and with other fleshly hurts. Whoever in this way before the great Judgement gives himself judgement is blessed and happy. For as the prophet says, *Non iudicabit Deus bis in idipsum*[a] – 'Our Lord does not wish that a man be judged twice for one thing.' It is not the same in God's court as it is in the shire court, where he who gives a good denial can escape, and he who confesses be the one condemned. Before God it is otherwise: *Si tu accusas, Deus excusat, et vice uersa*[b] – if you accuse yourself here, God will defend you there and clear you absolutely at the strict Judgement, as long as you judge yourself as I have taught you.

Confession must be bitter in return for the sin's once seeming sweet. 'Judith', which means 'confession', as I have often said,[c] was Merari's daughter, and Judah – that is, again, 'confession' – married Tamar. 'Merari' and 'Tamar' both mean one thing in the Hebrew language: 'bitterness'. Take note now carefully of the signification. I shall tell it briefly. Bitter pain and confession – the one must come of the other, as Judith did of Merari. And both are joined together, like Judah and Tamar. For either without the other is worth nothing – or little. They never give birth to Perez and Zerah. Judah begot Perez and Zerah of Tamar. *Phares diuisio, Zaram oriens interpretatur*,[c] which, spiritually, signifies separation from sin and grace arising in the heart afterwards. If a man thinks of them, four things which capital sin has done to him may make him sorrow and embitter his heart. This, look, is the first. If a man had lost in one hour of the day his father and his mother, his

---

a God will not give judgement twice on the same matter (see Nahum 1.9).
b If you accuse, God will excuse, and vice versa.
c Perez means 'division', Zerah 'rising'.

sisters and his brothers and all his relations, and all the friends that he ever had had unexpectedly died, would he not, above all men, be sorrowful and as sorry as he well might? God knows, a great deal more sorrowful may he be who has spiritually killed God within his soul. Not only has he lost the sweet father of heaven and Mary his precious mother, or Holy Church, now that he has nothing from her, large or small, and the angels of heaven and all the holy saints, whom he had before as friends, as brothers and as sisters – as far as he goes they are dead. As regards himself, he has killed them all, and, where they live for ever, he has hatred from them all, as Jeremiah testifies: *Omnes amici eius spreuerunt eam; facti sunt ei inimici*[a] – that is, 'All who loved him cry "Ssss!" on him, and they all hate him.' There is still more: his children, as soon as he sinned mortally, all died outright – that is, his good works, which are all lost. Further, as well as all this, he has himself been changed and has become, from being a child of God, the devil of hell's child, hideous to look upon, as God says himself in the Gospel: *Vos ex patre diabolo estis.*[b] Let each think of the condition in which he is or was, and he can see why he ought sorely to sigh. Therefore Jeremiah says: *Luctum unigeniti fac tibi, planctum amarum*[c] – 'Make a bitter lament, as a woman does for her child,' who only had it alone and sees it die unexpectedly in front of her. Now the second that I promised. A man who for an evil murder was sentenced to be burnt alive or shamefully hanged, how would things be with his heart? But you, unhappy sinner, when through deadly sin you murdered God's wife – that is, your soul – then you were sentenced to be hanged on the burning gibbet in the eternal flames[7] of hell. At that point you made an agreement with the devil about your death and said, in Isaiah, with the lost: *Pepigimus cum morte fedus, et cum inferno iniuimus pactum*[d] – that is, 'We have plighted troth with death, fixed an agreement with hell'; for this is the fiend's bargain: he is to give you sin, you him your soul, and your body as well, into woe and misery, world without end. Now the third briefly. Think: a man who had all the world in his power and because of his

a All her friends have despised her; they have become her enemies (Lamentations 1.2).

b You are of your father the devil (John 8.44).

c Make thee mourning as for an only son, a bitter lamentation (Jeremiah 6.26).

d We have entered into a league with death, and we have made a covenant with hell (Isaiah 28.15).

wickedness had lost it all in a moment, how he would mourn and be sorry? Then you ought to be a hundred times more sorry, who, through one capital sin, lost the kingdom of heaven, lost Our Lord who is a hundred times – yes, a thousand, thousand times – better than the whole world, both earth and heaven – _Que enim conuentio Christi ad Belial?_ [a] Now the fourth as well. If the king had entrusted his dear son to one of his knights to look after and a foreign people had taken off this child in his keeping, so that that child himself made war on his father with the foreign people, would not the knight be sorry and feel most miserably ashamed? We are all sons of God, the king of heaven, who has entrusted each of us to an angel for safe-keeping.[8] He is sorry, after his own fashion, when a foreign people takes us off, when we anger our good father with sin. Let us be sorry that we should ever anger such a father and grieve such a guardian, who guards and protects us all the time against the unblessed spirits – for otherwise things would be bad with us. But we drive him away when we do deadly sin, and they then leap to us as soon as he is gone. Let us keep him near us with the smell of good works – and ourselves in his keeping. Christ knows, each one of us pays too little honour to so noble a guardian and shows him too little thanks for his service. These, and many more, are reasons why a man may be bitterly sorry for his sins and weep most grievously – and it is well for him who can do so, for weeping is the soul's health. Our Lord acts towards us as one does towards a bad debtor, takes less than we owe him and is, nevertheless, well pleased. We owe him blood for blood, and even so, our blood in return for his blood, which he shed for us, would be a very unequal exchange. But you know what they say: 'From a bad debtor you take oats instead of wheat' – and Our Lord takes from us our tears in return for his blood, and is pleased. He wept on the cross, over Lazarus, over Jerusalem, for the sins of other men: if we weep for our own, it is no great wonder. 'Let us weep,' said the holy man in _Vitas Patrum_ [b] when they had long clamoured at him for a sermon. 'Let us shed tears,' he said, 'lest our own tears boil us in hell.'

Confession must be complete – that is, everything from childhood –

a   For what concord hath Christ with Belial (2 Corinthians 6.15).
b   _Lives of the Fathers_ (5.3, 9).

and said to one man.[9] The poor widow, when she wants to clean her house, collects all the largest bits into a heap first of all and then pushes it out. After that she comes back again, and again heaps together what was left before and pushes it out after. After that, if it is very dusty, she sprinkles water on the fine dust and after sweeps out all the rest. So must he who confesses push out the smaller after the large bits; if the dust of light thoughts blows up too much, let him sprinkle tears on them. Then they will not blind the heart's eye. Whoever conceals anything has said nothing by which to be the purer, but is like the man who has many deadly wounds on him and shows the doctor all of them and lets them be healed, except one, of which he dies – as he would have of them all. He is like men in a ship which has many holes where the water pours in, and they stop them all up except one, on account of which they are all drowned outright. They tell about a holy man who lay in his death-sickness and was loath to declare a sin of his childhood – and his abbot commanded him to declare it anyway. And he answered that there was no need because he was a little child when he did it. At last, though reluctantly, at the abbot's urging he declared it and died soon afterwards. After his death he came one night and showed himself to his abbot in snow-white clothes, as one who was saved, and said that assuredly, if he had not declared plainly in confession that thing which he had done in childhood, he would have been condemned as one of the lost. Also about another who was nearly condemned because he had once forced a man to drink and had died without having confessed it. Also about the lady, because she had lent a woman one of her garments for a wake. But whoever has carefully searched all the corners of his heart and can wring no more out, if anything is lurking there, it is, I hope, pushed out in confession with the rest – when it is not a case of heedlessness and he would readily say more if he knew it.

Confession must be naked – that is, made nakedly, not dressed in fine excuses or given elegant flavours, but the words should be shaped according to the deeds. It is a sign of hating that what is much hated is treated extremely badly. If you hate your sin, why do you speak of it in honourable terms? Why do you hide its filthiness? Speak shame on it in terms of ignominy and treat it extremely badly, in the same way that you strongly desire to put the devil to shame. 'Sir,' a woman says, 'I have had a lover', or 'I have been foolish about myself.' This is not

naked confession. Do not dress it up. Take away the trappings.
Uncover yourself and say, 'Sir, God's mercy, I am a foul stud mare, a
stinking whore.' Give your foe a foul name and call your sin foul. In
confession make it stark naked – that is, do not conceal anything of all
that has to do with it. However, one can speak too foully. One ought
not to name the foul deed by its own foul name, nor the shameful parts
by their own names. It is enough to speak in such a way that the holy
father confessor clearly understands what you wish to lament. Six
things which conceal it are set around sin (in Latin 'circumstances', in
English they can be called 'trappings'[10]): person, place, time, manner,
amount, cause. Person – who did the sin, or with whom it was done.
Uncover it and say, 'Sir, I am a woman and should by rights be more
ashamed at having spoken as I spoke or done as I did, because my sin is
greater than had it been a man's, for it became me worse. I am an
anchoress' (or 'a nun', or 'a married woman', or 'a maiden', or 'a
woman that was so well trusted', or 'a woman who has been burnt
before by a thing like this and ought to be the better on my guard').
'Sir, it was with this sort of man', and then say 'monk', or 'priest', or
'clerk', and about his order; 'a married man', or 'an innocent thing', or
'a woman, as I am'. This now is about the person. Likewise, about the
place: 'Sir, I fooled about or spoke like this in church,' or 'I joined in a
dance in the churchyard',[11] or 'I watched it' – or wrestling and other
silly games. 'I spoke like this or fooled about in front of men in the
world', or 'in front of a recluse in an anchor-house', or 'at another
window than I should have', or 'near a holy thing'; 'I kissed him there;
I touched him in such a place (or myself); in church I thought like this;
I watched him at the altar.' About the time likewise: 'Sir, I was of such
an age that I certainly ought to have watched myself more wisely.' 'Sir,
I did it in Lent; on fast days; on holy days; when others were at
church.' 'Sir, I was soon overcome, and the sin is greater than if I had
been thrown down with violence and many blows.' 'Sir, I was the start
of such a thing going on, because I came to such a place at such a time.'
'I considered very well before ever I did it how evil it was to do it, and
I did it none the less.' You should state the manner likewise – that is,
the fourth of the trappings. 'Sir, this sin I did thus and in this way.
Thus I first learned it, thus I first fell into it, thus I did it from then on,
in these several ways – thus foully, thus shamefully. Thus I sought

pleasure with which I might satisfy the burning of my desire' – and you should state the way in full. Amount is the fifth of the trappings. [You should tell in full how often it is done: 'Sir, I have done this this often, been accustomed to speaking like this and listening to this kind of talk and thinking this kind of thought, been careless about things or forgotten them – laughed, eaten, drunk less or more than was necessary. I have been angry this often since I last confessed – and for this kind of thing, and it lasted this long. I spoke lies this often, said this and that this often. I have done this this many times.' Cause is the sixth trapping.][12] Cause is why you did it or helped others to do it, or the means by which it began: 'Sir, I did it for pleasure; for evil love; for gain; for fear; for flattery.' 'Sir, I did it to cause evil, though none came of it.' 'Sir, my light answer, or my light behaviour, first enticed him to me.' 'Sir, from this word came another, from this deed anger and evil words.' 'Sir, the reason why the evil still continues is this.' 'My heart was weak in this way.' Each person should state his trappings in accordance with what he is – a man as it pertains to him, a woman what touches her. For here I have only said things to remind a man or a woman of what is appropriate to them through what is said here as it were at a sprint. In this way strip your sin of these six coverings and make it naked in your confession, as Jeremiah teaches: *Effunde sicut aquam cor tuum*[a] – 'Pour out your heart like water.' If oil is poured out of a vat, some of the liquid will still be left in it; if milk is poured out, the colour is left; if wine is poured out, the smell is left. But water all goes out together. Just so, pour out your heart – that is, all the evil that is in your heart. If you do not, look how terribly God threatens you, through Nahum the prophet: *Ostendam gentibus nuditatem tuam et regnis ignominiam tuam et proitiam super te abhominationes tuas*[b] – 'You were not willing to uncover yourself to the priest in confession, and I shall show your wickedness quite naked to all people and to all kingdoms your shameful sins, to the kingdom of earth, to the kingdom of hell, to the kingdom of heaven, and pack up all your shamefulness on to your own neck, as is done to the thief who is taken to be judged. And so with all

a Pour out thy heart like water (Lamentations 2.19).
b I will show thy nakedness to the nations and thy shame to kingdoms and I will cast thy abominations upon thee (Nahum 3.5 6).

the shame you will pack up and go – and tumble right into hell.' *O*, says St Bernard, *quid confusionis, quid ignominie erit quando dissipatis foliis et dispersis uniuersa nudabitur turpitudo. Sanies apparebit*[a] – 'Oh,' says St Bernard, 'what shame and what sorrow will there be at the Judgement, when all the leaves shall be scattered and all that filth shows itself and presses out that pus in front of all the wide world, dwellers on earth and in heaven – not only of deeds, but of omissions, of words and of thoughts which have not been atoned for here.' As St Anselm testifies: *Omne tempus impensum requiretur a uobis qualiter sit expensum*[b] – 'Each hour and moment will be reckoned up there – how it was spent here.' *Quando dissipatis foliis, et cetera* – 'When all the leaves,' says St Bernard, 'shall be scattered.' He considered how Adam and Eve, when they had sinned in the beginning, gathered leaves and made coverings from them for their shameful parts. Thus many do after them: *Declinantes cor suum in uerba malicie ad excusandas excusationes in peccatis.*[c]

Confession must be made often. Therefore in the Psalter it is *Confitebimur tibi, Deus, confitebimur.*[13][d] And Our Lord himself says to his disciples, *Eamus iterum in Judeam*[e] – 'Let us go again,' he said, 'into Judea.' 'Judea' means 'confession', and so we find that he often went out of Galilee into Judea. 'Galilee' means 'wheel' – to teach us that we should often go from the world's turbulence and the wheel of sin to confession. For this is the sacrament, after the sacrament of the altar, and the sacrament of baptism, most hateful to the fiend, as he has himself most unwillingly acknowledged to holy men. Will a piece of weaving be well bleached with one lot of water on one occasion? A soiled cloth well washed? You wash your hands two or three times in a single day, and you will not wash the soul, Jesus Christ's wife – and the whiter that is, the more the dirt shows on it, unless it is washed – you will often not wash it for God's embrace once in a week. *Confiteor*,[f]

a Oh, what confusion, what ignominy there will be when, with the leaves scattered and dispersed, all disgrace is laid bare. The pus will be visible (Geoffrey of Auxarre, *Declamations . . . from the Sermons of St Bernard* 50.61).

b An account will be required of you for all the time you have spent – how you have spent it (*Meditation* 1).

c Inclining their hearts to evil words, to make excuses in sins (see Psalm 140.4).

d We will confess to thee, God, we will confess (Psalm 74.1).

e Let us go into Judea again (John 11.7).

f I confess.

holy water, prayers, holy thoughts, blessings, kneelings, each good word, each good deed wash small sins, all of which we are not able to state. But confession is always the most important.

Confession must be made quickly. If sin happens at night, immediately, or in the morning. If it happens in the day, before one sleeps. Who would dare sleep while his deadly foe held a drawn sword above his head. Those who take a nap upon the brink of hell often tumble right in before they the least suspect it. Whoever has fallen into a burning fire, is he not more than mad if he lies and thinks about when he will get up? A woman who has lost her needle or a shoemaker his awl looks for it at once and turns over each straw until it is found – and God, lost through sin, shall lie unlooked for seven whole days! There are nine things that ought to hasten one to confession. The punishment that accrues as interest. For sin is the devil's money, which he loans with punishment as the interest, and the longer a man lies in his sin, so the interest grows – of punishment in purgatory, or here, or in hell: *Ex usuris et iniquitate, et cetera.*[a] The second thing is the great and pitiful loss which he suffers, in that nothing that he does is pleasing to God: *Alieni comederunt robur eius.*[b] The third is death, in that he does not know whether he will die suddenly that same day: *Fili, ne tardes, et cetera.*[c] The fourth is sickness, in that he cannot think properly, but only about his illness, nor speak as he should, but groan because of his aching and grunt – more because of his pain than his sin: *Sanus confiteberis et vivens.*[d] The fifth thing is the great shame it is after a fall to lie so long, and especially underneath the devil. The sixth is the wound, which gets worse all the time and is more difficult to heal: *Principiis obsta: medicina [sero] paratur cum mala per longas.*[e] The seventh thing is bad habit, which Lazarus signifies, who stank, so long had he lain in the earth; over whom Our Lord wept, as the Gospel tells, and shook and was troubled, and cried loud upon him before he raised him up, to show

a From usuries and iniquity, etc. (Psalm 71.14).
b Strangers have devoured his strength (Hosea 7.9).
c Son, delay not, etc. (Ecclesiasticus 5.8).
d Whilst thou art alive and in health thou shalt confess (Ecclesiasticus 17.27).
e Resist the beginnings: too late is the medicine prepared when the disease [has gained strength] by long [delays] (Ovid, *Remedies for Love* 91). 'Sero' is supplied from Ovid; it does not appear in the Corpus manuscript.

how difficult it is for one who rots in his sin to arise from bad habit. St Mary! Lazarus stank after four days. How does the sinner stink after four or five years! *Quam difficile surgit quem moles male consuetudinis premit*[a] – 'Oh,' says St Augustine, 'in what hardship does he arise who under the habit of sin has lain long.' *Circumdederunt me canes multi*[b] – 'Many dogs,' says David, 'have surrounded me.' When greedy dogs stand before the table, do you not need a stick? As often as any jumps at you and takes away your food, will you not as often strike it? Otherwise they would snatch from you all you had. And you also, then, take the stick of your tongue, and as often as the dog of hell snatches any good from you, strike him immediately with the stick of your tongue in confession, and strike him so violently that he may hate and fear to sneak up to you again. That blow of all blows is the most hateful blow to him. The dog which chews leather or tears the throat out of livestock is beaten immediately so that he may understand why he is beaten. Then he does not dare do the same again. Beat likewise the dog of hell immediately with your tongue's confession and he will be afraid to do you such an injury again. Who is so foolish as to say in the case of the dog that chews leather, 'Wait until the morning, don't beat him yet'? But beat immediately; beat, beat immediately. There is nothing in this world that stings him more painfully than does such beating. The deeper one wades into the fiend's swamp, the longer it takes to come out. The eighth thing is what St Gregory says: *Peccatum quod per penitentiam non diluitur mox suo pondere ad aliud trahit*[c] – that is, 'The sin that is not soon atoned for draws on at once another', and that, again, a third, and so each one gives birth to a greater and a worse offspring than the mother herself. The ninth reason is the sooner a man begins to do his penance here, the less he has to atone for in the pain of purgatory. This is now nine reasons – and there are many more – why confession ought always to be made quickly.

Confession ought to be humble, as the publican's was, not as the pharisee's was, who numbered his good deeds and put what was

---

a With what difficulty does a person on whom the bulk of a bad habit presses arise (*On St John's Gospel* 49.10, 24).

b Many dogs have encompassed me (Psalm 21.17).

c A sin which is not washed away through penance soon by its own weight draws to it another one (*Morals on Job* 25.9, 22).

healthy on show when he should have uncovered his wounds. Therefore, as Our Lord himself tells, he went out of the temple unhealed.[14]
Humility is like these cunning down-and-outs and their running sores
and their oozing boils which they are always putting forward and,
horrible as it is, they show it in front of rich men's eyes looking more
horrible still, so that they may have pity on them and give them some
good thing the more readily. They hide their good clothes and put on
the dirtiest possible rags, completely torn to pieces. In this same way
humility humbly beguiles Our Lord and gets some of his goods with
blessed cheating. She hides her goods and puts on show her poverty,
puts forward her ulcer, weeping and groaning before God's eyes. She
implores insistently by his harsh passion, by his precious blood, by his
five wounds, by his mother's tears, by those breasts that he sucked, the
milk that fed him, by all his saints' love, by the dear dalliance that he
has with his dear wife – that is, with the pure soul, or with Holy
Church – by his death on the cross, to help her. With constant
beseeching of this sort she implores some help for a distressed wretch,
to treat a sick person, to heal her ulcer. And Our Lord, so implored,
cannot for pity refuse her and grieve her with a refusal, especially so
since he is so immeasurably generous that nothing is dearer to him
than being able to find a reason to give. But whoever boasts of
his goodness, as these proud people do in confession, what need is
there to help them? Many have such a way of stating their sins that
it is as good as a secret boast and they hunt after praise for greater
holiness.

Confession ought to be full of shame. By the people of Israel going
out through the Red Sea, which was red and bitter, is signified that we
must pass to heaven through ruddy shame – that is, in true confession
and bitter penance. It is very right, Christ knows, that we should be
ashamed before men, we who forgot shame when we did the sin before
God's sight. *Nam omnia nuda sunt et aperta oculis eius ad quem nobis sermo*[a]
– 'For all that is, all is naked,' says St Paul, 'and open to his eyes, with
whom we must make account of all our deeds.' Shame is the greatest
part, as St Augustine says, of our penance: *Verecundia pars est magna*

a For all things are naked and open to his eyes, to whom our speech is (Hebrews 4.
13).

penetentie.[a] And St Bernard says that no precious gemstone so much delights a man to look at as the red of a man's face who states his sins properly does God's eye. Understand this saying well. Confession is a sacrament, and each sacrament has a likeness on the outside to what it does on the inside, as is the case in baptism. The washing on the outside signifies the washing of the soul within. Likewise in confession the lively red of the face makes us understand that the soul, which was black and had only a dead colour, has got a lively colour[15] and has become beautifully red. *Interior tamen penitentia non dicitur sacramentum, set exterior uel puplica uel solempnis.*[b]

Confession must be full of fear, so that you say with Jerome: *Quociens confessus sum, uideor michi non esse confessus*[c] 'As often as I confess, I always seem to myself not to have confessed' – for one or other of the trappings is always forgotten. Therefore St Augustine says, *Ve laudabili hominum uite si remota misericordia discutias eam*[d] that is, 'The best man in all the world, if Our Lord were to judge him completely in accordance with righteousness and not in accordance with mercy, there would be woe for him!' *Set misericordia superexaltat iudicium*[e] – 'But his mercy towards us always weighs more than strict justice.'

Confession must be full of hope. Whoever states as he is able and does all that he can, God asks no more. But hope and fear must always be mingled together. To signify this it was in the Old Law commanded that no one should separate the two grindstones. The lower, which lies still and carries a heavy load, signifies fear which holds man back from sin, and is heavily weighted here with the hard to be free of the harder. The stone on top signifies hope, which runs and busies itself in good deeds all the time with trust in a great reward. These two no one should part, for as St Gregory says, *Spes sine timore luxuriat in presumptionem. Timor sine spe degenerat in desperationem*[f] 'Fear without hope

---

a Shame is a large part of penance (Pseudo-Augustine, *True and False Penance* 10.25).
b Interior penance, however, is not called a sacrament, but rather exterior or public or solemn.
c Whenever I have confessed, I seem to myself not to have confessed.
d Woe to those of praiseworthy life if you remove mercy and put their life under scrutiny (*Confessions* 9.13, 34).
e But mercy exalts itself above judgement (James 2.13).
f Hope without fear runs riot into presumption. Fear without hope degenerates into despair.

makes a man lack trust, and hope without fear makes him trust too much.' These two vices, lack of trust and too much trust, are the devil's trists,[16] from which the wretched animal seldom escapes. A trist is where they sit with the greyhounds to look out for the hare, or set the nets for it. All his urging is towards one of these two, because there are his greyhounds, there are his nets. Lack of trust and too much trust are, of all the sins, nearest the gate of hell. With fear, without hope – that is, with lack of trust – were Cain's confession and Judas's, on account of which they perished. With hope, without fear – that is, with too much trust – is the saying of the unfortunate man who says in the Psalter, *Secundum multitudinem ire sue non queret*[a] – 'God is not,' he says, 'as fierce as you make him out.' 'No?' says David. 'Yes he is!' And then says, *Propter quid irritauit impius Deum? Dixit enim in corde suo: non requiret.*[b] First of all he calls the too trusting an unbeliever. On account of what does the unbeliever anger God? On account of his saying, 'He will not judge as strictly as you say.' Yes, to be sure, but he will. Thus these two vices are likened to fierce robbers: for the one – that is, too much trust – steals from God his judgement by rights and his righteousness. The other – that is, lack of trust – steals from him his mercy. And so they are out to destroy God himself. For God could not exist without righteousness, nor without mercy. Now then, which vices are equal to these that want to kill God in their foul way? If you are too trusting and consider God too soft to avenge sin, sin is pleasing to him by your account. But look at how he took vengeance on his high angel for a proud thought; how he took vengeance on Adam for the biting of an apple; how he sank Sodom and Gomorrah, man, woman and child, the famous cities, an entire great district, down into the bottom of hell, where the Dead Sea is now, in which there is nothing living; how he drowned all the world in Noah's flood, except for eight in the ark. How he avenged himself fiercely on his own people Israel, his darling, as often as they offended – Dathan and Abiram, Korah and his companions; the others also that he killed in their many thousands, often only for their complaining. On the other hand, look, if you lack

a According to the multitude of his wrath he will not seek (Psalm 9.25).
b Wherefore hath the wicked provoked God? For he hath said in his heart: he will not require [it] (Psalm 9.34).

trust in his immeasurable mercy, how easily and how soon St Peter, after he had forsaken him – and that for what a slut said – was reconciled to him; how the thief on the cross who had always lived badly in an instant got mercy from him by some good words. Therefore, between these two, lack of trust and too much trust, let hope and fear be always joined together.

Confession must further be wise and made to a wise man; of unfamiliar sins, not to young priests – I mean young in understanding – nor to foolish old ones. Begin with pride first and seek all the branches of it, as they are written above, which apply to you. Afterwards likewise with envy; and let us go down in this way row by row until the last is reached, and draw together all the brood under their mother.

Confession ought to be true: do not lie about yourself, for as St Augustine says, *Qui causa humilitatis de se mentitur fit quod prius ipse non fuit, id est, peccator*[a] – 'He who tells lies about himself through too much humility, he is made sinful, though he was not before.' St Gregory, though, says, *Bonarum mentium est culpam agnoscere ubi culpa non est*[b] – 'It is the nature of the good heart to be afraid of sin where often there is none', or to give its sin more weight than necessary on occasion. To give it too little weight is as bad or worse. The middle way of moderation is always golden.[17] Let us always fear, for often we intend to do a small evil, and do a great sin; often to do good, and we do something altogether wrong. Let us always then say with St Anselm, *Etiam bonum nostrum est aliquo modo corruptum, ut possit non placere aut certe displicere Deo. Paulus: Scio quod non est in me, hoc est in carne mea, bonum.*[c] No good in us is from us: our good is God's, but sin is from us and our own. 'God's good, when I do it,' says St Anselm, 'in some way my evil gnaws it away: either I do it uncheerfully or too early or too late, or think well of it though no one knows about it, or wish that someone knew about it, or do it heedlessly, or too unwisely – too much or too

a The person who for humility's sake tells lies about himself becomes what he was not before, a sinner (*Sermons* 181.4, 5).

b It is the mark of good souls to acknowledge fault where there is no fault (*Letters* 11.4, 64).

c Even our goodness is in some way corrupted, so that it may not please and may even displease God (*Meditation* 1). Paul: I know that good is not in me, that is, in my flesh (Romans 7.18).

little. Thus some evil always mingles with my good, which God's grace gives me, so that it can please God little and displease him often.' St Mary! When the holy man spoke like this about himself, how certainly can we speak it about our wretched selves!

Confession ought to be willing, that is, willingly given unrequested, not drawn out of you as if against your wishes. While you are able to say anything, say everything unasked. Nothing should be asked, except only when necessary, for evil may occur because of the asking, unless it is wise enough. Again, many a man waits to confess until the extremity of need. But often that trick lets him down, so that he can't when he wants who didn't want to when he could.[18] There is no greater stupidity than to set God a term, as though grace were one's own, as though one carried it in one's purse, and could take out some of the grace in it at the term, as one set it oneself. No, good friend, no. The term is in God's hand, not in your control. When God offers it you, reach out both your hands, for should he withdraw his hand, you can go looking for it! If sickness or something else forces you to confession, look what St Augustine says: *Coacta seruicia Deo non placent*[a] – 'Forced services do not please Our Lord.' However, 'O' is none the less better than 'No': *Numquam sera penitentia, si, tamen, uera*[b] – 'Repentance that is truly made is never too late,' he himself says afterwards. But David says it better: *Refloruit caro mea et ex uoluntate mea confitebor mei*[c] – 'My flesh has flowered, become all new, for I shall confess and praise God willingly.' Well does he say 'flowered' to signify 'willing confession', for the earth, quite unforced, and the trees also, open up and bring forth various flowers. *In Canticis: Flores apparuerunt in terra nostra.*[d] Humility, abstinence, the innocence of a dove and other such virtues are beautiful in God's eyes and in God's nose sweet-smelling flowers; of them make his lodging within yourself, for his delight, he says, is to dwell there: *Et delicie mee esse cum filiis hominum: in libro Prouerbiorum.*[e]

a Forced services do not please God (see Pseudo-Augustine, *Sermons to the Brothers in the Desert* 30).
b Penitence is never too late, if it is, nevertheless, true.
c My flesh hath flourished again and with my will I will give praise to him (Psalm 27.7).
d In Canticles (2.12): The flowers have appeared in our land.
e And my delights were to be with the children of men: in the Book of Proverbs (8. 31).

Confession ought to be one's own. One must only accuse oneself in confession, as far as one can. I say this because something may happen to a man or a woman such that they cannot fully reveal themselves unless they reveal others. But none the less they are not to mention them by name, although the father confessor may know well to whom it points. But 'a monk' or 'a priest', not 'William' or 'Walter', although there may be no one else.

Confession must be determined to keep to the penance and leave the sin, so that you say to the priest, 'I am determined in thought and in heart to abandon this sin and to do the penance.' The priest must not ask you if you will from then on renounce your sin. It is enough that you should say that you have it in your heart truly to do so, through God's grace, and if you fall into it again, you will rise at once, through God's help, and come to confession again. *Vade et amplius noli peccare*[a] – 'Go,' said Our Lord to a sinful woman, 'and have the will that you will not sin anymore.' Thus he did not ask for any other assurance.

Confession ought to be thought about long before. With your reason gather your sins with respect to five things: of all your ages   of childhood, of youth – gather them all together. After that, gather the places that you lived in; and think carefully what you did in each place separately and at each age. After that, seek right out and track down your sins with reference to your five senses. After that, with reference to all the parts of your body – in which you have sinned most and most often. Lastly, separately with reference to days and times.

Now you have had, as I understand it, all the sixteen parts as I promised to divide them, and I have broken them all up for you, my dear sisters, as they do for children who might die of hunger with unbroken bread. But many crumbs, as you know, have fallen from me. Seek and gather them, for they are the soul's food.

This sort of confession which has these sixteen parts like this has those great powers of which I spoke first[19] – three against the devil, three over ourselves and three against the world – precious above gold ore and gems from India.

My dear sisters, this fifth part, which is about confession, pertains to

a   Go and sin no more (John 8.11).

all people alike.[20] Therefore do not be surprised that I have not spoken with reference particularly to you in this part. Have for your benefit, however, this little final ending. All familiar sins, such as pride, a swollen or a high heart, envy, anger, sloth, heedlessness, idle speech, undisciplined thoughts, something idly listened to, some false happiness, or heavy mourning, hypocrisy, too much or too little food or drink, complaining, grim looks, silences broken, sitting long at the window, hours said wrong, or without the attention of the heart, or at the wrong time, something false said, swearing, fooling about, shaking with laughter, spilling crumbs or ale, letting things go mouldy, or rusty, or rotten, clothes unsewn, rained on, unwashed, breaking a cup or a dish, looking carelessly after anything being used or which ought to be taken care of, cutting and hurting through inattention, all the things that are in this rule which have been done wrong – let her confess all this sort of thing once each week at least. For none of these is so small that the devil does not have it recorded in his roll. But confession scrapes it off and makes him waste much of his time. But all that confession does not scrape off, all that he will on Judgement Day very certainly read to accuse you with it. Not one word will be wanting there. Now then, I advise, give him to write the least that ever you can, for no job is dearer to him, and whatever he writes, be out to scrape it clean off – with nothing can you frustrate him better. To every priest an anchoress may confess such outward sins as happen to everyone. But she must be very assured of the goodness of the priest to whom she shows in its entirety how she stands with respect to temptations of the flesh, if she is so tempted – unless in fear of death. However, it seems to me that she may speak like this: 'Sir, a temptation of the flesh which I have (or have had) is making too much headway with me through my consent. I am afraid that I go driving on my foolish thoughts – foul as well sometimes – too much. I might, through God's strength, often shake them off me, if I went at it vigorously and resolutely. I am very much afraid that the delight in the thought lasts too long, so that it comes close to the consent of reason.'[21] I cannot risk her confessing more deeply and more plainly to a young priest about this – and he would be easily enough outraged even at this. But let her pour all the pot out to her own father confessor, or to some man of holy life, if she can get him – spew out there all the outrageous facts, there, with foul words, ill-treat that filth quite outrageously, in accordance with what it is, so that she is afraid of hurting the ears of the person listening to her sins. If any anchoress does not know about this sort of thing, she should thank Christ heartily and keep herself in fear. The devil is not dead – let her know that – although he may be sleeping.

Atone for slight faults at once on your own like this (and, nevertheless, state them in confession, when you think of them as you speak with the priest); for the smallest of all, as soon as you notice it, fall to the earth before your altar in the shape of a cross and say, *Mea culpa*[a] – 'I am guilty – mercy, Lord.' The priest need not lay on you for any fault, unless it be great enough, other penance than the life that you lead in accordance with this rule. But after the absolution he must say, 'All the good that you ever do and all the evil that you ever endure for the love of Jesus Christ within your anchoress's walls, I enjoin it all on you, I lay it all upon you for the remission of these and for the forgiveness of all your sins.' And then he may lay upon you something small, such as a psalm or two, ten or twelve *Pater nosters* and *Aues*. Let him add disciplines, if it seems right to him. According to the trappings which are written above, he must judge the sin greater or less. A most forgivable sin may become most deadly through some evil trappings that are attached to it. After confession it is appropriate to speak of penance, that is, satisfaction; and so we have an entry out of this fifth part into the sixth.

a My fault.

PART SIX
Penance

All is penance – and severe penance – that you ever suffer, my dear sisters. All that you do which is good, all that you endure, is martyrdom for you in so harsh an order. For you are night and day upon God's cross. You can be happy about this, for as St Paul says, *Si compatimur, conregnabimus*[a] – 'As you partake with him of his pain on earth, so you will partake with him of his bliss in heaven.' Therefore St Paul says, *Michi absit gloriari, nisi in cruce Domini Iesu Christi.*[b] And Holy Church sings, *Nos opportet gloriari in cruce Domini nostri Iesu Christi*[c] – 'All our bliss must be in Jesus Christ's cross.' This saying applies especially to recluses, whose bliss ought to be entirely in God's cross. I shall begin higher[1] and so come down to here. Take good note, now, for it is nearly all St Bernard's views.

Three kinds of people – of God's chosen – live on earth. The first may be likened to good pilgrims, the second to the dead, the third to those hanged with their consent on Jesus's cross. The first are good; the second are better, the third best of all.

To the first St Peter cries earnestly, *Obsecro uos, tanquam aduenas et peregrinos, ut abstineatis uos a carnalibus desideriis que militant aduersus animam*[d] – 'I implore you,' he says, 'as foreigners and pilgrims, that you restrain yourselves from fleshly desires, which war against the

---

a If we suffer with him, we shall reign with him (2 Timothy 2.12).
b Let me not glory, save in the cross of Our Lord Jesus Christ, [by whom the world is crucified to me, and I to the world] (Galatians 6.14).
c We ought to glory in the cross of Our Lord Jesus Christ (introit of the Mass for the Feasts of the Finding and the Exaltation of the Cross).
d I beseech you, as strangers and pilgrims, to refrain yourselves from carnal desires which war against the soul (1 Peter 2.11).

soul.' The good pilgrim always keeps to his proper way forward. Though he may see or hear idle games and wonders at the wayside, he does not stop as fools do, but keeps on on his course and hurries towards his lodgings. He carries no treasure except his bare expenses, or clothes except only what he needs. Such are holy men who, though they are in the world, are in it as pilgrims and go with a good way of life towards the kingdom of heaven, and say with the Apostle, *Non habemus hic manentem ciuitatem, set futuram inquirimus*[a] – that is, 'We have no dwelling here, but we seek another.' They make do with the least that they can and take no account of any worldly comfort, although they are on a path in the world, as I said of the pilgrim. But they have their hearts always fixed on heaven – and well they ought to have. For other pilgrims go on very laborious journeys to seek the bones of one saint, such as St James or St Giles;[2] but these pilgrims who go towards heaven, they go to be made saints and to find God himself and all his saints living in bliss, and shall live with him in joy without end. They certainly find St Julian's[3] inn, which wayfarers earnestly seek.

Now these are good, but yet the second are better; for inevitably pilgrims, as I said before, though they may always go on and not become citizens in the world's city, sometimes they find pleasure in what they see by the wayside and stop a bit, though not completely, and many things happen to them by which they are hindered, so that, more's the pity, some come home late, some never again. Who then is purer and more out of the world than pilgrims – that is to say, than those who have worldly things and do not love them, but give them as they get them, and go easily without baggage, as pilgrims do, towards heaven? Who are better than these? God knows, those are better to whom the Apostle speaks and says in his epistle, *Mortui estis, et vita uestra abscondita est cum Christo in Deo. Cum autem apparuerit uita uestra, tunc et uos apparebitis cum ipso in gloria*[a] – 'You are dead, and your life is hidden with Christ; when he who is your life appears again and rises like the dawn after night's darkness, you also will rise with him,

a   We have not here a lasting city, but we seek one that is to come (Hebrews 13.14).
b   You are dead, and your life is hid with Christ in God. When Christ shall appear, who is your life, then you also shall appear with him in glory (Colossians 3.3 4).

brighter than the sun, into eternal joy.' The way of life of those who are now dead like this is higher. For many things trouble a pilgrim. It does not matter to the dead man though he lie unburied and rot above the earth. Praise him, blame him, treat him shamefully, speak of him shamefully – it is all equally welcome. This is a happy death which in this way makes a living man or a living woman be out of the world. But certainly, whoever is dead like this in herself – God lives in her heart. For this is what the Apostle says: *Viuo ego, iam non ego; viuit autem in me Christus*[a] – 'I live – not I myself, but Christ lives in me through his indwelling grace'; and it is as though he said, 'Worldly speech, worldly sight and every worldly thing find me dead, but what pertains to Christ, that I see and hear and do, full of life.' In just this way is every religious[4] dead to the world and alive, though, to Christ. This is a high step, but there is still, even so, a higher. And who ever stood on that? God knows, he who said, *Michi absit gloriari nisi in cruce Domini mei Iesu Christi, per quam michi mundus crucifixus est, et ego mundo.*[b] This is what I said above: 'Christ shield me from having any joy in this world, except in the cross of Jesus Christ my Lord, through whom the world is worthless to me and I am worthless to it, like a criminal who is hanged.' Ah Lord, he stood high who spoke in this way. And this is the anchoress's step, in that she should say like this, *Michi autem absit gloriari, et cetera* – 'May I find my joy in nothing except in God's cross, in that I endure woe now and am accounted worthless, as God was on the cross.' Look, dear sisters, how this step is higher than any of the others are. The pilgrim in the way of the world, though he goes on towards the home of heaven, he sees and hears foolishness – and speaks it sometimes. He gets angry at wrongs and many things can hinder him from his journey. To the dead person, shame matters no more than honour, hard than soft, for he feels neither – and therefore he deserves neither sorrow nor delight. But the person that is on the cross and has joy of it turns shame into honour and sorrow into delight, and therefore deserves reward on top of reward. This one is those who are never glad-hearted, except when they endure some sorrow or some

a I live, now not I; but Christ liveth in me (Galatians 2.20).
b Let me not glory [, save in the cross of Our Lord Jesus Christ, by whom the world is crucified to me, and I to the world] (Galatians 6.14).

shame with Jesus on his cross, for this is happiness on earth, when someone is able for God's love to have shame and hurt. Thus, look, true anchoresses are not only pilgrims, nor yet only dead people. But they are of this third sort, for all their joy is to be hung painfully and shamefully with Jesus on his cross. These may sing happily with Holy Church, *Nos opportet gloriari, et cetera*[a] – that is, as I said before, however it may be with others who have their joy, some of them in the flesh's pleasure, some in the world's deception, some in another's harm, we must of necessity find our joy in Jesus Christ's cross – that is, in shame and in sorrow, which he suffered on the cross. Many a man has been willing to endure hardship of the flesh in some way, but being accounted worthless, and shame, he could not endure. But he is only half upon Christ's cross if he is not prepared to endure them both.

Vilitas et asperitas[b] – abjectness and hardship, these two, shame and suffering, as St Bernard says, are the two ladder-uprights which are set up to heaven, and between these uprights are the rungs of all virtues fixed, by which one climbs to the joy of heaven. Because David had the two uprights of this ladder, although he was king, he climbed up and said boldly to Our Lord, *Vide humilitatem meam et laborem meum et dimitte uniuersa delicta mea*[c] – 'Behold,' he said, 'and see my humility and my toil and forgive all my sins together.' Note well these two words that David links together: toil and humility – toil in suffering and in grief, in hurt and in sorrow; humility in the face of the wrong of shame that a man suffers when he is accounted worthless. 'Both these behold in me,' said David, God's darling, 'I have these two ladder-uprights.' *Dimitte uniuersa delicta mea.* 'Leave behind me,' he said, 'and throw away from me all my offences, so that, lightened of their weight, I may lightly[5] ascend up to heaven by this ladder.' These two things, that is, grief and shame linked together, are Elijah's wheels, which were fiery, it says, and bore him up to paradise, where he still lives. Fire is hot and red. By the heat is understood every grief that afflicts the flesh; shame by the redness. But their being here wheeling[6] like wheels can do

a   We ought to glory, etc.
b   Abjectness and hardship.
c   See my abjection and my labour and forgive me all my sins (Psalm 24.18).

us well:[7] they soon go over and do not last a long while. The same thing is signified by the cherub's sword in front of the gate of paradise, which was of flame and wheeling and turning about. No man comes into paradise except through this flaming sword, which was hot and red, and on Elijah's fiery wheels – that is, through hurt and through shame, which goes over promptly and departs soon. And is not God's cross made ruddy and red, with his precious blood to show through his own case that suffering and sorrow and hurt must be coloured with shame? Is it not written of him, *Factus est obediens Patri usque ad mortem, mortem autem crucis*[a] – that is, 'He was obedient to his Father not only to death, but to death on the cross'? Through his saying first 'death', suffering is understood; through his saying afterwards 'death on the cross', shame is signified, for such was God's death on the precious cross, painful and shameful above all others. Whoever dies in God and on God's cross must suffer these two – shame and suffering – on his account. I call shame always being accounted worthless here, and begging one's livelihood like a down-and-out, if need be, and being another's bedesman[8] – as you are, my dear sisters; and you often endure the disdain of such as might at one time have been your serf. This is that blessed shame which I am talking about. Suffering will not fail you. In these two things, in which is all penance, rejoice and be glad, for in return for these, twofold blisses are prepared: in return for shame, honour; in return for suffering, delight and rest without end. *Ysaias: In terra, inquit, sua duplicia possidebunt*[b] – 'They shall,' says Isaiah, 'in their own land possess twofold bliss in return for the twofold woe which they suffer here.' 'In their own land,' says Isaiah, for just as the evil man has no share in heaven, so the good man has no share in earth. *Super Epistolam Iacobi: Mali nichil habent in celo, boni uero nichil in terra*[c] – 'In their own land they shall possess bliss, twofold kinds of reward in return for twofold sorrow', as though he said, 'Let them not think it at all strange, though they here endure, as in a strange land and in a strange country among foreigners, both shame

a He became obedient to the Father unto death, even to the death of the cross (Philippians 2.8).

b Isaiah (61.7): He says, They shall receive double in their land.

c On the Epistle of James (*Glossa Ordinaria* on James 1.2): The evil possess nothing in heaven, but the good nothing on earth.

and sorrow, for so does many a man of good family who is a stranger in a strange place.' One has to work hard when away: it's at home one must rest. And is he not a stupid knight who seeks rest in the fight and ease on the field? *Milicia est vita hominis super terram*[a] – 'All this life is a fight,' as Job testifies, but after this fight here, if we fight well, honour and rest are waiting for us at home in our own land – that is, the kingdom of heaven. Look now how certainly Our Lord himself testifies to it: *Cum sederit Filius hominis in sede maiestatis sue, sedebitis et uos iudicantes, et cetera. Bernardus: In sedibus, quies inperturbata, in iudicio, honoris eminencia commendatur*[b] – 'When I sit for judging,' says Our Lord, 'you shall sit with me and judge with me all the world that shall be judged, kings and emperors, knights and clerks.' By the seat, rest and ease are signified, in return for the toil that there is here; by the honour of the judgement that they shall give, eminence honourable beyond everything is understood, in return for the shame and lowness which they mildly endured here for God's love.

Now, then, to endure gladly is the only thing, for by God himself has been written, *Quod per penam ignominiose passionis peruenit ad gloriam resurrectionis*[c] – that is, 'Through shameful suffering he came to the glory of the blissful resurrection.' It is no wonder, then, if we wretched sinners endure suffering here, if we want on Judgement Day to arise joyfully – and that we may, through his grace, if we ourselves want. *Quoniam si complantati fuerimus similitudini mortis eius, simul et resurrectionis erimus.*[d] St Paul's saying, who always speaks so well: 'If we are engrafted in the likeness of God's death, we shall be in that of his resurrection.' That is to say, if we live in shame and suffering for his love – in which two things he dies – we shall be like his blissful resurrection, our bodies bright as his is, world without end, as St Paul testifies: *Saluatorem expectamus, qui reformabit corpus humilitatis nostre configuratum corpori*

a The life of man upon earth is a warfare (Job 7.1).

b When the Son of man shall sit on the seat of his majesty, you also shall sit on twelve seats judging [the twelve tribes of Israel] (Matthew 19.28). Bernard: In the seats, undisturbed rest is commended, in the judging, the eminence of honour (see Geoffrey of Auxerre, *Declamations . . . from the Sermons of St Bernard* 40.49).

c That through the torment of his ignominious passion he came to the glory of his resurrection.

d For if we have been planted together in the likeness of his death, we shall be also in the likeness of his resurrection (Romans 6.5).

claritatis sue[a] – 'Let others, who run on ahead, adorn their bodies; let us wait for our Saviour, who will adorn ours after the fashion of his own.' *Si compatimur, conregnabimus*[b] – 'If we suffer with him, we shall find our bliss with him.' Is this not a good bargain? Christ knows, he is not a good or true companion who will not share in the loss as afterwards in the gain. *Glosa: Illis solis prodest sanguis Christi, qui uoluptates deserunt et corpus affligunt*[c] – God shed his blood for all, but it only has value for those who flee the flesh's pleasure and torment themselves. And is that any wonder? Is not God our head and we all his members? But is not each member in pain with the suffering of the head? He is then not his member who does not have an ache beneath a head so painfully aching. When the head sweats a lot, the member that does not sweat – isn't this a bad sign? He who is our head sweats a sweat of blood[9] because of our sickness, to turn us away from that plague under which all lands lay, and many still lie. The member which does not sweat in laborious suffering for his love, God knows, it remains in its sickness, and there is nothing to be done but cut it off, although it may seem painful to God, for the finger is better off than aching all the time. Now, does he who, because he will not sweat, deprives God of the member he himself was please him well? *Oportebat Christum pati et sic intrare in gloriam suam.*[d] St Mary, mercy! 'It must so be,' it says, 'that Christ endure suffering and torment and so have entry into his kingdom.' Look, separate up what he says: 'So have entry into his kingdom' – so and no other way – and we sinful wretches want to go up with ease to heaven, which is so high above us and worth so very much? And one cannot put up a little cottage without labour, nor have two laced shoes without expense. Either they are fools, who think to buy eternal bliss with short measure, or the holy saints are, who bought it so dear. Were not St Peter and St Andrew stretched out on crosses for it, St Lawrence on the gridiron[10] and innocent maidens, their breasts torn off, whirled to bits on wheels, heads cut off?[11] But our foolishness is clear, and they

a We look for the Saviour, who will reform the body of our lowness, made like to the body of his glory (Philippians 3.20–21).

b If we suffer with him, we shall reign with him (2 Timothy 2.12).

c Gloss: The blood of Christ profits only those who have abandoned pleasures and afflict their body.

d It behoved Christ to suffer and so to enter into his glory (Luke 24.46, 26).

were like those cunning children who have rich fathers, who, willingly and wanting to, tear their clothes to pieces to get new ones. Our old tunic is our flesh, which we have from Adam, our first father; the new one we shall receive from God, our rich father, at the resurrection on Judgement Day, when our flesh shall shine brighter than the sun, if it is torn to pieces here with misery and with grief. Of those who tear their tunics to pieces in this way Isaiah says: *Deferetur munus Domino Exercituum a populo diuulso et dilacerato, a populo terribili*[a] – 'A people mutilated and torn to pieces, a terrible people,' he says, 'shall make to Our Lord a present of themselves' – a people mutilated and torn to pieces by a severe and harsh way of life. He calls the people terrible because the fiend is frightened and afraid of such. Because Job was like this, he complained and said, *Pellem pro pelle et uniuersa, et cetera*[b] – that is, 'He will give skin for skin, the old for the new', as though he said, 'I shall gain nothing by attacking him: he is of that people who are torn to pieces; he tears his old tunic and rends in pieces the old garment of his mortal skin'; for the skin is immortal which, at the new resurrection, shall shine seven times brighter than the sun. Ease and comfort of the flesh are the devil's emblems. When he sees these emblems on a man or on a woman, he knows the castle is his and goes boldly in where he sees such banners raised up, as is done in a castle. In that people torn to pieces he fails to find his emblems and sees in them God's banner raised up – that is, harshness of life – and has great fear of it, as Isaiah testifies.

'But, dear sir,' someone says, 'is it sensible to inflict such suffering on oneself?' Well then, you give me an answer as to which of two men is more sensible. They are both sick: the one gives up all that he likes by way of food and drink and drinks bitter infusions to recover his health; the other follows his inclination absolutely and fulfils his desires in the face of his sickness and soon loses his life. Which of these two is wiser? Which is his own friend better? Which loves himself more? And who is not sick with sin? God, on account of our sickness, drank poisonous drink on the cross – and we will not bite anything bitter on our own account. Nothing comes of that. His follower must certainly,

a A present shall be brought to the Lord of Hosts from a people rent and torn in pieces, from a terrible people (Isaiah 18.7).
b Skin for skin, and all [that a man has he will give for his life] (Job 2.4).

with the suffering of his flesh, follow his suffering. Let no one think to go up to heaven with comfort.

'But, sir,' says someone again, 'will God so vengefully avenge sin?' Oh yes! – for now look how he hates it very much. Now, how would the man beat the thing itself, wherever he found it, who for great hatred would beat the shadow of it and all that had any similarity to it? God the Father Almighty, how bitterly did he beat his precious Son Jesus Christ Our Lord, who never had any sin, only because he bore flesh like ours, which is full of sin – and we are to be spared, who bear on us his Son's death? The weapon which slew him, that was our sin, and he that had never had any sin except the shadow only was in that shadow so shamefully ill-treated,[12] so grievously tormented, that before it came to it, because of the threat of it only, he was so terrified of it that he prayed his Father for mercy: *Tristis est anima mea usque ad mortem. Pater mi, si possibile est, transeat a me calix iste*[a] – 'I am deeply afraid,' he said, 'of my great pain. My Father, if it may be, spare me at this time. Let your will, however, and not mine, always be fulfilled.' His precious Father did not on that account stop, but laid on him so violently that he began to cry in a piteous voice, *Heloy, heloy, lama zabatani*[b] – 'My God, my God, my precious Father, have you quite cast me away, your only Son? – you are beating me so hard.' For all this he did not cease, but beat so very long and so fiercely that he died on the cross. *Disciplina pacis nostre super eum,*[c] says Isaiah. Thus our beating fell on him, for he put himself between us and his Father, who threatened to strike us, as a mother full of pity puts herself between her child and the strict father when he is going to beat it. Our Lord Jesus Christ acted like this, received on himself death's blow to shield us by this – his mercy be thanked. Where there is so great a blow it recoils back on those who are standing nearby. Truly, whoever is near him who received so heavy a blow, it will recoil on him – and he will never complain, for that is the proof that he stands near him. And the recoil is easy to endure for the love of him who received so heavy a blow to save us from the devil's cudgel in the torment of hell.

a   My soul is sorrowful even unto death. My Father, if it be possible, let this chalice pass from me (Matthew 26.38–9).

b   My God, my God, why hast thou forsaken me? (Matthew 27.46).

c   The chastisement of our peace was upon him (Isaiah 53.5).

'Still,' say many men, 'how is God better off, though I torment myself for his love?' Dear men and women, God is concerned with what is good for us. It is good for us if we do what we ought. Take note of this illustration. A man who had journeyed far, and someone came and told him that his dear wife pined for him so very much that without him she had no pleasure in anything but, for thinking about his love, was lean and pallid, would it not please him better than if he was told that she made merry and played and went wild with other men and lived in pleasure? Just so Our Lord, who is the soul's husband, who sees all that she does though he sit on high – he is very well pleased that she pines for him and will hurry to her much the quicker with the gift of his grace, or fetch her wholly to him to glory and joy everlasting.

Let no one treat herself too softly so as to deceive herself. She will not, to save her life, keep herself completely pure or maintain her chastity properly without two things, as St Ælred the Abbot wrote to his sister.[13] The one is mortification of the flesh with fasts, with vigils, with scourgings, with hard clothing, a hard bed, with sickness, with great labours. The other is virtues of the heart: devotion, pity, right love, humility and other such virtues. 'But, sir,' you answer me, 'does God sell his grace? Is not grace a voluntary gift?' My dear sisters, though purity of chastity may not be a purchase from God but a gift of grace, ungratefully do they stand against it and make themselves undeserving of holding so high a thing who are not willing gladly to endure labour for it. Amidst pleasures and ease and the comfort of the flesh who was ever chaste? Who ever bred within her a fire so as not to be burned? A pot which is boiling fast, will it not spill over unless cold water is poured in and brands taken away? The belly-pot which boils with food and drink is so close a neighbour to that undisciplined member that it shares with it the fire of its heat. But many, more's the pity, are so fleshly-minded and so exceedingly afraid in case their head aches, in case their body gets too weak, and guard their health in such a way that the spirit loses strength and sickens in sin. And those who should only treat their soul with repentance of heart and mortification of flesh degenerate into physicians and doctors of the body. Did St Agatha[14] do so, who answered Our Lord's messenger, who brought ointment for her breasts in God's name, *Medicinam carnalem corpori meo nunquam adhibui*[a] – that is, 'I never took fleshly medicine'? Have you not heard tell of the three holy men?[15] One of them, though, was accustomed, because of his cold stomach, to make use of hot spices and was fussier about food and drink than the other two, even if they were sick, and they never took any care about what was healthy or what unhealthy to eat or to drink, but always took straight away whatever God sent them, and never worried about ginger or zedoary[16] or cloves. One day, when the three of them had fallen asleep – between these two lay the third one that I spoke of – the queen of heaven came and two maidens with her. One, so it seemed, carried a syrup, the other a golden spoon. With the spoon Our Lady took some of the syrup and put it in the mouth of one of them, and the maidens went on to the one in the middle. 'No,' said Our Lady, 'he is his own doctor, go along to the third.' A holy man stood a way off and watched all this. When a sick man has to hand something that will do him good, he may certainly use it. But to be so concerned about it – especially a religious – is not pleasing to God. God and his disciples speak of the soul's doctoring, Hippocrates and Galen of bodily health.[17] The person who was most learned in Jesus Christ's doctoring[18] says the wisdom of the flesh is death to the soul – *Prudencia carnis, mors. Procul odoramus bellum*,[b] as Job says. We so fear the disease of the flesh – often before it comes – that the disease of the soul comes on, and we endure the disease of the soul to escape the disease of the flesh, as though it were better to endure lust's burning than a headache or the complaining of an upset stomach. And which is better, in sickness to be God's free child or in health of the flesh to be a slave under sin? And I do not say this so that sense and moderation – which are mother and nurse of all virtues – should be completely overlooked. But we often call that sense which is none, for true sense is always to put the health of the soul before the health of the flesh,[19] and, when one cannot keep both together, to choose injury to the body before the suffering of the soul because of too strong temptation. Nicodemus brought to anoint Our Lord[20] a hundred measures of myrrh and of aloes, which are bitter spices and signify bitter

a I have never used fleshly medicine for my body (second antiphon, Lauds for the Feast of St Agatha).
b The wisdom of the flesh is death (Romans 8.6). We smell the battle afar off (see Job 39.25).

labours and mortifications of the flesh. A hundred is a complete number and denotes perfection,[21] that is, a completed deed, to show that one must take on completely the torment of the flesh as far as ever nature may endure. By the measure is signified sense and moderation – each man should with sense measure what he can do and be not so exceedingly in the spirit that he neglects the body, nor again so soft with his flesh that it becomes undisciplined and makes the spirit a slave. Now this is nearly all said about outer bitterness: let us now say something about inner bitterness; for of these two bitternesses awakes sweetness – even now here in this world, not only in heaven.

As I said just now that Nicodemus brought ointments to Our Lord, so the three Marys bought precious spices to anoint his body. Take careful note now, my dear sisters. These three Marys signify three bitternesses, for this name, 'Mary', like 'Meraht' and 'Merari', of which I spoke above,[22] means 'bitterness'. The first bitterness is in repentance of sin and in penance, when the sinner is turned first to Our Lord. And this is understood in the first Mary, Mary Magdalene – and with good reason. For she, with much repenting and bitterness of heart, left her sins and turned to Our Lord.[23] But because someone might, through too much bitterness, fall into despair, 'Magdalene', which means 'tower's height', is linked to 'Mary', through which is signified hope of high mercy and of heaven's joy. The second bitterness is in wrestling against and resisting temptations. And this is signified in the second Mary, Mary Jacobi, for 'Jacob' means 'wrestler'. This wrestling is very bitter to many who are far forward on the path to heaven, for they still, in temptations which are the devil's throws, lose their balance and have to wrestle back with stern resistance; for as St Augustine says, *Pharao contemptus surgit in scandalum*.[a] All the time the people of Israel were in Egypt under Pharaoh's hand, he never led an army against them, but when they fled from him, then with all his power he went after them. Therefore bitter fighting is always necessary against Pharaoh – that is, against the devil – for as Ezechiel says, *Sanguinem fugies, et sanguis persequetur te*[b] – 'Flee sin and sin will always follow after.' Enough has been said above about why the good person is never clear from all

---

a When Pharaoh is defied, he rises against the offence.
b Thou shalt flee blood, and blood shall pursue thee (Ezekiel 35.6).

temptations. As soon as he has overcome the one, let him watch out straight away for another. The third bitterness is in longing for heaven and in the weariness of this world – when anyone is so high that he has heart's rest as regards the war with vices and is, as it were, in heaven's gates, and all worldly things seem bitter. And this third bitterness is understood in Mary Salome, the third Mary; for 'Salome' means 'peace', and even those who have the peace and rest of a clean conscience have in their hearts bitterness at this life which holds them back from the bliss which they long for, from God whom they love. Thus, look, in each condition bitterness rules: first in the beginning, when one is reconciled with God, in the progress of a good life, and in the final end. Who is there then on God's side, who wants ease or comfort in this world?

But take note now, my dear sisters, how after bitterness comes sweetness. Bitterness buys it, for, as the Gospel tells, those three Marys bought sweet-smelling spices to anoint Our Lord. Through spices which are sweet is understood the sweetness of a devout heart. These Marys buy it – that is, through bitterness one comes to sweetness. (By this name, 'Mary', always understand 'bitterness'.) Through Mary's prayer was water turned to wine at the marriage[24] – which is to be understood as meaning that through the prayer of bitterness which one suffers for God, the heart that was watery, tasteless, and which sensed no flavour of God any more than in water, shall be turned to wine – that is, a taste found in him sweet above all wines. Therefore the Wise Man[25] says: *Vsque in tempus sustinebit paciens, et postea redditio iocunditatis*[a] – 'The patient person may endure the bitter for a while; he shall soon afterwards have the recompense of joy.' And Anna in Tobit says of Our Lord, *Qui post tempestatem tranquillum facit, et post lacrimationem et fletum exultationem infundit*[b] – that is, 'Blessed be you, Lord, who make a calm after a storm and after the waters of weeping give cheerful happiness in return.' *Salomon: Esuriens etiam amarum pro dulci sumet*[c] – 'If you are hungry for the sweet, you must first assuredly bite on the bitter.' *In*

a A patient man shall bear for a time, and afterwards joy shall be restored to him (Ecclesiasticus 1.29).
b Who makes a calm after the tempest, and after tears and weeping pours in joyfulness (see Tobit 3.22).
c Solomon: A soul that is hungry shall take even bitter for sweet (Proverbs 27.7).

Canticis: Ibo michi ad montem myrre, ad colles turis[a] - 'I shall,' says God's dear bride, 'go to the hill of incense, by the mountain of myrrh.' Look what the way is to the sweetness of incense – by the myrrh of bitterness; and after in the same love-book, *Que est ista que ascendit per desertum sicut uirgula fumi ex aromatibus myrre et thuris?*[b] One makes fragrances from myrrh and incense. But he puts myrrh first and incense comes after: *Ex aromatibus myrre et thuris.* Now someone complains that she can have no sweetness from God, or sweetness within. Let her not wonder at all if she is not Mary, for she must buy it with bitterness outside – not with every bitterness, for some tend away from God, such as every worldly hurt which is not for the health of the soul. Therefore in the Gospel the three Marys are written of in this way: *Vt uenientes ungerent Iesum, non autem recedentes*[c] – 'These Marys,' it says, 'these bitternesses, were coming to anoint Our Lord.' Those which we endure for his love are the ones coming to anoint Our Lord, who stretches himself towards us as a thing that is anointed and makes himself tender and soft to handle. And was he not himself a recluse in Mary's womb? These two things pertain to an anchorite, confinedness and bitterness. For the womb is a confined dwelling, where Our Lord was a recluse enclosed. And this word, 'Mary', as I have often said, means 'bitterness'. If you then endure bitterness in a confined place, you are his fellows, recluse as he was in Mary's womb. Are you constrained within four wide walls – and he in a confined cradle, nailed on the cross, closed in tight in a stone tomb? Mary's womb and this tomb were his anchor-houses. In neither was he a worldly man, but, as it were, out of the world, to show anchoresses that they must not have anything in common with the world. Yes, you answer me, but he went out of both. Yes, you will go likewise out of both your anchor-houses, as he did without breakage and left them both intact – that will be when the spirit goes out at the end without breakage or blemish from its two houses. The one is the body, the other is the outer house, which is like the outer wall around the castle.

a In Canticles (4.6): I will go to the mountain of myrrh and to the hill of frank-incense.
b Who is she that goeth up by the desert, as a pillar of smoke of aromatical spices, of myrrh and frankincense? (Canticles 3.6).
c That coming they might anoint Jesus (Mark 16.1), not going away.

All that I have said about mortification of the flesh, my dear sisters, is not for you, who sometimes endure more than I would wish, but is for people who will, like enough, read this, who treat themselves too softly. None the less, one surrounds young saplings with thorns in case animals eat them while they are tender. You are young saplings set in God's orchard. The hardships of which I have spoken are thorns, and it is necessary for you to be surrounded with them, so that the animal of hell, when he sneaks up to you to bite you, may hurt himself on the sharp bits and be scared off back again. As well as all these hardships, be glad and well pleased if there is little said about you, if you are not valued. For a thorn is sharp and not valued. Be surrounded with these two things. You ought not to allow bad things to be said about you. Scandal is a capital sin – that is, a thing so said or done that people can justifiably turn it to evil, and afterwards sin because of it, in wicked thought, in evil speech, about this one or that one, and sin also in deed. But you ought to allow nothing to be said of you any more than about the dead and be cheerful at heart if you endure the disdain of Slurry the cook's boy, who washes and wipes the dishes in the kitchen. Then are you mountains raised up towards heaven. For look how the lady in the sweet love-book speaks: *Venit dilectus meus saliens in montibus, transiliens colles*[a] – 'My beloved comes leaping,' she says, 'on the mountains, [overleaping the hills.' The mountains signify those who lead the highest life, the hills are the lower people. Now, she says that her beloved leaps on the hills][26] – that is, treads them down, disfigures them, allows them to be trodden down, to be quite atrociously ill-treated, shows on them his own footprints so that one can follow his track in them, to find how he was trodden down, as his footprints show. These are the high mountains, such as Mount Jove,[27] or the mountains of Armenia. The hills, which are lower, these, as the lady says herself, he leaps over and does not have as much faith in them because of their weakness – and they could not endure such treading down – and he leaps over them, avoids them and turns aside until they grow higher, from hills into mountains. His shadow, at least, goes over them and covers them while he leaps over them – that is, he lays on

a   My beloved cometh leaping upon the mountains, skipping over the hills (Canticles 2.8).

them some likeness of his life on earth, as though it were his shadow. But the mountains receive his own footprints and show in their life what his way of life was, how and where he went, in what abjectness, in what grief he led his life on earth. Of mountains like this the good Paul spoke and humbly said, *Deicimur set non perimus, mortificationem Iesu in corpore nostro circumferentes, ut et uita Iesu in corporibus nostris manifestetur* [a] – 'All grief,' he said, 'and all shame we endure. But it is our blessedness that we bear on our bodies the likeness of Christ's death, so that it may be made clear in us what his life on earth was like.' God knows, they who do this prove to us their love for Our Lord. Do you love me? – make it known, for love wants to show itself in outer acts. *Gregorius: Probatio dilectionis, exhibitio est operis.* [b] Be a thing never so hard, true love lightens it and softens it and sweetens it – *Amor omnia fatilia reddit.* [28c] What do men and women endure for false love and for foul love – and would endure more? And what greater wonder is there than that love sure and true and sweet beyond all other cannot master us so completely as does the love of sin? Nevertheless, I know a certain person who wears both together a heavy coat of mail and a hairshirt bound hard with iron round middle, thigh and arms with broad thick bands, so that the sweat caused by it is torment to endure. He fasts, keeps vigil, labours and, Christ knows, he complains that it does not pain him at all, and often asks me to teach him something with which he could torment his body. All that is bitter, for Our Lord's love, it all seems sweet to him. God knows, he still weeps to me in the most grief-stricken fashion and says God forgets him because he does not send him any great sickness. God knows, it is love that does this, for, as he often says to me, not for anything that God could do to treat him badly – though he were to cast him into hell with the lost – could he ever, it seems to him, love him the less: if any man should suspect any such thing of him, he is more confounded than a thief caught with his thievings. I know also a certain woman who endures little less. But we

a We are cast down but we perish not, bearing about in our body the mortification of Jesus, that the life also of Jesus may be made manifest in our bodies (2 Corinthians 4.9 10).
b Gregory: The proof of love is the manifestation of the deed (*Homilies on the Gospels* 2.30, 1).
c Love makes everything easy.

can only thank God for the strength he gives them and acknowledge humbly our weakness. Let us love their good, and in this way it is our own. For, as St Gregory says, of such great strength is love that it makes another's good, without labour, our own, as is said above.[29] Now it seems to me we have come on to the seventh part, which is entirely about love, which makes the heart pure.

PART SEVEN

The Pure Heart and the Love of Christ

St Paul testifies that all outer hardships – all mortifications of the flesh and bodily labours – all is as nothing in comparison with love, which purifies and brightens the heart: *Exercitio corporis ad modicum ualet; pietas autem ualet ad omnia*[a] – that is, 'Bodily effort is of little value, but a sweet and pure heart is good for all things.' *Si linguis hominum loquar et angelorum, et cetera; si tradidero corpus meum ita ut ardeam, et cetera; si distribuero omnes facultates meas in cibos pauperum, caritatem autem non habeam, nichil michi prodest*[b] – 'Though I knew,' he says, 'men's languages and angels', though I laid on my body all the torture and torment that a body might endure, though I gave to the poor all that I had, if I did not have love as well, for God and for all men in him and for him, all would be wasted.' For, as the holy abbot Moses[1] said, all the grief and all the hardship which we endure in the flesh, and all the good that we ever do, all such things are nothing except as tools with which to cultivate the heart. If the axe did not cut, or the spade dig, or the plough furrow, who would bother to keep them? Just as no one loves tools for themselves, but does so for the things that are done with them, so no suffering of the flesh is to be loved, except in so far as God may the sooner look that way with his grace and make the heart pure and bright of vision – which no one can have with a mixing in of vices or with earthly love of worldly things, for this mixing in so troubles the eyes of the heart that they cannot recognize God or rejoice at the

a Bodily exercise is profitable to little; but godliness is profitable to all things (1 Timothy 4.8).
b If I speak with the tongues of men and of angels, etc.; if I should deliver my body to be burned, etc.; if I should distribute all my goods to feed the poor, and have not love, it profiteth me nothing (1 Corinthians 13.1, 3).

sight of him. Two things, as St Bernard says,[2] make a pure heart – that you should do all that you do either for love of God alone or for the good of another and for his advantage. In all that you do, have one of these two intentions – or both together, for the latter comes in under the former. Always have a pure heart in this way, and do all that you want: have a troubled heart, and all affects you badly. *Omnia munda mundis; coinquinatis uero nichil est mundum – Apostolus. Item, Augustinus: Habe caritatem, et fac quicquid uis,*[3] *uoluntate uidelicet rationis.*[a] Therefore, my dear sisters, above all things busy yourselves about getting a pure heart. What is a pure heart? I have said it before: it is that you should not desire or love anything except God alone and those things, for God, that help you towards him. For God, I say, love them, and not for themselves (as with food or clothing, man or woman by whom you are benefited). For as St Augustine says, and he is speaking in this way to our God, *Minus te amat qui preter te aliquid amat quod non propter te amat*[b] – that is, 'Lord, less do they love you who love anything except you, unless they love it for you.' Purity of heart is love of God alone. In this is all the strength of all religious professions, the end of all orders. *Plenitudo legis est dilectio*[c] – 'Love fulfils the law,' says St Paul. *Quicquid precipitur, in sola caritate solidatur*[d] – 'All God's commandments,' as St Gregory says, 'are rooted in love.' Love alone is to be put in St Michael's balance.[4] Those who love most are to me most blessed, not those who lead the hardest life, for love outweighs it. Love is the steward of heaven because of her great generosity; for she holds back nothing, but gives all that she has, and herself also – otherwise God would have no regard for what she did.

God has earned our love in all sorts of ways. He has done much for us and promised us more. A great gift draws forth love; but he gave us all the world in Adam, our first father, and cast everything that is in the world, the animals and the birds, under our feet before we were

a All things are clean to the clean, but to them that are defiled nothing is clean – the Apostle (Titus 1.15). Again, Augustine: Have love and do whatever you wish – with a rational will, that is (see *On the Epistle of John* 7).

b He loves you the less who loves anything apart from you which he does not love on account of you (*Confessions* 10.29).

c Love is the fulfilling of the law (Romans 13.10).

d Whatever is commanded is established in love alone (Gregory, *Homilies on the Gospels* 2.27).

convicted of sin: *Omnia subiecisti sub pedibus eius, oues et boues uniuersas, insuper et pecora campi, uolucres celi, et pisces maris, qui perambulant semitas maris.*[a] And even now all that is, as has been said above, serves the good to the benefit of their souls: even the evil are served by earth, sea and sun.[5] He did still more – gave us not only his, but gave us himself, all in all. So high a gift was never given to such low wretches. *Apostolus: Christus dilexit ecclesiam et dedit semet ipsum pro ea*[b] – 'Christ,' St Paul says, 'loved his beloved so much that the price he gave for her was himself.' Now take good note, my dear sisters, of why he ought to be loved. First, like a man who woos, like a king who loved a poor lady of good family living in a country far off, he sent his envoys before him (they were the patriarchs and prophets of the Old Testament) with sealed letters. In the end he came himself and brought the Gospel like letters patent[6] and wrote in his own blood salutations to his beloved – a love-greeting to woo her with and win her love. There is a story to do with this, a parable with a hidden meaning.

A lady was closely besieged by her enemies, her land completely devastated and she utterly destitute inside a castle of earth.[7] A powerful king, though, had fallen so extravagantly in love with her that to woo her he sent her his envoys, one after another, often many of them at once, sent her much beautiful jewellery, assistance in provisions, the help of his fine army in holding her castle. She received it all as if she did not care, and so hard-hearted was she that he could never get any closer to winning her love. What more do you want? He came himself in the end, showed her his beautiful face (he being of all men the most beautiful to look at),[8] spoke so very sweetly and in words so joyful that they could raise the dead to life, worked many wonders and performed many mighty acts in her sight, showed her his power, told her about his kingdom, offered to make her queen of all he possessed. All this was no use. Was not this contempt an extraordinary thing? – for she was never worthy to be his maidservant. But because of his graciousness love had so overcome him that in the end he said this: 'Madam, you are

a Thou hast subjected all things under his feet, all sheep and oxen, moreover the beasts also of the fields, the birds of the air and the fishes of the sea that pass through the paths of the sea (Psalm 8.8–9).
b The Apostle: Christ loved the Church and delivered himself up for it (Ephesians 5.25).

under siege and your enemies are so strong that without my help there is no way for you to escape capture by them and prevent them putting you to a shameful death after all your misery. Because of my love for you I shall take up the fight myself and set you free from those who want to kill you. I know, though, for certain that in combat with them I shall be fatally wounded – and I desire that heartily, so as to win your heart. Now, then, I implore you, for the love that I declare to you, that you at least love me after the deed when I am dead, even though you would not when I was alive.' This king did exactly so: he set her free from all her enemies and was himself atrociously ill-treated and finally put to death. Through a miracle he arose, though, from death to life. Would not this lady indeed come of a wicked race, if she did not love him above anything else after this?

This king is Jesus, God's Son, who in just this way wooed our souls, which devils had besieged.[9] And he, like a noble wooer, after many messengers and many acts of kindness, came to prove his love and showed by his knightliness that he deserved to be loved, as knights once used to do. He entered the tournament and for the love of his beloved had every part of his shield, like a brave knight, pierced in battle. His shield, which covered his divinity, was his dear body, which was spread out on the cross, wide at the top, like a shield, where his arms were stretched out, and narrow at the bottom, where one foot (so many suppose) was placed on top of the other.[10] That this shield has no sides is to signify that his disciples, who ought to have stood by him and have been his sides, all ran away and left him like a stranger, as the Gospel says: *Relicto eo, omnes fugerunt.*[a] 'This shield is given us against all temptations,' as Jeremiah testifies: *Dabis scutum cordis, laborem tuum.*[b] Not only does this shield shield us from all evils, but it does still more – crowns us in heaven *scuto bone uoluntatis.*[c] 'Lord,' David says, 'you have crowned us with the shield of your good will' – 'shield of good will', he says, for he suffered willingly all that he suffered: *Isaias: Oblatus est quia uoluit.*[d]

'But, Lord,' you say, 'what for? Could he not have set us free with

a All leaving him, they fled (Matthew 26.56).
b Thou shalt give [them] a buckler of heart, thy labour (Lamentations 3.65).
c With a shield of good will (Psalm 5.13).
d Isaiah (53.7): He was offered because it was his own will.

less pain?' Oh yes, of course, very easily – but he did not want to. And why? So as to deprive us of any excuse we could offer him for not giving him our love, which he had bought so dear. You buy cheap what you do not much care for. He bought us with his heart's blood – never was payment dearer – so as to draw to himself our love, which cost him so painful a price. In a shield there are three things, the wood, the leather and the painting; just so in this shield – the wood of the cross, the leather of Christ's body, the painting of the red blood which coloured it so beautifully. After this, the third reason:[11] after the death of a brave knight, his shield is hung up in church in his memory; just so this shield – that is, the crucifix – is put in the church in a place where it can most easily be seen, so through it people may think of the knightliness of Jesus Christ on the cross. His beloved should look at it and see how he bought her love, let his shield be pierced, his side opened to show her his heart, to show her openly how fervently[12] he loved her, and to draw her heart to him.

Four chief loves are found in this world: between good friends, between man and woman, between a woman and her child, between body and soul. The love that Jesus Christ has for his beloved surpasses these four, goes beyond them all. Is he not reckoned a good friend, who lays a pledge with the Jews to get his friend out of debt? God Almighty laid himself as a pledge with the Jews[13] and put down his dear body to get his beloved out of the Jews' hands. Never did a friend do such a favour for his friend.

There is often much love between a man and a woman. But, even if she were married to him, she could become so wicked and she could for such a long time whore about with other men that, even if she wanted to come back again, he would not take any notice of her. Therefore Christ loves more, for even if the soul, his wife, whores about with the devil in capital sin for years on end, his mercy is always ready for her when she wants to come home and leave the devil. All this he says himself through Jeremiah: *Si dimiserit uir uxorem suam, et cetera. Tu autem fornicata es cum multis amatoribus. Tamen reuertere ad me, dicit Dominus.*[a]

---

a If a man put away his wife [, and she go from him and marry another man, shall he return to her any more? Shall not that woman be polluted and defiled?] But thou hast prostituted thyself to many lovers. Nevertheless, return to me, saith the Lord (Jeremiah 3.1).

Still he cries all day long, 'You who have acted so wickedly, turn and come back! – you will be welcome to me.' *Immo et occurrit prodigo uenienti*[a] – 'He even runs,' it says, 'to meet her as she comes back and throws his arms about her neck.' What greater mercy is there? Yet here is a still more joyful wonder. However many deadly sins his beloved may have whored about with, as soon as she comes to him again, he makes her a new virgin. For, as St Augustine says, so great is the difference between God's approach and a man's to a woman that a man's approach makes a woman out of a virgin and God makes a virgin out of a woman.[14] *Restituit, inquit Job, in integrum.*[b] Good works and true faith – these two things are virginity in the soul.

Now on the third love. A child who had an illness of such a kind that it had to have a bath of blood[15] before it could be cured, the mother who was willing to make this bath for it would love it a great deal. This Our Lord did for us who were so sick with sin and so sullied with it that nothing could heal us or cleanse us except his blood alone – for so he wanted it. His love makes us a bath of it – may he be blessed for ever. He prepared three baths for his dear beloved to wash herself in so white and so beautiful that she would be worthy of his clean embraces. The first bath is baptism; the second is tears, inner or outer, if after the first bath she sullies herself; the third bath is Jesus Christ's blood,[16] which sanctifies both the others, as St John says in the Apocalypse: *Qui dilexit nos et lauit nos in sanguine suo.*[c] That he loves us more than any mother does her child he says himself through Isaiah: *Nunquid potest mater obliuisci filii uteri sui? Et si illa obliuiscatur, ego non obliuiscar tui*[d] – 'May a mother,' he says, 'forget her child? And even if she does, I can never forget you.' And he tells the reason after: *In manibus meis descripsi te*[e] – 'I have,' he says, 'painted you in my hands.' He did this with red blood on the cross. One knots one's girdle to remind oneself of something, but Our Lord, because he did not wish ever to forget us, put pierce-marks, to remind him of us, in both his hands.

a He even runs to meet the prodigal as he comes (see Luke 15.20).
b He makes whole again, says Job (12.23).
c Who hath loved us and washed us from our sins in his own blood (Apocalypse 1.5).
d Can a mother forget the son of her womb? And if she should forget, yet will not I forget thee (Isaiah 49.15).
e I have graven thee in my hands (Isaiah 49.16).

Now the fourth love. The soul loves the body very much indeed, and that is evident at their separation – for dear friends are sorry when they have to separate. But Our Lord willingly separated his soul from his body so as to join ours both together, world without end, in the joy of heaven. Thus, look, Jesus Christ's love for his dear wife – that is, Holy Church, or the pure soul[17] – passes and overcomes all the four greatest loves that are found on earth. With all of this love he still woos her in this way:

'Your love,' he says, 'either it is to be given outright, or it is to be sold, or it is to be seized and taken by force. If it is to be given, where might you bestow it better than upon me? Am I not the most beautiful of things? Am I not the richest of kings? Am I not the highest born? Am I not the wisest of the wise? Am I not the most courteous of men? Am I not the most generous of things? For so it is said of a liberal man that he has his hands pierced, as mine are. Am I not the sweetest and most fragrant of all things? Thus you can find in me all the reasons why love ought to be given, especially if you love chaste purity – for no one may love me unless she preserves that. But it is threefold: in widowhood, in wifehood, in maidenhood, the highest.[18] If your love is not to be given, but you want it to be bought – to be bought? how? Either with love or with something else. Love is well sold for love, and it ought to be sold like this and for nothing else. If yours is to be sold like this, I have bought it with a love above all others, for of the four greatest loves, I have shown towards you the greatest of them all. If you say that you do not want to put such a low price on it but want still more, state what it is to be. Put a price on your love. You'll not say so much that I don't want to give more. Do you want castles, kingdoms? Do you want to rule all the world? I want to do better by you – make you, with all this, queen of the kingdom of heaven. You shall yourself be seven times brighter than the sun. No evil shall come near you, no joy shall be lacking to you. All your will shall be done in heaven and also in earth – yes, and even in hell.[19] Never shall heart think of such happiness that I don't want to give for your love immeasurably, incomparably, infinitely more. All the wealth of Croesus,[20] who was the richest of kings; the radiant beauty of Absalom,[21] who as often as his hair was cut sold the clippings – the hair which he cut off – for two hundred shekels of silver weighed out; the swiftness of Asahel,[22] who ran races against deer; the strength of Samson, who killed a thousand of his foes all on a single occasion, and on his own without a friend;[23] the generosity of Caesar;[24] the fame of Alexander;[25] the health of Moses[26] – wouldn't a man give everything he owned for one of these? And all of them together in comparison to my person aren't worth a needle. If you're so obstinate and so out of your mind that you, for no loss, refuse such a gain, with all kinds of happiness – look, I hold here a cruel sword over your head to part your life and your soul and sink them both into the fire, to be the devil's whore shamefully and sorrowfully, world without end. Answer now and guard yourself, if you can, against me, or grant me your love, which I long for so much – not for my but for your great benefit.'

Thus, look, Our Lord woos. Is she not too hard-hearted, whom a wooer like this cannot turn to his love, if she thinks carefully about these three things: what he is and what she is, and how great is the love of one so high as he is for one so low as she is? Therefore the Psalmist says, *Non est qui se abscondat a calore eius*[a] – 'There is no one who can hide away so that she doesn't have to love him.' The true sun was at the third hour mounted up on high on the high cross for this, to spread hot beams of love everywhere. So driven was he – and is until this day – to kindle his love and his beloved's heart, and he says in the Gospel, *Ignem ueni mittere in terram, et quid uolo nisi ut ardeat?*[b] – 'I came to bring,' he says, 'fire into the earth' – that is, burning love into earthly hearts – 'and what else do I long for, but that it should blaze?' Lukewarm love is hateful to him, as he says through St John in the Apocalypse: *Vtinam frigidus esses aut calidus; set quia tepidus es incipiam te euomere de ore meo*[c] – 'I wish,' he says to his beloved, 'that you were in loving me either altogether cold or entirely hot, but because you are, as it were, lukewarm, in between the two, neither hot nor cold, you make me feel sick, and I will spew you out, unless you become hotter.'

Now you have heard, my dear sisters, how and why God is to be loved very much. To kindle yourselves well, gather wood for it with

a There is no one that can hide himself from his heat (Psalm 18.7).

b I am come to cast fire on the earth, and what will I but that it be kindled? (Luke 12.49).

c I would thou wert cold or hot; but because thou art lukewarm I will begin to vomit thee out of my mouth (Apocalypse 3.15–16).

the poor woman of Sarepta, the city which means kindling. *En, inquit, colligo duo ligna: Regum iii*[a] – 'Lord,' she said to Elijah the holy prophet, 'look, I am gathering two pieces of wood.' These two pieces of wood signify the one piece that stood upright and the other that went crosswise on the dear cross. From these two pieces of wood you must kindle a fire of love within your heart. Look at them often. Think whether you ought not readily to love the king of joy, who so spreads out his arms towards you and bows down his head as if to offer a kiss. I say this with certainty: if the true Elijah – that is, God Almighty finds you busily gathering these two pieces of wood, he will take lodgings with you and multiply in you his precious grace, as Elijah did her livelihood when he lodged with her whom he found gathering the two pieces of wood in Sarepta.

Greek fire[27] is made from a red man's blood[28] and nothing can quench it, so they say, except urine and sand and vinegar. This Greek fire is the love of Jesus Our Lord, and you must make it from a red man's blood – that is, Jesus Christ, reddened with his own blood on the dear cross – and he was naturally very red also, so it is thought.[29] This blood, shed for you on the two pieces of wood mentioned before, will make you Sareptans – that is, kindled with this Greek fire, so that, as Solomon says, no waters – that is, worldly tribulations – no temptations, either inner or outer, can quench this love. Now in the end, then, you have only to guard yourselves carefully against everything that quenches it, that is, urine and sand and vinegar, as I said before. Urine is the stench of sin. On sand no good thing grows, and it signifies idleness. Idleness cools and quenches this fire. Bestir yourselves vigorously in good works always, and that will heat you and kindle this fire against the burning of sin; for just as one nail drives out another,[30] so the burning of God's love drives the burning of foul love out of the heart. The third thing is vinegar – that is, a heart sour with spite or with envy. Understand what is being said here. When the spiteful Jews offered to Our Lord this sour present on the cross, then he said that pitiful saying: *Consumatum est.*[b] 'Never,' he said, 'before now was I fully tormented' – not by the vinegar, but by their envious spite which the

---

a   Behold, she said, I am gathering two sticks: 3 Kings (17.12).
b   It is finished (John 19.30).

vinegar they made him drink signified; and that is as though a man had laboured long and in the end missed, after long labour, his reward. Just so Our Lord, for more than thirty-two years, toiled in pursuit of their love, and for all his heavy labour wanted nothing except love as wages. But at the end of his life, which was, as it were, in the evening when workmen are paid their day's wages, look how they paid him, instead of a cordial of honey love, vinegar of sour envy and gall of bitter spite. 'O,' said Our Lord then, *'consumatum est'* – 'All my labour on earth, all my torment on the cross, does not grieve me or distress me at all in comparison with this – that I should give all that I have done to this end. This vinegar that you offer me, these sour wages, complete my torment.' This vinegar of sour heart and bitter thought above every other thing quenches Greek fire – that is, the love of Our Lord – and whoever bears it in her breast towards a woman or a man is a partner of the Jews. She offers God this vinegar and completes, as regards herself, Jesus's pain on the cross. People throw Greek fire on their foes and so overcome them. You must do likewise when God raises up for you from some foe any strife. How you must throw it, Solomon teaches: *Si esurierit inimicus tuus, ciba illum; si sitierit, potum da illi: sic enim carbones ardentes congeres super caput eius*[a] – that is, 'If your foe is hungry, feed him, for his thirst give him drink' – which is to be taken as meaning, if he has a hunger or thirst for your harm, give him the food of your prayers that God may have mercy on him; give him the drink of tears, weep for his sins. 'In this way you will,' says Solomon, 'heap on his head burning coals' – that is to say, in this way you will kindle his heart to love you, for the heart, in Holy Writ, is understood by 'head'. God will speak like this at the Judgement: 'Why did you love that man or that woman?' 'Sir, they loved me.' 'Yes,' he will say, 'you paid back what you owed. There is nothing much for me to pay you back here.' If you could answer, 'They caused me all kinds of suffering and I owed them no love, and, sir, I loved them for love of you' – that love he owes you, for it was given him, and he will pay it you back.

Urine, as I said, which quenches Greek fire, is the stinking love of the flesh, which quenches spiritual love, which Greek fire signifies. On

a If thy enemy be hungry, give him to eat; if he thirst, give him to drink: for thus thou shalt heap hot coals upon his head (Proverbs 25.21–2; see also Romans 12.20).

earth what flesh was as sweet and as holy as Jesus Christ's flesh was? And, nevertheless, he said to his disciples, *Nisi ego abiero, Paraclitus non veniet ad uos*[a] – that is, 'Unless I part from you, the Holy Ghost – that is, my love and my Father's – cannot come to you; but when I am gone from you I will send him to you.' When Jesus Christ's own disciples, while they loved him in the flesh when he was near them, forwent the sweetness of the Holy Ghost and could not have both together, judge for yourselves – is he not mad (or she) who loves too much her own flesh, or any man in the flesh, so that she longs too much to see him or hear him? And let it never seem a wonder if she should lack the Holy Ghost's comfort. Now let everyone choose which of these two things – earthly consolation and heavenly – she will hold on to; for she must let the other go. For if there is a mixing of the two, she cannot any more have purity of heart, which is, as we said before, the goodness and the strength of all religious professions and in each order. Love makes her pure, peaceful and clean. Love has a power beyond all others, for all that she touches, she turns it all to her and makes it all her own: *Quemcumque locum calcauerit pes uester, pes videlicet amoris, uester erit.*[b] Many people would buy at a high price a thing of such a kind that everything they touched with it would be their own. And did it not say a long way above that simply by loving the good that is in another, with the touching of your love, without other labour, you make his good your own good, as St Gregory testifies?[31] Look now how much good the envious lose. Stretch your love to Jesus Christ and you have won him. Touch him with as much love as you have at some time felt for some person, and he is yours to do with all you wish. But who loves a thing and lets it go for less than it is worth? Is not God incomparably better than all that is in the world? Charity is the cherishing[32] of a loved and precious thing. He makes God unprecious and altogether too unvalued who lets go of his love for any worldly thing – for nothing can love rightly, but he alone. So exceedingly does he love love that he makes her his equal; still more I dare to say – he makes her his master and does all that she commands as though he had to. Can I prove this? Yes, certainly, I can – by his own words. For he speaks like this to Moses,

a If I go not, the Paraclete will not come to you (John 16.7).
b Every place that your foot shall tread upon – the foot, that is, of love – shall be yours (Deuteronomy 11.24; explanation between dashes added by author).

who of all men loved him the most: *In Numeri: Dimisi iuxta uerbum tuum. Non dicit preces*[a] – 'I had,' he said, 'meant to wreak my wrath on this people. But you say I must not – let what you say be fulfilled.' They say that love binds: certainly love binds Our Lord, so that he cannot do anything except with love's leave.[33] Now a proof of this, for it seems a wonder. *Ysaias: Domine, non est qui consurgat et teneat te*[b] – 'Lord, you will strike,' says Isaiah. 'Alas, well you may; there is no one to hold you', as though he said, 'If anyone loved you right he could hold you and prevent you from striking.' *In Genesy, ad Loth: Festina, et cetera. Non potero ibi quicquam facere, donec egressus fueris illinc*[c] – that is, when Our Lord wanted to sink Sodom, where his friend Lot was, 'Hurry away,' he said, 'for while you are among them, I cannot do anything to them.' Was not this being bound by love? What more do you want? Love is his chamberlain, his counsellor, his wife, from whom he cannot conceal anything but tells all that he thinks. *In Genesy: Num celare potero Abraham que gesturus sum?*[d] – 'Can I,' said Our Lord, 'conceal from Abraham the thing that I think to do? No, not at all.' Now he who speaks like this and acts like this to all who fervently trust and love him knows how to love. The joy which he is preparing for them, as it is incomparable with all worldly joys, so it is also indescribable by worldly tongues. *Ysaias: Oculus non uidit, Deus, absque te que preparasti diligentibus te. Apostolus: Oculus non uidit, nec auris audiuit, et cetera.*[e] You have something written elsewhere about these joys.[34] This love is the rule that rules the heart.[35] *Confitebor tibi in directione, id est, in regulatione cordis. Exprobratio malorum: generatio que non direxit cor suum.*[f] This is the lady rule:[36] all the others serve her, and the command to

---

a In Numbers: I have forgiven according to thy word (14.20). He did not say 'prayers'.

b Isaiah (64.7): Lord, there is none that riseth up and taketh hold of thee.

c In Genesis (19.22) to Lot: Hurry, etc. I cannot do anything till thou go out from there.

d In Genesis (18.17): Can I hide from Abraham what I am about to do?

e Isaiah (64.4): The eye hath not seen, God, besides thee what things thou hast prepared for them that love thee. The Apostle: The eye hath not seen, nor the ear heard, etc. (1 Corinthians 2.9).

f I will praise thee with uprightness of heart (Psalm 118.7), that is, in the ruling of the heart. The reproach of the wicked: a generation that set not their heart aright (Psalm 77.8).

love them is made only for her sake. I consider them of little significance as long as this one is lovingly kept. You have them in brief, however, in the eighth part.

PART EIGHT
The Outer Rule

I said before at the beginning that you should not in any way as under a vow promise to keep any of the outer rules.[1] I say the same again. And I do not write them for anyone except you alone. I say this so that other anchoresses should not say that I am, in my presumption, making them a new rule. And I do not ask that they should keep them – but you also may change these whenever you wish for better ones. In comparison with the things before they have little significance.

Of sight and of speech and of the other senses, enough has been said. Now this last part, as I promised at the beginning,[2] is divided up and separated into seven small sections.

One cares less about a thing that one has often. Therefore you must only receive communion, as our brothers do,[3] fifteen times a year: (i) Midwinter Day; (ii) Twelfth Day; (iii) Candlemas Day; (iv) a Sunday midway between that and Easter, or Our Lady's Day, if it is near the Sunday, because of its dignity; (v) Easter Day; (vi) the third Sunday after that; (vii) Holy Thursday; (viii) Whit Sunday; (ix) Midsummer Day; (x) St Mary Magdalene's Day; (xi) the Assumption; (xii) the Nativity; (xiii) St Michael's Day; (xiv) All Saints' Day; (xv) St Andrew's Day.[4] In preparation for all these make a clean confession and receive disciplines[5] – never, though, from anyone but yourself – and forgo your pittance[6] for one day. If anything goes wrong so that you do not receive communion at these set times, let it be the next Sunday or if the following time is near, wait till then.

You must eat twice each day from Easter until Holy Cross Day (the later one, which is in harvest)[7] except on Fridays, Ember Days, Rogation Days and vigils.[8] On those days and in Advent you must not eat white food[9] unless need makes you. The other half-year you must fast all the time except Sundays only, when you are healthy and completely strong; but the rule does not apply to the sick or those who have been let blood.

You must not eat meat or fat[10] except on account of a severe illness – or if someone is very feeble. Eat vegetable stew contentedly and accustom yourselves to little drink. None the less, dear sisters, it has often seemed to me that your food and your drink are less than I would wish. Do not fast on any day on bread and water unless you have leave.

Some anchoresses take their meals with their guests outside. That is too much friendliness; for of all orders it is most unnatural to and most against the order of an anchoress, who is dead to the world. One has often heard that the dead have spoken with the living, but that they have eaten with the living I have never yet found.

Do not offer hospitality and do not encourage unknown down-and-outs to come to the gate: though there were no other harm except their immoderate noise, it would sometimes hinder heavenly thoughts. It is not right for an anchoress to be generous with another person's charity. Would not a beggar who invited people to a feast be laughed loudly to scorn? Mary and Martha were sisters together, but their ways of life split apart.[11] You anchoresses have set yourselves to Mary's part, which Our Lord himself praised: *Maria optimam partem elegit*[a] – 'Martha, Martha,' he said, 'you are greatly troubled. Mary has chosen better and nothing shall take her part away from her.' To be a housewife is Martha's part. Mary's part is quietness and peace from all the world's noise, so that nothing may hinder her from hearing the voice of God. And look what God says – that nothing shall take this part away from you. Martha has her job: let her be. You should sit with Mary stone-still at God's feet and listen to him alone. Martha's job is to feed and clothe the poor as the lady of a house does. Mary ought not to be at all concerned with this. If anyone reproaches her, God himself defends her on all occasions, as Holy Writ testifies: *Contra Symonem: Duo debitores, et cetera; contra Martham: Maria optimam partem, et cetera; contra Apostolos, murmurantes, vt quid perditio hec? Bonum, inquit, opus, et cetera.*[b] Again, an

---

a   Mary hath chosen the best part (Luke 10.42).
b   Against Simon: [A certain creditor had] two debtors, etc. (Luke 7.36ff.); against Martha: Mary [has chosen] the best part, etc. (Luke 10.42ff.); against the Apostles, who were complaining, 'To what purpose is this waste?' he said '[She hath wrought] a good work [upon me]', etc. (Matthew 26.8ff.).

anchoress should only take in moderation what is necessary to her, so what can she be generous with? She must live on charity as moderately as ever she can and not gather in order to give – she is not a housewife, but a church anchoress. If she can spare any poor scraps, let her send them quite secretly out of her house. Under the semblance of good, sin is often hidden. And how are these rich anchoresses who till fields or have fixed incomes going to give charity secretly to their poor neighbours? Let her not want to have a reputation as a generous anchoress, nor, so as to give much, be any greedier to have more. Whenever greediness is the root of such gathering, all the boughs that grow from it are bitter with its bitterness. To beg a thing so as to give it away is not an anchoress's right. From an anchoress's courtesy, from an anchoress's generosity have often come sin and shame in the end.

As for the women and children and particularly the anchoress's maids who come and have taken trouble for you, even if you have to do without it yourself, or beg, or borrow, behave charitably and give them something to eat and invite them to stay.

Let no man eat in your presence unless by your director's leave – either general or special (general in the case of Friars Preacher and Friars Minor, special in the case of all others).[12] Do not invite anyone else to eat or drink unless also with his leave. 'Pleasy!' they say, 'is easy.'[13] I do not at all want you to be reputed gracious anchoresses because of such invitations. Always, though, take the utmost care that no one leaves you scandalized because of your bad manners.[14]

Take from good people all that you need, but look out that you do not get a name as acquisitive anchoresses. From someone you mistrust because of his foolish manner or empty talk do not take anything, great or small. Need must drive you to beg for anything; however, humbly make known to good men and women your difficulties.[15]

You, my dear sisters, unless need drives you and your director advises, must not keep any animal except a cat. An anchoress who has livestock seems more like a housewife, as Martha was, and she cannot easily be Mary, Martha's sister, with serenity of heart, because then she has to think about the cow's fodder and the herdsman's pay, coax the hayward,[16] curse him when he impounds the cow and pay the damages even so. It is a hateful thing, Christ knows, when complaints are made in the village about an anchoress's livestock. So, then, if anyone has of necessity to have a cow, she should make sure that it does not bother or harm anyone and that her thoughts are not at all fixed on it An anchoress ought not to have anything that draws her heart outwards.

Do not do any trading. An anchoress who is a tradeswoman – who buys so as to sell for a profit – trades her soul to the tradesman of hell. Things, though, that she makes she may, on her director's advice, sell to meet her needs: holy people formerly have lived by their hands.[17]

Do not, dear daughters, keep other people's things in your house – not livestock, or clothes, or boxes, or charters; no tallies or indentures, not the church vestments or the chalices, unless need or force makes you, or great fear. From such keeping much evil has often come about.

Do not let any man sleep within your walls.

If some very great necessity means that your house is broken open, all the time it is broken open have in it with you a woman of pure life, day and night.

Because men do not see you, nor you them, it does not matter whether your clothes are white or black as long as they are plain, warm and well made – skins well cured; and have as many as you need for your bed and to wear.

Next to the skin no one must wear linen clothing unless it be of hard and coarse flax. Whoever wants may have a stamin;[18] whoever wants may do without.

You must sleep in a robe and with a belt on – loosely enough, though, for you to be able to put your hands under it. Let no one put on any kind of belt unless by her confessor's leave, nor wear any iron, or hair, or hedgehog skins, nor beat herself with these or with a leaded scourge, nor draw blood from herself with holly or brambles, without her confessor's leave; let her not sting herself with nettles anywhere, nor beat herself on her front, nor do any cutting, nor take at one time over-harsh disciplines to extinguish temptations. Do not, as a cure for natural illnesses, have faith in or try any unnatural treatment unless your director gives permission, in case you get worse.

Let your shoes in winter be soft, roomy and warm; in summer you have leave to walk and sit barefoot, or to wear light shoes.

Let anyone who wishes lie down in stockings without feet. Do not sleep with shoes on, or anywhere except in bed. Some women are ready enough to wear breeches of haircloth very well knotted on, the legs very tightly laced down to the feet. But always best is the sweet and fragrant heart: I would rather you bore a harsh remark well than a harsh hairshirt.

If you can do without wimples[19] and are quite willing to, wear warm caps and over them white or black veils. Some anchoresses sin in their wimpling no less than ladies. But, however, someone says that it is naturally proper for every woman to wear a wimple. No. Holy Writ does not mention 'wimple' or 'head-cloth' either, but only 'covering': *Ad Corinthios: Mulier uelet caput suum*[a] – 'A woman,' says the Apostle, 'must cover her head.' 'Cover', he says, not 'wimple'. She must cover her shame as sinful Eve's daughter in remembrance of the sin which destroyed us all at the beginning, and not turn the covering into adornment and finery. Again, the Apostle wishes that a woman should cover her face as well in church in case evil thoughts should arise through her being seen. *Et hoc est propter angelos.*[20][b] Why, then, you church anchoress, do you wear a wimple and uncover your face to the eye of a man? The Apostle is speaking against you who see men, if you do not conceal yourself. But if anything covers your face from a man's eye, be it a wall, be it a cloth in a well-closed window, an anchoress can well do without other wimpling. The Apostle is speaking against you who act like this, not against the others whom their own wall covers from every man's sight. Often weak thoughts are awakened from this – and sometimes deeds. Whoever wants to be seen, it is no surprise if she adorn herself, but in God's eyes she is more lovely who is for love of him unadorned outside.

Do not have a ring or a brooch or a girdle with plates, or gloves or any such thing which it is not right for you to have. In hot summer you may wear a light gown.

The plainer the things you make, the better I like it.

Do not make any purses to gain friends with except for those people your director gives you leave for, or caps or bandages of silk or girdles without leave. But cut out and sew and mend church vestments and

a To the Corinthians: Let a woman cover her head (1 Corinthians 11.6).
b And this is because of the angels (1 Corinthians 11.10).

poor people's clothes. You must not give anything of this sort without your confessor's leave, any more than accept what you do not tell him about before, as with other things – relations and friends   how often you should receive them, how long you should have them to stay. It is not proper for an anchoress to be soft about relations. There was a man of religion, and his brother in the flesh came to him for help and he directed him to his third brother, who was dead and buried. He answered, surprised. 'No,' he said, 'isn't he dead?' 'And I,' said the holy man, 'am spiritually dead. Let no friend in the flesh ask me for consolation in the flesh.'[21] Ladies in the world can perfectly well make amices and parures;[22] and if you make them, do not make a show about it. Vainglory poisons all virtues and all good works. None of you must do sieve-work,[23] for love or for payment. I do not forbid silk borders, if someone is trimming a surplice or an alb. She should not do other trimmings, especially over-ornate ones, except out of great need.

Help yourselves with your own labour, as far as ever you can, to clothe and feed yourselves, if need be – and those who serve you.

As St Jerome teaches,[24] do not ever be long or lightly altogether idle, not doing anything; for immediately the fiend offers his work to her who does not labour at God's work and whispers to her at once. For while he sees her busy, he thinks like this, 'I'd come near her now for nothing; she cannot pay attention to listen to my lore.' From idleness there awakes much temptation of the flesh: *Iniquitas Sodome saturitas panis et ocium* [a] – that is, 'Sodom's wickedness came from idleness and a full stomach.' Iron that lies still soon gathers rust; water that does not move quickly stinks.[25]

An anchoress must not degenerate into a school-teacher or turn the anchor-house into a children's school. Her maid may teach another maid for whom it would be dangerous to take lessons with men or with boys, but an anchoress ought only to attend to God alone, though on her director's advice she may guide and help someone to learn.

You must not send letters or receive letters or write[26] without leave.

You must be cropped or, if you want, shaved four times a year, to lighten your head (let anyone who prefers it so have their hair trimmed) and be let blood as often, and if there is need, more often. Anyone who

---

a   The iniquity of Sodom [was] fullness of bread and idleness (Ezekiel 16.49).

can do without, I am ready to allow it. When you have just been let blood, you shall do nothing that troubles you for three days, but talk to your maids and entertain one another with virtuous stories. You may do so often when things seem heavy to you, or you are upset or ill for some worldly thing – though every worldly consolation is worthless to an anchoress.

Look after yourself so sensibly during your blood-letting and take things so easily that you can long afterwards labour the more manfully in God's service – and also when you feel ill at all. It is great stupidity to lose for the sake of one day ten or twelve.

Wash yourself wherever there is need as often as you want, and your things, too – filth was never dear to God, though poverty and plainness are pleasing.

Always understand about all these things that none is a command or a prohibition, being of the outer rule, which is of little significance provided that the inner rule is well kept, as I said at the beginning.[27] This can be changed wherever any need or any reason requires it, according as she best may serve the lady rule as her humble handmaiden – but, assuredly, the lady comes to grief without her.

An anchoress who does not have her food to hand needs two women, one to stay at home all the time, another to go out when need presses; and this one should be very plainly dressed without any adornment – either a little handmaiden or else of a fair age. As she goes on her way she should chant her prayers and not hold conversations with men or with women and neither sit nor stand, except the least that ever she may, before coming home. She should go nowhere else, except where she is sent, without leave; and let her not eat or drink when out. Let the other be inside all the time and not go outside the gates without leave. Let both be obedient to their mistress in all things – except in sin alone. Let them have nothing which she does not know about, nor accept anything, nor give anything either without her leave. Let them not allow any man in and let the younger not speak with any man without leave, and let her not go out of the village without a reliable companion, if that is possible, nor spend the night out. If she cannot read, let her say her hours with *Pater nosters* and with *Aues* and do what she is told without grumbling. Let her always have her ears open to hear her mistress. Let neither of these women take from her mistress or bring to her any idle stories or items of news, nor between themselves sing or speak any worldly talk, nor laugh or fool around so that any man that sees it might interpret it in a bad way. Above all things, let them hate lies and wicked words. Let their hair be cut short, their head-cloths come low down. Let each sleep by herself. Let their necklines be stitched up high without a brooch. Let no man see them cloakless or bare-headed. Let them keep their eyes down. They shall not kiss any man, neither friend nor relation, nor embrace out of friendship, nor wash their heads, nor look fixedly at any man, nor tussle or fool around with them. Let their clothes be of such a shape and all their attire such that it is clear to what life they have turned. Let them look carefully to their behaviour, so that none may reproach them, in the house and out of the house. Let them in all ways avoid angering their mistress and as often as they do it, before they eat or drink, let them make their *Venie*[a] down on their knees before her and say *Mea culpa*[b] and accept the penance that she lays upon them, bowing low to her. Let the anchoress after that never again rebuke that fault, however angry she may be – unless she falls into the same again soon – but put it entirely out of her heart. If any strife arises between the women, let the anchoress make them make their *Venie* to one another on their knees on the ground and let them raise one another up and kiss one another finally; and let the anchoress lay on each some penance – more on the one who was more greatly at fault. This is a thing, let them well know, most dear to God – concord and unity – and most hateful to the fiend; and so he is always bent on raising up some hatred. Now the traitor sees well that when a fire is well ablaze and one wants it to go out one separates the brands – and he does just the same. Love is Jesus Christ's fire, which he wants to blaze always in your heart, and the devil blows so as to puff it out. When his blowing gains nothing, he brings up some evil remark or some other trifle through which they recoil one from another, and the Holy Ghost's fire is quenched when the brands are separated through anger. Therefore let them hold fast together in love, and let it be nothing to them when the fiend blows, especially if many are joined together and well kindled with love. Though the anchoress may lay

a Pardons.
b My fault.

penance on her maids for open faults, let them none the less confess to the priest when there is need – but always, though, with leave.

If they do not know the meal graces, let them say instead of them *Pater noster* before and *Aue Maria*, and after the meal also, and a *Credo*,[a] too, and lastly say this: 'Father, Son and Holy Ghost, Almighty God, give our mistress his grace always more and more and grant her, and us as well, to have a good end. Reward all those that do us good and have mercy on the souls of those who have done us good – their souls and all Christian souls.'

Between meals let them not nibble – neither fruit nor anything else – nor drink without leave; and let leave be easily got in all that is not sin. At the meal no speaking, or little and that softly. Also, after the anchoress's Compline until Prime,[28] let them not do or say anything through which her silence might be disturbed.

No anchoress's servant ought by right to ask set wages, except food and clothing which she can get by with and God's mercy. Let no one mistrust God, whatever may happen to the anchoress, and think that he will fail her. The maids outside, if they serve the anchoress just as they ought, their wages will be the high joy of heaven. Whoever has the eye of hope on such high wages will gladly serve and endure all misery and all trouble. With ease and comfort one does not buy bliss.

You anchoresses ought to read this last section to your women once each week until they know it. And it is very necessary that you pay much attention to them, for you can be greatly benefited by them and greatly harmed. In addition, if they sin through your heedlessness, you will be called to account for that before the High Judge. And therefore, as is very necessary for you and still more for them, diligently teach them to keep their rule, both for you and for themselves – gently and lovingly, for such ought women's teaching to be: loving and gentle and seldom stern. It is right that they should fear and love you both, and also that there should be more of love than of fear. Then things will go well. Oil and wine both must be poured into wounds according to God's teaching, but more of soothing oil than of biting wine; that is, more of gentle words than of cutting, for of that comes the best of

a I believe.

things   that is, love-dread. Easily and sweetly forgive them their faults when they acknowledge them and promise to make amends.

As far as you can, in food and in clothes and in other things that the need of the flesh requires, be generous towards them, though you be strict and hard on yourselves. He acts like this who blows well   turns the narrow end of the horn to his own mouth and the wide one outwards. And you should do likewise, as you want your prayers to trumpet well and resound in Our Lord's ears, not only to your own but to all people's salvation – as Our Lord grant, through the grace that is his, that it may be so. Amen.

When your sisters' maids come to you to comfort you, come to them at the window in the morning and the afternoon once or twice and go back soon to your spiritual occupation; and do not before Compline sit beyond the right time on their account, so that their coming may be no loss to your religious observance, but spiritual profit. If anything is said which might hurt feelings, it should not be carried away or brought to another anchoress who is easily hurt. It must be told to him who sees to all of them. Two nights is enough for anyone to stay, and that should very seldom be. Do not break silence at the meal for them, nor for blood-letting, unless some great good or need makes you. Let the anchoress and her maid not play worldly games at the window nor ticky-touch[29] together, for, as St Bernard says,[30] a thing unworthy of every spiritual person is every such fleshly solace   and especially of the anchoress   and it takes away the spiritual – that is, supreme mirth without measure – and that is a bad exchange, as is said above.

Read from this book each day, when you are at leisure, less or more. I hope that, if you read it often, it will be very profitable to you through God's great grace – otherwise I have wasted the long time I spent on it. I would rather, God knows, start off for Rome than begin to do it again. If you find that you do as you read, thank God earnestly. If you do not do it, pray for God's mercy and in future work at keeping it better according to your strength.

May Father, Son and Holy Ghost, one Almighty God, keep you under his watch. May he gladden you and comfort you, my dear sisters, and, for all that you suffer and endure for him, may he give you nothing less than himself completely. May he be exalted from world into world always, eternally. Amen.

As often as you have read anything in this, greet the Lady with an *Aue*, for him who laboured at it. I am moderate enough in asking so little! [31]

Explicit. [a]

Think about your scribe in your prayers, sometimes, no matter how little. It turns to your good that you pray for others.

i The end.

Notes

Introduction

1. *The Ancren Riwle*, ed. James Morton, Camden Society 57 (London, 1853), p. 1. The title *Ancrene Riwle* (Rule for Anchoresses) is a modern invention. The one medieval title for any of the versions of this work is *Ancrene Wisse*, a title found only in the Corpus Christi College Cambridge manuscript. It has come to be conventional to distinguish this Corpus version from other versions of the work by the title *Ancrene Wisse*, but I use *Ancrene Wisse* of the work in any of its versions.

2. The Corpus text here translated is a good copy of what seems to be a definitive authorial revision of previous versions. On this see E. J. Dobson, 'The Affiliations of the Manuscripts of *Ancrene Wisse*', *English and Medieval Studies presented to J. R. R. Tolkien*, ed. Norman Davis and C. L. Wrenn (London, 1962), pp. 128–63. For other editions and translations see Further Reading.

3. *Ancrene Wisse: Parts Six and Seven*, ed. Geoffrey Shepherd (London, 1959; rev. Exeter, 1985), p. ix.

4. Shepherd, *op. cit.*, p. ix.

5. A monk, however, might take up a life of enclosure.

6. See p. 70. In *The Origins of Ancrene Wisse* (Oxford, 1976) E. J. Dobson suggests that *Ancrene Wisse* moves between imagining the situation of a typical anchoress with a cell of her own and thinking in terms of the actual establishment of the three sisters for whom it was originally produced, an establishment in which, in Dobson's view, they

lived together (pp. 252–5). This view contrasts with that of Robert W. Ackerman and Roger Dahood, as expressed in their edition of part of *Ancrene Wisse, Ancrene Riwle: Introduction and Part 1* (Binghamton, N.Y., 1984), who envisage (p. 16) the sisters living in three separate cells.

7. See R. M. Clay, *The Hermits and Anchorites of England* (London, 1914), pp. 82–4. This work is the source of much of the information presented in the Introduction. For other works on anchorites in medieval England see Further Reading.

8. See Ackerman and Dahood, *op. cit.*, pp. 36ff. This work gives very full information on the devotions.

9. Shepherd, *op. cit.*, p. ix.

10. For this, see Ann K. Warren, *Anchorites and their Patrons in Medieval England* (Los Angeles and Berkeley, 1985).

11. See, for instance, Matthew 6.16–18 for fasting and Matthew 26.41 for keeping vigil.

12. See below, p. 54.

13. For rites of enclosure, see, for example, F. D. Darwin, *The English Mediaeval Recluse* (London, 1944), pp. 71–8. Clay, *op. cit.*, pp. 193–8. gives a translation of the Sarum Rite of Enclosure.

14. See below, p. 160.

15. See, for example, 1 Corinthians 9, 25–7.

16. See below, p. 168.

17. James 4.3–4.

18. James 1.27.

19. See below, pp. 32 and 86, for example.

20. *The Rule of St Benedict*, ed. Justin McCann (London, 1952), p. 15.

21. Darwin, *op. cit.*, p. 8, cites the listing of anchorites before abbots in the list of benefactors of the *Book of Life* of Durham as evidence of the esteem in which anchorites were held. See also Clay, *op. cit.*, p. xix.

22. *Felix's Life of Saint Guthlac*, ed. Basil Colgrave (Cambridge, 1956), pp. 101–5 (Colgrave's translation).

23. See Clay, *op. cit*, p. 118f., for *loricati*; p. 119 for cold water. See also Ackerman and Dahood, *op. cit.*, p. 15, for Wulfric and the recitation of the Psalter.

24. See *The Book of Margery Kempe*, trans. Barry Windeatt (Harmonds worth, 1989). For Julian, see pp. 77–9. It is possible that this refers to someone other than the Julian who was the author of the *Shewings*.

25. See Warren, *op. cit.*, pp. 18ff.

26. See below, p. 46.

27. See below, p. 193.

28. As recorded in the *Book of Llandaff*, cited by Clay, *op. cit.*, pp. 7–8.

29. See particularly Part Eight. 'Solitaries' often lived in touch with others of the same vocation (see Sharon K. Elkins, *Holy Women of Twelfth-Century England* (Chapel Hill, 1988) pp. 38ff.). There was a view that complete isolation was spiritually dangerous; two 'solitaries' to-gether safeguarded one another's spiritual well-being.

30. This passage occurs in the Nero text of *Ancrene Wisse*, on p. 85 of the Early English Text Society edition (EETS 225), ed. Mabel Day (London, 1952). There is no equivalent in the Corpus text.

31. See Warren, *op. cit.*

32. Cited by Clay, *op. cit.*, pp. 91–2.

33. *The Eremitical Life* (also known as *The Order of Recluses*), written probably between 1160 and 1162. This has been translated by Mary Paul MacPherson in the volume of Ælred's works entitled *Treatises and the Pastoral Prayer*, Cistercian Fathers Series 2 (Kalamazoo, 1971).

34. *The Eremitical Life* 1.

35. Quoted by Darwin, *op. cit.*, p. 29. The incident is from a much later period (mid-fifteenth century) than either Ælred's or *Ancrene Wisse*'s, but it would be surprising if Ælred's comments, or the fears expressed

in *Ancrene Wisse*, were completely without grounding in the reality of their own times.

36. See below, pp. 33–4 and 58.

37. Shepherd, *op. cit.*, p. xxxi. See also Linda Georgianna, *The Solitary Self: Individuality in the Ancrene Wisse* (Cambridge, Mass., 1981).

38. This is from the passage in the Nero text of which part was quoted above, p. xv. 'Desired by many' – in marriage, no doubt, presumably at some time in the past.

39. See below, pp. 24 and 114.

40. See Angela M. Lucas, *Women in the Middle Ages* (Brighton, 1983), p. 140.

41. For the expanded community, see below, p. 119.

42. The religious reform movement of the eleventh century produced certain communities of clerks in northern Italy and southern France who sought to live a common life of poverty, chastity and obedience. Their way of life was given official Church sanction and it came to be widely adopted in the following century. Such communities came to be known as canons regular, and gradually the Rule of St Augustine (probably drawn up in the mid-fifth century by one of Augustine's followers) became the core for the canonical rule of life.

43. Bella Millett, 'The Origins of *Ancrene Wisse*: New Answers, New Questions', *Medium Aevum*, 61 (1992), pp. 206–28.

44. See below, p. 119. Also, see Millett, *op. cit.*, pp. 218ff.

45. On the date and dialect, besides Millett, *op. cit.*, see J. R. R. Tolkien, '*Ancrene Wisse* and *Hali Meiþhad*', *Essays and Studies*, 14 (1929), pp. 104–26; Shepherd, *op. cit.*, pp. xxi–xxv; E. J. Dobson, 'The Date and Composition of *Ancrene Wisse*', *Proceedings of the British Academy*, 52 (1967), pp. 181–208; and Roger Dahood, '*Ancrene Wisse*, the Katherine Group and the *Wohunge* Group', *Middle English Prose: A Critical Guide to Major Authors and Genres*, ed. A. S. G. Edwards (New Brunswick, N.J., 1984) 1–33 (pp. 8–11).

46. In *The Origins of Ancrene Wisse* (p. 138), Dobson pleasingly suggests that the three sisters for whom *Ancrene Wisse* was in the first instance produced bore the names of these saints and were complimented in the choice of these three saints for literary treatment.

47. For comparative analysis see Bella Millett, '*Hali Meiþhad*, *Sawles Warde* and the Continuity of English Prose', *Five Hundred Years of Words and Sounds: A Festschrift for Eric Dobson* (Cambridge, 1983), pp. 100-108.

48. See Shepherd, *op. cit.*, pp. li-lii. *Ancrene Wisse* may also be indebted to manuals on confession, which proliferated following the decree of the Fourth Lateran Council (1215) that all Christians should make an annual confession. See Alexandra Barratt, 'The Five Wits and their Structural Significance in Part II of *Ancrene Wisse*', *Medium Aevum*, 56 (1987), pp. 12-24.

49. Shepherd, *op. cit.*, pp. xxvi-xxvii.

50. See below, p. 6.

51. See below, pp. 108, 100ff. and 179ff. respectively.

52. The author occasionally uses technical rhetorical terms. See below, pp. 2 and 41.

53. See Sr Agnes Margaret Humbert, *Verbal Repetition in the Ancrene Riwle* (Washington, 1944).

54. See R. W. Chambers, *On the Continuity of English Prose from Alfred to More and his School* (Oxford, 1933).

55. On the debt to Latin literature see Millett, '*Hali Meiþhad . . .*', and Elizabeth Salter, *English and International: Studies in the Literature, Art and Patronage of Medieval England* (Cambridge, 1988), Part 1, and especially pp. 70-74.

56. See below, pp. 157f.

Preface

1. Canticles (The Song of Songs) is probably an anthology of secular love songs, but it has been from early times interpreted allegorically.

Christian exegetes understood it as dealing with the relationship between God and the Church or between God and the individual soul.
This latter interpretation was brought to prominence in the twelfth
century by St Bernard of Clairvaux (1090–1153) in his set of eighty-
six homilies on Canticles. The idea of the soul as the Bride of Christ
is an important theme in *Ancrene Wisse*, where the erotic imagery
acquires added force and resonance in virtue of the work's being
addressed to women committed to virginity in what we nowadays,
begging a question, might call the 'real' world.

2. This remark exploits different possible meanings of the Latin *recti*:
(i) the righteous; (ii) the ruled.

3. The Apostle is St Paul, often so designated in medieval writings.

4. Antonomasia is a rhetorical principle of substitution, such that here
boni, 'good', is substituted for 'who direct all their willing according to
the rule of the divine will'. This makes the point that being good is
identical with acting according to God's will – you can actually call
those who do the latter good. This is one of the points at which the
author puts his knowledge of the technicalities of rhetoric on display.
See also p. 41.

5. The expository material between the quotations is to be found in *On
the Psalms* by Peter Lombard (*c.*1100–1160), the standard medieval commentary on the Psalms, which itself made heavy use of Augustine's
Expositions on the Psalms.

6. *Inwit* is the Middle English word here rendered 'inner judgement'
and glossed in the text itself at this point by the Latin *consciencia*. This
translation normally renders *inwit* 'conscience', for which it is the usual
term in the text, though the French-derived *consience* also appears. The
appearance of the Latin gloss here perhaps suggests that the author did
not consider *inwit* an exact equivalent of *consciencia*.

7. St Bernard's *Precept and Dispensation* may be the source of this phrase.

8. Lack of hope and lack of trust are extensively treated later. See
below, pp. 153–5.

9. See, for example, Mark 6.3 for James as 'God's brother'. There was
no Order of St James among the proliferating orders of the twelfth

century. The author invokes it as a way of sidestepping sterile arguments about the merits of different kinds of religious professions.

10. The two kinds of religious are those in the active and contemplative life. The author here follows traditional exegesis, as he does with his allegorizing of the works of mercy, so that visiting the widows and fatherless becomes helping them with 'the food of holy teaching'.

11. Different orders wore different coloured habits, for instance, the Cistercians white and the Benedictines black.

12. The saints mentioned here are representatives of the early flowering of Christian eremiticism in the deserts of Egypt beginning in the third century; the author looks back to this time as a golden age for the solitary ideal. Their lives are recorded in *Lives of the Fathers*, a compilation the origins of which can be traced back to the fourth century and which is laid under heavy contribution by *Ancrene Wisse*. Paul (d. 342) was traditionally the first hermit.

13. Antony the Great, 'the Father of Monks', was born in Egypt, *c*.251; *c*.269 he gave away his possessions and, after years of ascetic living, retired to the desert *c*.285, where his holiness attracted a number of disciples whom he eventually (*c*.305) organized into a community of hermits. He died in 356. His *Life* was written by St Athanasius. Stories about Antony and the saints who follow in the text are conveniently available in *The Sayings of the Desert Fathers*, translated by Benedicta Ward (Oxford, 1975).

14. Arsenius (d. 450) was of senatorial rank and, because of his great learning, appointed by Theodosius the Great tutor to his sons. After ten years in this post he left the court at Constantinople for Alexandria and eventually retired into the desert.

15. Presumably Macarius the Great (the Egyptian), who was born *c*.300 and, according to Cassian (*c*.360 435), whose *Conferences* record his conversations with the monks of the Egyptian desert, was 'the first who found a way to inhabit the desert of Scetis'.

16. Sarah was said to have waged war (successfully) for thirteen years against sexual temptation. This incident is mentioned in the text (see below, p. 110).

17. Syncletica (d. *c*.400) was a woman of Greek parentage who refused an illustrious marriage and lived a life of self-mortification instead. On receiving a large inheritance she distributed her riches to the poor. She eventually retired with her blind sister to a burial chamber on the estate of one of her relatives, where she was consulted by many.

18. *Destinctiuns* is the Middle English word. Theological treatises and commentaries were often divided into *distinctiones* in the Middle Ages.

19. One of several remarks which indicate the author's self-consciousness about the shaping of his material.

PART ONE: *Devotions*

1. The devotions in this first part are modelled on the regimen of prayer in monasteries, as classically formulated by St Benedict (*c*.480–*c*.550). The hours are the traditional monastic services: Matins, Lauds, Prime, Terce, Sext, None, Vespers, Compline. The hours are made up of psalms, hymns, lessons, antiphons, versicles, responses and prayers. The anchoresses said the hours according to the Office of Our Lady. The Office of the Holy Ghost might also be recited, and some hours from the Office of the Dead were prescribed. For full information on the devotions, see *Ancrene Riwle: Introduction and Part 1*, ed. Robert W. Ackerman and Roger Dahood (Binghamton, N.Y., 1984). I have expanded some abbreviations in the Latin texts.

2. A famous and much-used hymn.

3. i.e. the Apostles' Creed.

4. That is, of the church on to which the anchor-house abutted. The altar would have been visible through a window.

5. Passages printed as verse in this translation are not so lineated in the manuscript.

6. These lines are taken (with variations, including appropriate feminine forms in *sanas* and *egras*) from a hymn attributed to Adam of St Victor (d. *c*.1192).

7. Probably kneel, rather than fall prostrate.

8. Not in fact a psalm, but a canticle based on part of the Song of the Three Children (Shadrach, Meshach and Abednego) in the burning fiery furnace, found in the Septuagint version of Daniel (3.57ff.).

9. i.e. the Nicene Creed.

10. An indication that the anchoresses – at least the original addressees – had some considerable degree of competence in liturgical Latin.

11. September 14th, the Feast of the Exaltation of the Cross (as opposed to the Feast of the Invention of the Cross, commemorating the finding of the true cross by St Helena, celebrated on May 3rd). The division of the year into summer and winter at these dates is in accordance with monastic practice.

12. This psalm verse began the service of Preciosa that had come to be attached to Prime.

13. i.e. Vespers.

14. This came to designate Vespers in the Office of the Dead.

15. The Matins of the Office of Our Lady usually had one nocturn and therefore three lessons, but on a feast day it had three nocturns and therefore nine lessons. A nocturn, a division of Matins, is composed of psalms with their antiphons, a versicle, lessons and various prayers.

16. This came to designate the Matins and Lauds of the Office of the Dead.

17. Suffrages are intercessory prayers. The Commendation is a form of prayers for the dead.

18. 'We' being the religious order to which the author belongs, probably the Dominicans. See Introduction, pp. xviii – xix and note 43.

19. Having outlined the hours, the author now treats extraneous material. The Seven Penitential Psalms (traditionally supposed to have been written by David in remorse for his affair with Bathsheba) are 6, 31, 37, 50, 101, 129, 142. The Litany of the Saints requests mercy and

deliverance of the Trinity and intercession of the saints and other classes of holy person.

20. The fifteen Gradual Psalms are 119–33. Jerome rendered the Hebrew title each of these bears *canticum graduum* (song of ascents). What the title means is not clear.

21. Christ was held to have suffered on the cross from noon till 3.00 p.m.

22. i.e. priests not in religious orders (not monks, canons, etc.).

23. This division of aspects of the Trinity is not in fact biblical. It is classically stated in St Augustine of Hippo's (354–430) *The Trinity* and became very widespread thereafter.

24. *Alpha et Omega* is the opening phrase of a hymn to the Trinity by Hildebert of Lavardin (1056–1133).

25. A common devotional theme in the Middle Ages, the spread of which owes much to St Bernard.

26. Cruces were prayers focusing on the cross.

27. For the gifts, see Isaiah 11.2.

28. The seven day-time hours, Matins being said at night, a pattern established with reference to Psalm 118.164 ('Seven times a day I praise thee') and 62 ('At midnight I rise to praise thee').

29. The Our Father was commonly analysed in terms of the seven petitions it contains.

30. The seven 'capital and deadly sins' are pride, envy, anger, avarice, sloth, gluttony and lechery. *Ancrene Wisse* does not seem to operate a distinction between capital and deadly sins (for which, see Morton Bloomfield, *The Seven Deadly Sins* (East Lansing, Michigan, 1952), pp. 43–4). Its preferred term is *heaued*, capital.

31. For the Beatitudes ('Blessednesses'), see Matthew 5.3ff.

32. See 1 Corinthians 13.4–7.

33. The six corporal works of mercy are feeding the hungry, giving

drink to the thirsty, harbouring the stranger, clothing the naked, visiting the sick, ministering to prisoners. See Matthew 25.35–6. To these might be added a seventh, burying the dead.

34. This refers to the qualities of the resurrected body (imperishable-ness, glory, power and being spiritual rather than physical) as described by St Paul at 1 Corinthians 15.42–4. These are seen as marriage-gifts given by Christ to his bride, in line with the idea that the soul is the bride of Christ which runs through *Ancrene Wisse*.

35. The nine, as classically formulated by Dionysius 'the Areopagite' (*c.* 500) in his *Celestial Hierarchy*, are Seraphim, Cherubim, Thrones, Dominations, Virtues, Powers, Principalities, Archangels, Angels.

36. This Latin section is based on St Augustine's *Confessions* 1.2, 5 and 6.

37. i.e. at the Peace ('The peace of the Lord be always with you') in the Mass.

38. A passage which invites thought about the relation between the spirituality of the anchorites of *Ancrene Wisse* and 'mysticism'. In *Anchorites and their Patrons in Medieval England* (Los Angeles and Berke-ley, 1985), pp. 113–24, Ann K. Warren finds that the pursuit of mystical experience became central to anchoritism in England in the fourteenth and fifteenth centuries, but that before this the ideal was 'ascetic'. In 'The Methods and Objectives of Thirteenth-century Anchor-itic Devotion', *The Medieval Mystical Tradition in England, Exeter Sympo-sium* IV, ed. Marion Glasscoe (Cambridge, 1987), pp. 132–53, Nicholas Watson accepts a distinction between later mysticism and the spirituality of the anchorites in *Ancrene Wisse*, but suggests it might be possible to regard this latter as in some sense mystical: certainly the anchorites are engaged in a difficult and sophisticated spiritual practice. (Watson rightly registers the slipperiness of the term 'mysticism'.)

39. i.e. those from *Adoramus te* to *O crux lignum* on pp. 10–11, above.

40. A sequence of prayers centred on the Five Joys of the Virgin begins. The five joys here are the Annunciation, the Nativity, the Resurrection, the Ascension, the Assumption. The joys of the Virgin

are very commonly treated in medieval devotional writings.

41. The question being whether the contact with the Divinity purified Mary's body or whether her bodily purity made her a fit recipient of the Godhead.

42. Traditional doctrine.

43. The hymn *Alma Redemptoris Mater* dates from the eleventh century.

44. *O sancta Virgo uirginum* is the beginning of the Prayer to St Mary by Marbod of Rennes (*c.*1035–1123).

45. M.A.R.I.A. – the initial letters of the five psalms, in one case a canticle – beginning with the *Magnificat* (the Canticle), on pp. 20–21.

46. This bilingual competence (trilingual, if Latin be included) indicates high social status.

47. See below, p. 195, for discussion of how the devil finds work for idle hands.

48. There was an Office of the Holy Ghost.

49. i.e. those being said by the priest in the church to which the cell or cells were annexed. Secular priests (those not in religious orders) came to emulate monastic practice in saying a full daily office.

50. This hymn is not found in the standard collections, though there are similar ones. The crosses are in the manuscript.

51. Penitential acts involving bowing, genuflexion or prostration.

52. What is here translated 'these following rules' may rather mean 'these rules (just presented)'. But the author's remarks about the comparative unimportance of the outer rule and his insistence (p. 190) that he is not trying to make a rule of outer observance for anchoresses other than those who have asked him for a rule seem to indicate that the reference is to the more important inner rule, treatment of which follows.

PART TWO: *Protecting the Heart through the Senses*

1. See below, p. 30. *Ehþurl*, here translated 'eye-window', can mean simply 'window'; the author makes play with the literal meaning of the first element of the word. (In the next sentence the word translated 'windows' is the simple *þurl*.) There is more word-play with windows below, pp. 32–3.

2. See Canticles 1.15.

3. *Ancrene Wisse* has several of these alliterating doubletons, in which the impact of the sound seems more important than the precise semantic difference between the two terms.

4. The idea that anchoritic enclosure was a kind of dying was standard. See Introduction, pp. ix–x.

5. Although the author usually addresses his 'dear sisters', on occasion the form of address is singular.

6. The idea of Eve's leaps, which condemn mankind to hell, seems to be a kind of ironic parallel of the traditional notion of the leaps of Christ as, to save mankind, he moved from heaven to earth and then to hell and back to heaven. See R. E. Kaske, 'Eve's "Leaps" in the *Ancrene Riwle*', *Medium Aevum*, 29 (1960), pp. 22–4.

7. See Genesis 34.1ff.

8. See 2 Kings 11.

9. Showing he is a cleric.

10. The name David was commonly interpreted 'desirable' or 'beloved son', hence 'God's darling'.

11. Here two leaves of the Corpus manuscript have been lost. The text within square brackets, which continues until p. 34, is supplied from the Nero manuscript and then from the Anglo-Norman version in the somewhat damaged BL Cotton MS Vitellius F. vii for an added passage originally in the Corpus version of *Ancrene Wisse* and now surviving only in the Anglo-Norman.

12. See Exodus 21.33–4.

13. That is, cause to shake.

14. A little earlier the source of sin was said to be Eve's eyesight, and her looking at the apple was paralleled to the anchoresses' looking at men. See p. 29.

15. *Eiþurles* and *eilþurles*. *Eil* means harm, but *eilþurl* is used in a text associated with *Ancrene Wisse*, *Seinte Margarete*, to mean simply 'window', so the author may not only be playing with the two words *eiþurles* and *eilþurles*, but also with the elements of the latter – as he may be with those of the former (see note 1 to this Part).

16. The author of Ecclesiasticus was in fact Jesus, son of Sirach, but our author elsewhere attributes quotations from Ecclesiasticus to Solomon. Solomon was reputed to be the author of Proverbs, Canticles, Ecclesiastes and the Wisdom of Solomon, so-called 'wisdom literature' of the Bible and the Apocrypha.

17. In this context windows seem to be both literal windows and the eyes. However, in *The Origins of Ancrene Wisse* (p. 265), Dobson takes the words here translated as 'before' and 'afterwards' as referring to spatial arrangements, to windows in front and behind, and thinks that the author is referring to a reasonably large building housing members of a community which has expanded beyond the three original anchoresses and their anchor-house. The passage translated from the Vitellius manuscript begins at the start of this sentence.

18. Fire damage has caused gaps in the text here.

19. The story is found in the *Dialogues* of Sulpicius Severus (2.12). It is also mentioned by Ælred of Rievaulx in his treatise on the anchoritic life, a text used by *Ancrene Wisse*. See Introduction, pp. xvi–xvii.

20. See below, pp. 46 ff.

21. The word in the text here translated 'jackdaw' is *kaue* (related to modern 'chough'). It is not clear exactly what bird or birds this term covered.

22. The Friars Preacher are the Dominicans, the Friars Minor the

Franciscans. The former arrived in England in 1221, the latter in 1224. A date after which the Corpus version of *Ancrene Wisse* must have been written is therefore provided. The early enthusiasm for the Friars here in evidence contrasts with a rampant scepticism about their real spirituality in later medieval writers such as Chaucer and Langland.

23. 'Eye towards the wood-glade' – a line from a love song. See below, p. 49, at which point the Nero text quotes a further line (see note 45).

24. A confession book very likely to have been provided for the anchoresses by the centre at which the first copies of *Ancrene Wisse* were made, and perhaps even compiled by the author himself. See p. 114 for a reference to a *Life* of St Margaret, which was probably also written for the same centre and which seems likely to be the *Life* of that saint still surviving among the texts associated with *Ancrene Wisse*.

25. For the story of Joseph and Potiphar's wife see Genesis 39.6ff.

26. i.e. the deceit practised by Potiphar's wife.

27. Ember weeks are the weeks in which Ember Days occur. Ember Days follow St Lucy's Day (December 13th), Ash Wednesday, Whitsunday and Holy Cross Day (September 14th).

28. The week before Easter.

29. Attribution in the Middle Ages was often inaccurate. This seems likely to come from Rabanus Maurus (?776–856), not Anselm (1033–1109).

30. Perhaps ultimately, though it does not have the statement exactly, from Seneca's *Letter* 40.14. The Roman writer Seneca (4 B.C.–A.D. 65) came to be much revered as a moral authority in the Middle Ages. He was supposed to have corresponded with St Paul.

31. See Job 2.13.

32. For the marriage at Cana, see John 2.1–11.

33. See Luke 2.48 for Mary's words to her son on finding him in the temple at Jerusalem after the Feast of the Passover. The third and fourth occasions on which Mary spoke seem to come in the wrong order.

34. The *Oxford English Dictionary* defines hypallage as 'a figure of speech in which there is an interchange of two elements of a proposition, the natural relations of these being reversed'. Here the reversal is supposed to occur with *uias* 'ways' and *lingua* 'tongue'. See note 4 to the Preface.

35. This would seem to be a maxim from a treatise on rhetoric or preaching.

36. i.e. erased from the text of the rule, scraped off the parchment on which the rule is imagined written.

37. In *Lying* 9.13.

38. *Clauus* is used by Latin writers of a growth in the eye. The author is perhaps aware of this medical sense. The same sense is attested for the English 'pin' (which is what the Middle English word *preon* in the text here means) in the fifteenth century.

39. The twelfth century saw a great development of various aids to the interpretation of Scripture, including compilations on the etymology (often falsely derived) of Hebrew names which drew on earlier works such as Isidore of Seville's (*c*.560–636) *Etymologies* and the *Book of Names* incorrectly attributed to St Jerome.

40. A proverb, testifying to a common perception of anchor-houses as anything but places of retreat from society.

41. Proverbial.

42. For Jacob's blindness, see Genesis 48.10; for Toby's, the apocryphal Book of Tobit 5.16.

43. Gifts given to the bride by the husband after the first night of their marriage.

44. i.e. Psalm 50.

45. The Latin text here gives the English, indicating that this is a quotation from an English text, evidently a love song. The Nero text quotes a further line, 'in which is the one I love'. See above, p. 36 and note 23.

46. 2 Timothy 2.17.

47. See Genesis 34.1ff., as above, p. 30.

48. Translating the alliterating phrase *wah oper wal*, the two terms in which are equivalent in meaning.

49. Christ weeps at Luke 19.41 (over Jerusalem), at John 11.35 (over Mary at the death of Lazarus), and is said to have shed tears at Hebrews 5.7.

50. The text around this point seems faulty. I have emended it at points to make a translation. For instance, the words in square brackets do not appear in the original text.

51. The text reads ʒe, 'you', but 'we' gives much better sense.

52. See below, p. 184.

53. See Job 3.21–2.

54. See below, pp. 60–61.

55. Here, as elsewhere, 'linctus' translates *healewi*, 'healing water'.

56. Anchorites were often buried in their cells.

PART THREE: *Birds and Anchorites: the Inner Feelings*

1. The *Distichs of Cato* was a collection of pithy sayings in verse and prose, probably written in the third century A.D. In medieval times students memorized the *Distichs* as part of their early education in Latin. Not surprisingly, therefore, the work had considerable currency in the Middle Ages.

2. This quotation from Horace became proverbial.

3. Proverbial.

4. St Andrew was held to have been martyred by crucifixion at Patras in Greece in A.D. 60. The tradition that his cross was X-shaped may not go as far back as *Ancrene Wisse*.

5. According to a tradition now widely rejected by scholars, St Lawrence was martyred in 258 in the persecution under the Emperor Valerian by being slowly roasted on a gridiron.

6. For Stephen's martyrdom, see Acts 6–7.

7. *Lives of the Fathers* 7.3.

8. Recorded in a selection from Bernard's sermons made by Geoffrey of Auxerre, *Declamations . . . from the Sermons of St Bernard* (36.43).

9. Proverbial.

10. Further treatment of thinness and physical debility occurs in Part Six. See, for example, p. 169.

11. Christ is not – at least not apparently – thinking of anchorites when he makes this remark. But for many medieval exegetes the allegorical meanings of biblical texts, quite as much as the literal ones, are God's word.

12. There was much interest in the putative magical properties of gemstones in the Middle Ages, an important work on the subject being written by Marbod, Bishop of Rennes, in the eleventh century. An agate was regarded as a protection against poison and snakes.

13. According to the apocryphal Book of Judith, the Assyrian general Holofernes besieges the Israelites in Bethulia. Judith, a beautiful widow, promises to deliver her people and to this end makes her way into the enemy camp. Holofernes, aroused by Judith, takes too much drink and is beheaded by her, as a result of which the siege is lifted.

14. A common idea, involved with which is a pun on *sapor* (flavour) and *sapientia* (wisdom).

15. This perhaps derives from *Against Maximus* 2.25 (used just previously see footnote a).

16. A Greek word meaning 'night-*korax*', *korax* usually being translated 'raven' but what the species referred to is is unclear.

17. The etymology here is false. For the correct etymology, see the Introduction, p. viii.

18. St Anselm's treatment of the Judgement in this Meditation was very influential. See also pp. 141f., 155f.

19. See Exodus 4.6.

20. i.e. leprosy.

21. See Genesis 32.22ff.

22. For Moses in solitude, see Exodus 3 4 and 19, for Elijah, 1 Kings 19.

23. This hymn is for Matins of the Feast of the Nativity of John the Baptist.

24. 'Threeness' here translates *þrumnesse*, which was the standard early Middle English term for the Trinity.

25. St Hilarion (*c.*291–371) was the founder of the anchoritic life in Palestine, to which he returned having been converted to Christianity at Alexandria and after spending some time in the Egyptian desert, where he retired under the influence of St Antony. St Benedict of Nursia (*c.*480–*c.*550), writer of the rule which is the foundation of Western monasticism, began his career of retirement by withdrawing to a cave at Subiaco in around 500. For the other figures see the Preface, p. 5, and the accompanying notes. In Part One, p. 18, the anchoresses are envisaged as making God give them whatever they ask.

26. St Jerome's dates are in fact *c.*342–420; only questionably is he 'more recent'. He was a hermit for some years in the Syrian desert and ended his life presiding over the men's monastery at Bethlehem.

27. Not traced in Jerome, but quoted as his by Peter Cantor.

28. For John's divinely thwarted attempts to marry, see the apocryphal *Acts of John*, composed no later than the mid second century and attributed to one Leucius, ch. 113 (p. 269 in M. R. James's edition of *The Apocryphal New Testament* (Oxford, 1924)).

29. Precise source untraced. See John 19.26–7.

30. The true sun is Christ, a common idea.

31. See p. 48.

32. Esther 7.3ff.

33. See p. 49.

34. The 'at some time' suggests that the anchoresses are designated 'God's thieves' not because their anchoritic life makes them thieves on God's behalf (stealing from the world, perhaps, what might be regarded as its due of normal, secular living), but rather as offenders against God, who hope to escape the consequences of their sin by flight to the sanctuary of the anchor-hold, which involves the complete dedication of their lives to God.

35. This harks back to the quotation with which Part Two opens.

36. i.e. epilepsy.

37. That is to say that humility is maintained by an abiding consciousness of the physical and moral infirmity of the body. 'The lady' is the soul.

PART FOUR: *Fleshly and Spiritual Temptations and Comforts and Remedies for Them*

1. In this sentence 'temptations' translates the French-derived *temptatiuns* and 'trials' the native *fondunges*, but there does not seem to be any distinction of meaning, and *fondunge* in the next sentence and elsewhere (it is more common in this text than *temptatiun*) is translated 'temptation'.

2. 'Long-suffering' here translates *polemodnesse*, a native word which glosses the French-derived *patience*. Again, there does not seem to be any distinction of meaning, and *polemodnesse* (the usual word for the idea in this text) is translated 'patience' below.

3. See Ecclesiasticus 3.6 and Job 23.10.

4. Proverbial.

5. 1 Thessalonians 5.15.

6. See Matthew 27.39–43.

7. See above, pp. 53–4.

8. 'Displeasure' is supplied from the Nero text.

9. The classification of sin into seven major types and subdivisions of these types is extremely common in medieval devotional writings; its origins though are much earlier, a particularly influential work (cited frequently in *Ancrene Wisse*) being Gregory the Great's *Morals on Job*.

10. This threefold classification becomes very common following its introduction by St Bernard. This seems to be the first use of the classification in a text written in English.

11. Beginning at the last paragraph of this page.

12. 'Lechery' renders *leccherie*, 'lust' *galnesse*, as elsewhere in this translation.

13. The rather awkward change of gender occurs in the original text. In this passage the author seems to oscillate between thinking of a general audience and thinking specifically of the female recluses.

14. 'Airs and graces' translates *supersticiuns*, perhaps incorrectly. I take this term in a sense derived from its component elements 'above' and 'standing'.

15. This version in fact increases the number to ten.

16. See note 13.

17. Proverbial.

18. In fact, the text goes on to specify seven foals.

19. i.e. to do good.

20. Lending money at interest was officially condemned by the Church in the medieval period.

21. 'Kindred in the spirit' would include godparents and confessors (spiritual fathers).

22. The official Church teaching on sex was that it was only legitimate

within marriage and in modes which permitted procreation to occur. Pursuit of sexual pleasure for its own sake was wrong.

23. 'Inertia' translates the original's *accidie*, the English version of Latin *accidia*. *Accidia* means 'sluggishness', 'torpor'. It looks as though the author thought *accidie* rather technical (hence my latinate 'inertia') and in need of glossing as 'sloth'.

24. 'Din' renders imperfectly the text's *dream*, a word which can mean 'music', 'melody' (also, probably at this time, 'joy', 'rejoicing'), and so carries further the musical imagery of the proud as trumpeters.

25. See Ephesians 5.14.

26. 'Ashbum' is an attempt to render the text's *eskibah*, on which see J. Turville-Petre's article, 'Two Etymological Notes: 'Ancrene Wisse' *eskibah, hond þet ilke*', in *Studia Neophilologica*, 41 (1969), pp. 156–61. The term seems to be contemptuous, having reference apparently to feeble-minded people who would sit about uselessly on the hearth, fiddling with the ashes.

27. A manciple was a purchaser of provisions for an institution such as a college or a monastery.

28. This would seem to be an attack on what the author sees as the acceptability in aristocratic circles of sexual licence. The sardonic point would be that people prepared to be seen as lovers (a socially acceptable designation) are in fact nothing but lechers.

29. See *Lives of the Fathers* 6.3.

30. Referring back to the beginning of Part Four. See above, p. 86.

31. Medieval moral and religious teaching often enforced its points with such illustrations, or *exempla*.

32. Literally, 'turns the grim (fierce) tooth on (her)'.

33. *Wið liste*, here translated 'pleasurably', can also mean 'with art', 'skilfully'.

34. The plural 'slight and hidden temptations' is in the original, despite the preceding 'slight and hidden temptation' in the singular.

35. *Lausiac History* 44. This record of early monasticism was written by Palladius (*c*.365–425) about the year 419 for Lausus, chamberlain of Theodosius II. It became attached to *Lives of the Fathers* as Book 8.

36. *Lives of the Fathers* 6.4.

37. *Lives of the Fathers* 5.7.

38. Compare 1 Corinthians 10.12.

39. 'Mummy' may not be quite right as a rendering of the text's *dame*, which could certainly be used as a formal and dignified designation. But the child's situation is hardly formal or dignified.

40. *Lives of the Fathers* is here presumably indebted to 4 Kings 6.16, where Elisha, surrounded in Dothan by troops of the King of Syria, says this to his servant.

41. For Sarah, see note 16 to the Preface.

42. For Antony, see note 13 to the Preface, for Benedict, note 25 to Part Three.

43. *On the Book of Jesus (Joshua), Son of Nave (Nun)* 15.6. Origen (*c*.185–*c*.254) was an Alexandrian exegete and theologian.

44. Perhaps in the *Seinte Margarete* which is one of the surviving texts associated with *Ancrene Wisse*, where a version of the first four lines of this mnemonic occurs. A *Life* of St Margaret, probably this *Seinte Margarete*, was possessed by the anchoresses, as the reference on p. 114 indicates.

45. The idea that this world is an insubstantial shadow of higher reality is, in the West, ultimately Platonic.

46. Perhaps the author of *Ancrene Wisse* himself.

47. 'Anxious' translates the text's *ancreful*; there is a play here with the word for anchorite/anchoress, *ancre*.

48. See *Lives of the Fathers* 6.2.

49. See note 44.

50. See above, p. 18.

51. I have rendered the feminine pronoun in the Middle English with a feminine. As with 'heart' below (p. 137), it is not quite clear whether there is indeed a personification here, though I think that the context suggests that there is. (Elsewhere, however, I have rendered feminine pronouns referring to 'heart' with the neuter 'it'.) See also note 84.

52. The reference may be to Bernard's thirty-first sermon on Canticles.

53. 'Fake stock' translates the text's *eapeware*, a word which connects with the old ape (*eape*) of the next sentence.

54. i.e. leprosy.

55. This passage testifies to the expansion of the anchoritic community beyond the three sisters for whom *Ancrene Wisse* was originally written. The passage was added in the Corpus revision.

56. i.e., it would seem, towards the border with Wales.

57. See above, p. 116.

58. See Luke 24.1.

59. According to the *Oxford English Dictionary*, a pittance was originally 'a pious donation or bequest to a religious house or order, to provide an additional allowance of food, wine, etc. . . . hence, the allowance or dole itself'.

60. The repetition renders the *re* in *recogitate*.

61. The bracketed passage has been supplied from the Nero text.

62. The doctrine of transubstantiation seems to be referred to here, though the Eucharist is seen as effecting a change in Christ rather than in the consecrated elements.

63. Jehoshaphat, King of Judah, offered the prayer to which reference is made when threatened by the Moabites and Ammonites. See 2 Chronicles 20.

64. i.e. in the Mass.

65. For nocturns, see note 15 to Part One.

66. Ishbosheth was Saul's son and King of Israel, David being King of Judah contemporaneously. The unfriendly relations pertaining between David and the house of Saul caused Ishbosheth's killers to think they would be pleasing David in murdering Ishbosheth, but they were instead executed by David for their crime. See 2 Kings 4.

67. See pp. 115, 126.

68. See p. 92.

69. The indicative is in the original, although we might have expected a subjunctive parallel to 'hurt'.

70. A moralizing commonplace.

71. 'Lack of wisdom and lack of awareness' translates the text's alliterating doubleton *unwisdom and unweotenesse*.

72. See above, p. 106.

73. On pride here Bernard is quoting St Augustine's *The Literal Meaning of Genesis* 11.14.

74. See *Lives of the Fathers* 3.129.

75. In fact, it seems to be from Augustine's *Expositions on the Psalms* 92.3 (Psalm 92, verse 1).

76. Moral writers in the Middle Ages often drew on lore about animals, such as is found in the Bestiaries, compilations of stories (going back ultimately to a Greek work dating from early in the Christian era) in which moral and religious instruction was derived from the supposed characteristics of real and imaginary animals.

77. See above, p. 115.

78. See above, p. 89.

79. This comment seems obtrusive and has been taken as a punning reference to Limebrook, a religious house for which an association with *Ancrene Wisse* has been claimed. See Introduction, pp. xviii–xix. One wonders, however, whether play is being made with the whiteness of lime (in English), so as to highlight the brightening action of the file.

80. 'Ieronimus' repeats the citation of source already made in 'Therefore St Jerome says'.

81. This high valuation of reading seems consonant with the care the author expends on creating a text to be read.

82. That is to say, a language more immediate than Latin to the anchoresses, through which the proper affective response might be more quickly produced within them.

83. The crucifix is a shield in Part Seven. See p. 181.

84. The feminine pronouns here reflect the feminine forms of the Middle English. However, it is not certain that the Middle English gender is anything other than grammatical (though grammatical gender has largely been replaced by natural gender in *Ancrene Wisse*): there may be no attempt to personify the heart. See note 51.

85. See Gregory's *Dialogues* 2.2. The 'rolling about' was in thorns.

86. Self-flagellation, which the text's *discepline* presumably indicates, was a common practice among the devout in medieval times.

87. I take it that the author is thinking of a state in which the person does not consent to the act, but does not fight against the pleasurable imagining of it. This failure to fight would mean that the pleasure was *morosa*, lingering about in the mind too long.

88. Proverbial; see below, p. 156.

89. See p. 6.

PART FIVE: *Confession*

1. See above, Part Three, especially pp. 68ff.

2. For Judith as 'confession', see above, p. 68.

3. The section in brackets is supplied from the Nero text.

4. See above, p. 71, and below, pp. 155ff., where other quotations from Anselm's *Meditation* on the Last Judgement are used.

5. See note 6 to the Preface.

6. See, for example, above, p. 139 and note 2 to this Part.

7. 'Flames' (plural) here and later in this passage renders the original's singular noun.

8. The belief that God assigns every person an angel as guardian of body and soul was already held in pre-Christian times by pagans and Jews. Relevant New Testament texts are Acts 12.15 and Matthew 18.10.

9. That is to say that on any occasion of confession one must confess all the sins one recollects from childhood onwards to the person to whom one is confessing (though the confessor may be different on different occasions – as other passages in the text imply).

10. 'Trappings' translates the text's *totagges*, which means 'things tagged on, attached'.

11. There is other contemporary evidence that churchyards were used for dancing. Some of the situations specified in this passage are not relevant to anchoresses, as the work moves beyond its immediate audience, a movement it acknowledges below, pp. 157–8.

12. The section in brackets is supplied from the Nero text.

13. The repetition of *confitebimur* is held to demonstrate the need for frequent confession.

14. See Luke 18.10–14.

15. 'Lively' translates the text's *cwic*, which also means 'alive' and which therefore is in more direct opposition to 'dead' than is 'lively'. The imagery suggests spiritual life and death.

16. 'Trists' (*tristen* in the text) are appointed stations in hunting. There seems to be an etymological pun here involving *tristen* and the words rendered 'lack of trust' and 'too much trust', *untrust* and *ouer-trust*.

17. The idea of the golden mean (*aurea mediocritas*) is ultimately Aristotelian.

18. Proverbial; see above, p. 138.

19. See above, pp. 139ff. – though the powers against the world are not, in fact, spoken of earlier, nor anywhere specified.

20. An indication that the author sees his work as of relevance to, and likely to reach, a general audience.

21. See above, p. 137.

PART SIX: *Penance*

1. In *Anchoritic Spirituality* (New York, 1991), p. 393, Anne Savage and Nicholas Watson suggest that 'higher' here means further up in the text of St Bernard (his seventh Sermon in Lent) on which the opening of this Part of *Ancrene Wisse* draws heavily. The citation of the Galatians text occurs in Bernard after the treatment of the three ways of life which the author now proceeds to describe, working back to Galatians at p. 162.

2. The shrine of St James the Great is at Compostela in northern Spain. St Giles (?eighth century) is supposed to have lived in a hermitage at the mouth of the Rhone. The town of St Gilles grew up near his grave and, like Compostela, became a popular destination for medieval pilgrims.

3. St Julian was the patron saint of wayfarers and innkeepers.

4. i.e. all people in religious orders.

5. 'Lightly' translates the text's *lihtliche*, the primary meaning of which in this context is probably 'easily'. 'Lightly' is used to retain the text's contrast of lightness and weight.

6. 'Wheeling' translates the text's *hweolinde*. Play is probably being made on this word and *hwilinde*, meaning 'for a while', 'temporary'.

7. 'Can do us well' renders the apparently colloquial phrase *wel mei duhen*.

8. i.e. one who says prayers for other people.

9. See Luke 22.44.

10. According to tradition, Peter was crucified upside-down. For Andrew and Lawrence see notes 4 and 5 to Part Three.

11. Legend has it that the virgin martyr St Agatha was a Sicilian of noble birth executed in 253 at Catania. She was supposed to have had her breasts torn off (see below, p. 169) before being beheaded. The three saints whose lives are recorded in texts associated with *Ancrene Wisse* (see Introduction, p. xix), Katherine, Margaret and Juliana, were all beheaded, Katherine having suffered first on the wheel.

12. The shadow of sin is Christ's flesh, according (ultimately) to an interpretation of Lamentations 4.20. Christ was unsinning, but had the shadow of sin because he possessed human corporeality - the body of man, in its conflict with the spirit, being understood as a repository of sin (see, for example, Romans 7.22–4, with its 'Who will deliver from this body of death?' (24), or Romans 8.6, cited later in this part at p. 170).

13. On this, see the Introduction, p. xvi and note 33.

14. See note 11.

15. According to Shepherd (in *Ancrene Wisse: Parts Six and Seven*, p. 44), very probably a story of Cistercian origin. Shepherd cites Cistercian analogues.

16. Zedoary has properties like ginger.

17. Hippocrates, a Greek of the fifth century B.C., has the title 'the Father of Medicine'. Galen practised as a doctor at Alexandria and Rome in the late second century A.D. Galen's works and those attributed to Hippocrates were fundamental to medical science in the Middle Ages.

18. i.e. St Paul.

19. See 1 Timothy 4.8.

20. See John 19.39.

21. See Gregory, *Morals on Job* 30.25, 74.

22. See p. 143.

23. See Luke 8.2.

24. See John 2.1-11.

25. i.e. presumably Solomon. See Part Two, note 16.

26. The section in brackets is supplied from the Nero text.

27. This is apparently a name for the Alps in general.

28. Adapted from the seventieth sermon of St Augustine (section 3). The idea was commonplace in the twelfth century.

29. See pp. 131f.

PART SEVEN: *The Pure Heart and the Love of Christ*

1. The holy abbot Moses (probably a Libyan of the fourth century) figures as an important speaker in the *Conferences* of John Cassian (*c.*360-435). For this saying, see *Conferences* 1.7. Cassian visited the ascetics of the Egyptian desert and introduced their brand of monasticism into France. In the *Conferences* the aim of the monastic life is conceived as being purity of heart. Cassian's writings found particular popularity in the twelfth century.

2. See *Tractate on the Office and Duty of Bishops* 3.

3. This Augustinian sentiment was popular in the twelfth century. The author seems to hedge against the dangers of the idea with his reference to reason's controlling influence.

4. i.e. at the Last Judgement, where the archangel Michael will superintend the weighing of souls and their good and bad deeds.

5. See Matthew 5.45.

6. Letters patent from the sovereign proclaimed publicly the grant of some privilege. They are here opposed to the letters addressed to

specific persons, which would be closed and sealed. God's salvation, announced to the Jews in the Old Testament, and announced somewhat darkly (the letters are sealed), is in the Gospel, the record of Christ's saving acts, proclaimed openly and made available to all men.

7. The castle is said to be of earth to reflect the existence of an immaterial soul (the lady) within a material body. The fact that the castle is built of earth (rather than stone) indicates its weakness, and here the author is registering the moral dubiety of the body.

8. See Psalm 44.2. The Psalmist's words were often applied to Christ.

9. The idea of God or Christ as a king wooing the soul is ancient (see Shepherd, *Ancrene Wisse: Parts Six and Seven*, p. 55). Shepherd points out that new chivalric and courtly conventions colour the representation of the traditional theme in *Ancrene Wisse*.

10. Sometime after about 1200 it became fashionable to represent Christ's feet as fixed to the cross by a single nail, rather than by two nails, so providing a better likeness of a shield tapering to a point.

11. Probably the third reason why we should love God, the first being that he is an honourable and worthy suitor, the second that he has done so much for us. Possibly, though, the reference is to ways of interpreting the shield, in which case the use of the shield as memorial would be in addition to its use as defence and as a means of 'crowning us in heaven'.

12. There is a play in the Middle English involving an opposition between *openliche* and *inwardliche*, which the translation of the latter word as 'fervently' cannot communicate.

13. Jews had an important role in finance in the Middle Ages, since Church law forbade Christians to lend at interest. The twelfth century saw an increase of anti-Semitic feeling in England, which eventually culminated in the expulsion of the Jews from the country in 1290.

14. Possibly a reference to St Augustine's discussion of the violation of virgins in *The City of God* 1.16ff.

15. The motif of a healing bath of blood occurs in several medieval stories.

16. The classification is based on 1 John 5.8.

17. See note 1 to the Preface.

18. Medieval writers commonly rank virginity as the highest possible grade of chastity, followed by widowhood and then marriage.

19. The point being that the saved will what God wills.

20. The figures which follow were standard exemplars in the Middle Ages of certain desirable attributes. Croesus was king of Lydia in the sixth century B.C.

21. See 2 Kings 14.25–6.

22. See 2 Kings 2.18.

23. See Judges 15.14–17.

24. i.e. Augustus Caesar (27 B.C. – A.D. 14).

25. Alexander the Great (356–323 B.C.).

26. See Deuteronomy 34.7.

27. Greek fire, a liquid incendiary based on naphtha, pitch and sulphur, was used by defenders in siege warfare.

28. 'Red man's blood' may be an alchemical secret name, perhaps for sulphur, though Shepherd (in *Ancrene Wisse: Parts Six and Seven*, p. 65) cites one recipe for Greek fire which apparently involves actual blood from a red-complexioned man.

29. There was a tradition that Christ was red-complexioned.

30. Proverbial. The same idea is also found with fire, or love, instead of the nail.

31. See pp. 131–2 and 176.

32. 'Charity is the cherishing' is an attempt to retain the text's word-play in its *chearite is cherte*. Shepherd (in *Ancrene Wisse: Parts Six and Seven*, p. 67) suggests that though *chearite* and *cherte* are etymologically identical, the author is opposing religious and commercial meaning. *Vndeore* and *unwurth* ('unprecious' and 'unvalued') in the next sentence seem commercial in register.

33. The notion that love binds is a commonplace and the idea that love binds God is widespread in the twelfth century.

34. Possibly in *Hali Meiþhad* and *Sawles Warde*. See Introduction, p. xix.

35. The author here creates a link with the opening of *Ancrene Wisse*, where the rule which governs the heart is 'the charity of a pure heart and clean conscience and true faith' (p. 1).

36. This refers to the distinction between inner rule (lady) and outer rule (handmaiden) in the Preface (see pp. 2–3).

PART EIGHT: *The Outer Rule*

1. See above, pp. 3–4.

2. See above, p. 7.

3. 'Our brothers' are presumably lay brothers of the author's order (probably the Dominican Friars: see Introduction, pp. xviii–xix). Many of the prescriptions of *Ancrene Wisse*'s outer rule can be paralleled in the regulations of the Dominicans. See Bella Millett, 'The Origins of *Ancrene Wisse*: New Answers, New Questions', *Medium Aevum*, 61 (1992), pp. 206–28.

4. Midwinter Day is Christmas Day; Twelfth Day, the Feast of Epiphany (January 6th); Candlemas, the Feast of the Purification of the Virgin and the Presentation of Christ in the Temple (February 2nd); Our Lady's Day, the Feast of the Annunciation (March 25th); Holy Thursday, Ascension Day (fifth Thursday after Easter); Midsummer Day, the Feast of the Nativity of John the Baptist (June 24th); the Feast of St Mary Magdalene, July 22nd; the Feast of the Assumption of the Virgin, August 15th; the Feast of the Nativity of the Virgin, September 8th; Michaelmas Day, September 29th; the Feast of All Saints, November 1st; the Feast of St Andrew, November 30th.

5. The author presumably has flagellation, a common ascetic practice, in mind.

6. See note 59 to Part Four.

7. The Feast of the Exaltation of the Cross on September 14th.

8. For Ember Days, see note 27 to Part Two. Rogation Days were prescribed days of prayer and fasting in the early summer (April 25th and the three days before Ascension Day). A vigil here is the day and night before a feast.

9. *Hwit*, 'white [food]', is food made with milk (also, perhaps, with eggs).

10. i.e. animal fat. Not eating meat was a standard form of fasting.

11. Mary was commonly understood to represent the contemplative and Martha the active life.

12. For the Friars, see note 22 to Part Two.

13. A rendering of *liht is . . . leaue*. The phrase is taken in this sense by Millett and Wogan-Browne, but others have thought it means 'leave is easily granted'.

14. The *Oxford English Dictionary* gives 'discredit to religion occasioned by the conduct of a religious person' as a definition of scandal.

15. See above, p. 122.

16. The hayward was an official of manor, town or parish who, among other duties, had charge of fences and enclosures. He would have had to see that the cattle on common pasturage did not break through into cultivated fields.

17. St Paul, who according to Acts 18.3 made tents, might be cited as an example.

18. A stamin was an undergarment of coarse worsted, often used by ascetics.

19. The wimple was folded in such a way as to envelop the head, chin, sides of the face and neck.

20. *Angelos* here was sometimes explained as referring to the priests. (Some versions of the Latin Bible read *uelamen*, 'covering', rather than

potentiam, 'power', at 1 Corinthians 11.10, which explains how the text can appear relevant in this context.)

21. See Cassian, *Conferences* 24.9.

22. An amice is an ecclesiastical linen scarf; parures are decorative panels for ecclesiastical vestments.

23. 'Do sieve-work' translates *criblin*. The kind of needlework envisaged would be something like lace.

24. *Letter* 125.11.

25. Both these remarks are proverbial.

26. Copying books is probably meant, but 'write' (*writen* in the text) could cover composing books as well.

27. See above, p. 190; also pp. 2, 6.

28. On the hours see note 1 to Part One.

29. Rendering *ticki* in the text. There is still a children's touching game called 'ticky' in the area in which *Ancrene Wisse* was written.

30. Possibly a reference to *Letter* 462 of those ascribed to St Bernard.

31. In *The Origins of Ancrene Wisse* (Oxford, 1976), pp. 327ff., E. J. Dobson argues that there is a cryptogram in this sentence identifying the author as Brian of Lingen. See Introduction, pp. xviii–xix.

Discover more about our forthcoming books through Penguin's FREE newspaper...

Penguin

Quarterly

It's packed with:

- exciting features
- author interviews
- previews & reviews
- books from your favourite films & TV series
- exclusive competitions & much, much more...

Write off for your free copy today to:
Dept JC
Penguin Books Ltd
FREEPOST
West Drayton
Middlesex
UB7 0BR
NO STAMP REQUIRED

READ MORE IN PENGUIN

In every corner of the world, on every subject under the sun, Penguin represents quality and variety – the very best in publishing today.

For complete information about books available from Penguin – including Puffins, Penguin Classics and Arkana – and how to order them, write to us at the appropriate address below. Please note that for copyright reasons the selection of books varies from country to country.

In the United Kingdom: Please write to *Dept. JC, Penguin Books Ltd, FREEPOST, West Drayton, Middlesex UB7 0BR*

If you have any difficulty in obtaining a title, please send your order with the correct money, plus ten per cent for postage and packaging, to *PO Box No. 11, West Drayton, Middlesex UB7 0BR*

In the United States: Please write to *Penguin USA Inc., 375 Hudson Street, New York, NY 10014*

In Canada: Please write to *Penguin Books Canada Ltd, 10 Alcorn Avenue, Suite 300, Toronto, Ontario M4V 3B2*

In Australia: Please write to *Penguin Books Australia Ltd, 487 Maroondah Highway, Ringwood, Victoria 3134*

In New Zealand: Please write to *Penguin Books (NZ) Ltd, 182–190 Wairau Road, Private Bag, Takapuna, Auckland 9*

In India: Please write to *Penguin Books India Pvt Ltd, 706 Eros Apartments, 56 Nehru Place, New Delhi 110 019*

In the Netherlands: Please write to *Penguin Books Netherlands B.V., Keizersgracht 231 NL–1016 DV Amsterdam*

In Germany: Please write to *Penguin Books Deutschland GmbH, Friedrichstrasse 10–12, W–6000 Frankfurt/Main 1*

In Spain: Please write to *Penguin Books S. A., C. San Bernardo 117–6° E–28015 Madrid*

In Italy: Please write to *Penguin Italia s.r.l., Via Felice Casati 20, I–20124 Milano*

In France: Please write to *Penguin France S. A., 17 rue Lejeune, F–31000 Toulouse*

In Japan: Please write to *Penguin Books Japan, Ishikiribashi Building, 2–5–4, Suido, Tokyo 112*

In Greece: Please write to *Penguin Hellas Ltd, Dimocritou 3, GR–106 71 Athens*

In South Africa: Please write to *Longman Penguin Southern Africa (Pty) Ltd, Private Bag X08, Bertsham 2013*

READ MORE IN PENGUIN

A CHOICE OF CLASSICS

Aeschylus	**The Oresteian Trilogy**
	Prometheus Bound/The Suppliants/Seven Against Thebes/The Persians
Aesop	**Fables**
Ammianus Marcellinus	**The Later Roman Empire (AD 354–378)**
Apollonius of Rhodes	**The Voyage of Argo**
Apuleius	**The Golden Ass**
Aristophanes	**The Knights/Peace/The Birds/The Assemblywomen/Wealth**
	Lysistrata/The Acharnians/The Clouds
	The Wasps/The Poet and the Women/ The Frogs
Aristotle	**The Art of Rhetoric**
	The Athenian Constitution
	Ethics
	The Politics
	De Anima
Arrian	**The Campaigns of Alexander**
St Augustine	**City of God**
	Confessions
Boethius	**The Consolation of Philosophy**
Caesar	**The Civil War**
	The Conquest of Gaul
Catullus	**Poems**
Cicero	**The Murder Trials**
	The Nature of the Gods
	On the Good Life
	Selected Letters
	Selected Political Speeches
	Selected Works
Euripides	**Alcestis/Iphigenia in Tauris/Hippolytus**
	The Bacchae/Ion/The Women of Troy/ Helen
	Medea/Hecabe/Electra/Heracles
	Orestes/The Children of Heracles/ Andromache/The Suppliant Women/ The PhoenicianWomen/Iphigenia in Aulis

READ MORE IN PENGUIN

A CHOICE OF CLASSICS

Hesiod/Theognis	**Theogony** and **Works and Days/ Elegies**
Hippocrates	**Hippocratic Writings**
Homer	**The Iliad**
	The Odyssey
Horace	**Complete Odes and Epodes**
Horace/Persius	**Satires** and **Epistles**
Juvenal	**Sixteen Satires**
Livy	**The Early History of Rome**
	Rome and Italy
	Rome and the Mediterranean
	The War with Hannibal
Lucretius	**On the Nature of the Universe**
Marcus Aurelius	**Meditations**
Martial	**Epigrams**
Ovid	**The Erotic Poems**
	Heroides
	Metamorphoses
Pausanias	**Guide to Greece** (in two volumes)
Petronius/Seneca	**The Satyricon/The Apocolocyntosis**
Pindar	**The Odes**
Plato	**Early Socratic Dialogues**
	Gorgias
	The Last Days of Socrates (Euthyphro/ The Apology/Crito/Phaedo)
	The Laws
	Phaedrus and **Letters VII and VIII**
	Philebus
	Protagoras and **Meno**
	The Republic
	The Symposium
	Theaetetus
	Timaeus and **Critias**

READ MORE IN PENGUIN

A CHOICE OF CLASSICS

Plautus	**The Pot of Gold/The Prisoners/The Brothers Menaechmus/The Swaggering Soldier/Pseudolus**
	The Rope/Amphitryo/The Ghost/A Three-Dollar Day
Pliny	**The Letters of the Younger Pliny**
Pliny the Elder	**Natural History**
Plotinus	**The Enneads**
Plutarch	**The Age of Alexander** (Nine Greek Lives)
	The Fall of the Roman Republic (Six Lives)
	The Makers of Rome (Nine Lives)
	The Rise and Fall of Athens (Nine Greek Lives)
	Plutarch on Sparta
Polybius	**The Rise of the Roman Empire**
Procopius	**The Secret History**
Propertius	**The Poems**
Quintus Curtius Rufus	**The History of Alexander**
Sallust	**The Jugurthine War** and **The Conspiracy of Cataline**
Seneca	**Four Tragedies** and **Octavia**
	Letters from a Stoic
Sophocles	**Electra/Women of Trachis/Philoctetes/Ajax**
	The Theban Plays
Suetonius	**The Twelve Caesars**
Tacitus	**The Agricola** and **The Germania**
	The Annals of Imperial Rome
	The Histories
Terence	**The Comedies (The Girl from Andros/The Self-Tormentor/TheEunuch/Phormio/The Mother-in-Law/The Brothers)**
Thucydides	**The History of the Peloponnesian War**
Virgil	**The Aeneid**
	The Eclogues
	The Georgics
Xenophon	**Conversations of Socrates**
	A History of My Times
	The Persian Expedition